THE LAST
HEROES

AUT SI QUID EST IN VITA IN AETERNUM RESONAT

WHAT WE DO IN LIFE ECHOES IN ETERNITY

From when I began the 'Debt of Gratitude' project, *The Last Heroes*, in mid 2014, my on-going motivation and mission have remained the same, to write a book and subsequent work from the heart which is:

About veterans
For veterans
To honour veterans
Because to remember is to honour.

Gary Bridson-Daley

THE LAST
HEROES

VOICES OF BRITISH AND COMMONWEALTH VETERANS

GARY BRIDSON-DALEY

To my beautiful mother Sylvia June
Bridson, who was very proud of
The Last Heroes but who sadly passed
before its release.
For you Mum.
26 March 1942–27 January 2017

I would like to further dedicate this book to the memory of some
wonderful people who touched many lives including mine in a very
special, caring and lovely way: Brenda Griffin, Nancy Teacher, Violet
Meltzer and Tony Parkinson. Thank you for your friendship and
kindness; it will always be remembered.

First published 2017, this revised paperback edition published 2020

The History Press
97 St George's Place, Cheltenham,
Gloucestershire, GL50 3QB
www.thehistorypress.co.uk

British Library Cataloguing in Publication Data.
A catalogue record for this book is available from the British Library.

ISBN 978 0 7509 9434 7

Typesetting and origination by The History Press
Printed and bound in Great Britain by TJ International Ltd

Contents

Dedications   6

Foreword by Dame Vera Lynn   7

Author's Note   8

Second World War Timeline   9

Scale of the Conflict   12

Diversity of Those Who Served   15

THEATRES OF WAR

1   Army and the War on Land   17

2   Navy and the War at Sea   93

3   Air Force and the War in the Air   132

4   Intelligence and the Secret War   189

5   Home and the War on the Home Front   206

Connecting with History   247

Veterans' Poetry and Songs   249

Casualties of War   276

For Those Who Never Returned   279

D-Day 75   280

V.E. Day   281

Sacrifices Never Forgotten   283

Hope for a Better Future   285

Acknowledgements   286

Dedications

This book is dedicated firstly to all veterans, servicemen and servicewomen from the United Kingdom and Commonwealth countries from all backgrounds and cultures who served this country in any and every capacity during the Second World War, who when called upon to help in a time of peril and danger answered that call selflessly to be part of the fight against evil in order to preserve our freedom and way of life. It is this conflict and generation that my book is focusing on; this book has been written to represent and thank all veterans of that conflict.

Additionally and very importantly, I also wish to extend this dedication to all the men and women who have ever served this country and those who do so until this present day in order to give us that same freedom, safety and democracy that we and our families and our nation still enjoy. This freedom was bought at a very high price, mentally, physically and emotionally, and it still is. It is for these reasons that I feel remembrance is such a necessary and valuable thing to undertake and something that hopefully the nation will always continue to do.

This book also pays tribute to those who have made vital contributions in civilian life; those from the past through to those who currently perform their duties as part of the essential civilian services, such as the police, fire, medical services, mountain and sea rescue and all others.

To all these men and women, military and civilian, this is truly dedicated to you as a real debt of gratitude which you all deserve.

'They were a wall unto us both by night and day' – 1 Samuel 25:17

Foreword
by Dame Vera Lynn

I believe it is our shared vision to honour veterans from all the services – Army, Navy, Air Force, Intelligence and Home Front – and keep alive both now and for future generations what these amazing people did for us and our country, and the freedom they gave us through their selfless actions and contributions which we and our families still enjoy to this very day.

'A Debt of Gratitude' [*The Last Heroes*] brings to life the voices of World War Two veterans, from the United Kingdom and Commonwealth Countries, all with their own unique contribution and each heroes in their own way, and not only covers many aspects of the conflict but also includes poignant veterans' poetry.

This book by Gary Bridson–Daley could well become an integral part of our country's historical library.

Dame Vera Lynn DBE, LLD, M.Mus
April 2016

Author's Note

All information given to me by veterans during the interviews and at all stages during the making of this book has been taken on trust and comes mainly from memory on their part and from resources provided by them. It must be remembered that each veteran has supplied personal accounts from their own experiences that are more than seventy years old and therefore should be treated, enjoyed and respected as factual human interest stories that have been gathered in order to capture and preserve those vitally important narratives before they were lost forever. I have, when and where possible, researched Second World War material from many additional resources in order to check and reinforce the accounts within this book.

The different material that was combined to compile the veterans' profiles came from the following varied and extensive sources: the stories told and information imparted to me directly both face to face and in conversations over the telephone with veterans; additional supplementary information shared by spouses, family and friends of the veteran; and material resources I was allowed to view or take copies or pictures of, such as service records, log books, pay books, identification documents and miscellaneous documents from many sources. The information also comes from the videos made during the interview process, written and audio accounts given to me, and additional notes taken during the interviews plus veterans' wartime and other photos. On the odd occasion, original quotations from the veterans have been lightly edited for the sake of clarity. Further resources came from helpful veteran- and military-related associations and organisations, Ministry of Defence requests, online research and various materials kindly loaned to me.

Second World War Timeline

Although the Second World War officially began in September 1939 there were many events over a number of years leading up to that point that influenced and were directly and indirectly responsible for it happening from 1931 onwards when Japanese aggression in Manchuria began, and later with the rise and expansion of the fascist regimes of Italy, Germany and Spain and their aggressive expansionist policies. In time all of these combined would lead to the much bigger cataclysmic events of the Second World War, of which the main battles and events are shown here;

1939

1 September	Germany invades Poland, Second World War begins.
3 September	Great Britain and France declare war on Germany.
30 November –12 March 1940	U.S.S.R and Finland Winter War.

1940

9 April–10 June	Germany invades Denmark and Norway.
10 May–22 June	Germany attacks Western Europe.
10 June	Italy enters the war, invading southern France on 21 June.
10 July–31 Oct	The Battle of Britain.
27 September	Germany, Italy and Japan sign the Tripartite Pact creating the 'Axis Triangle'.

1941

February	The German Afrika Korps arrives in North Africa.
6 April–1 June	Germany and Axis allies invade Yugoslavia Greece and Crete.
22 June	Operation Barbarossa, Nazi Germany invades the Soviet Union.
7 December	Japan bombs the American Pacific Fleet at Pearl Harbour in Hawaii.
8 December	The United States declares war on Japan, entering the Second World War.

11–13 December Nazi Germany and its Axis partners declare war on the United States.
December
  – Mid 1942   Extensive Japanese offensives throughout S.E Asia and Pacific.

1942

4–8 May	Japanese Navy lose the Battle of the Coral Sea.
30 May	The first 1,000-bomber raid when the RAF bombs Cologne.
May–August	Germans advance in North Africa and in June take Tobruk.
3–7 June	Battle of Midway, another U.S victory in the Pacific.
June–September	German offensive in Southern Russia reaches Stalingrad on the River Volga.
23 October	
–11 November	Battle of El Alamein in Egypt, 'Turning Point' in the Desert War.
8 November	Operation Torch. U.S and British troops land in Algeria and Morocco.

1943

2 February	German 6th Army at Stalingrad surrenders to the Russians.
13 May	All Axis forces in North Africa surrender to the Allies.
5–15 July	Kursk offensive in the Soviet Union and biggest tank battles in history.
10 July–17 August	U.S and British invasion of Sicily.
3 & 9 September	Allies invade Italy at Calabria and Salerno.

1944

17 January– 18 May	Monte Cassino battles in Italy.
22 January	Allied troops land near Anzio, south of Rome.
6 June	Operation Overlord, D-Day, France, Allied invasion of Western Europe.
22 June	Operation Bagration. Russian offensive destroys German Army Group Centre.
15 August	Operation Dragoon. Allied forces land in southern France.
20 October	U.S troops land in the Philippines as the strategic Island hopping campaign in the Pacific continues.
16 December	Battle of the Bulge last Significant German offensive, defeated by Jan 1945.

1945

12 January –Mid April	U.S troops cross the Rhine River at Remagen.
7 March	Soviet offensive liberates Warsaw and pushes on into Germany.
16 March	U.S take the Japanese island of Iwo Jima.
16 April	Soviet final offensive, encircling Berlin, heart of the Third Reich.
30 April	Hitler commits suicide in his bunker in Berlin.
7 May	Germany surrenders to the Western Allies. The war in Europe is over.
8 May	Victory in Europe (VE Day). Celebrated by countries all over Europe.
22 June	U.S take Okinawa, last island stop before the Japanese islands.
6 August	The United States drops the first atomic bomb (Little Boy) on Hiroshima.
9 August	The United States drops the second atomic bomb (Fat Man) on Nagasaki.
14 August	Japan unconditionally surrenders.
2 September	Japan formally surrenders on the USS *Missouri* in Tokyo Bay, ending the Second World War.

Credit to the United States Holocaust Museum website for the main text used in the timeline.

Scale of the Conflict

The Second World War was a completely global conflict and the sheer scale of it is truly mindboggling: no corner of the planet was left untouched by it. During the six years that it raged it would encompass almost every type of terrain within its theatres of war, from the deserts of North Africa to the jungles of Burma, from the icy steppes of Russia and the skies above Europe to every ocean of the world and deep below them.

It would lead to the mobilisation and inclusion of nearly every country in the world directly or indirectly, and would pull into it hundreds of millions of personnel who served in one way or another in the many and varied roles that their nations needed, both on the battle fronts and the home fronts. They would be locked in a deadly life and death struggle using every means of warfare, from conventional to those of intelligence, sabotage and deception and many other aspects, including the development of new technologies and secret weapons that eventually led to the use of the most destructive of these, the A-bomb.

It was a war that was also fought on another level and dimension, one that had not existed before. It was against evil ideologies that all those engaged against it understood had to be defeated in order to preserve all the rights that good men and good nations believed in and stood for, such as freedom, democracy, liberty and the right to peaceful self-determination. Had Nazi Germany, Imperial Japan and their allies won the war, the outcome and alternative, which was already evident in occupied lands, would have been enslavement, oppression, totalitarian rule, tyranny, fear and, for many, death.

The Second World War also differed from other previous conflicts in that civilian deaths were for the first time more than double those of combatants. As a result of starvation, disease, bombing, forced labour, extermination programmes and other causes, more than 50 million civilians lost their lives, compared with approximately 20 million combatants. In comparison, the total number of combined casualties for the First World War was around 20 million. It is also important to remember that behind each one of these statistics there was a real person, a story, a life lost and a family that grieved his or her passing.

The nature of warfare had changed and knew no boundaries. This is reflected in the figures shown below for comparison between the two world wars:

	Proportion of dead	
	Military	**Civilian**
First World War	95%	5%
Second World War	33%	67%

For most, this really was the 'Second' World War in many ways because it was the second conflict that they had seen, fought or been involved in, and sadly in just over twenty years. It brought back painful memories, both mentally and physically, and of those who had survived the First World War, for a variety of reasons, many would not survive the Second.

The anguish experienced and the self-sacrifice and courage that was shown was equal to, and in many cases surpassed, that of wars and conflicts that had gone before it, both for the combatants and for civilians that were embroiled in it. Also, the frightful advances in weapons and tactics and the means of killing on an even bigger industrial scale than had been seen previously all added to the terrible experiences of people on both sides.

A rallying call to the nation from the Minister for Aircraft Production.

Another aspect that further reflects the scale of this conflict was the huge variation in roles and contributions of our servicemen and women to help bring about victory. It is this interesting variation that is reflected within the book alongside the personal recollections of the veterans and it is intended to capture and show as many of these different aspects as possible.

The scale of the conflict is further shown by the chart below that lists most of the countries involved, the sides they were on and their situation. Others not listed here mainly but not solely came under the United Kingdom as its Commonwealth and what were then essentially considered countries and possessions of the British Empire.

Allied and Axis Alliances in the Second World War, plus Occupied and Neutral Countries

Axis	Allied	Occupied	Neutral
Bulgaria	Argentina	Albania	Andorra
Croatia	Australia	Belgium	Ireland
Finland	Bolivia	Czechoslovakia	Liechtenstein
Germany	Brazil	Denmark	Portugal
Hungary	Canada	Estonia	Spain
Italy	China	Ethiopia	Sweden
Japan	Chile	France	Switzerland
Romania	Columbia	Greece	Turkey (until February 1945)
	Costa Rica	Latvia	Uruguay
	Cuba	Lithuania	Vatican City
	France	Luxembourg	
	India	The Netherlands	
	Iraq	Norway	
	Lebanon	Philippines	
	Mexico	Poland	
	New Zealand	Yugoslavia	
	Paraguay		
	South Africa		
	Soviet Union		
	United Kingdom		
	United States		

Diversity of Those Who Served

A further indication of the size and scope of the Second World War is the number of Commonwealth countries and islands that answered Great Britain's call for help in her hour of need, and who in most cases volunteered to stand by us. In doing so, many paid the ultimate price for a country they had never even seen. These invaluable contributions should always be recognised and remembered with the same amount of respect and reverence that we give to the memory of our own veterans from the United Kingdom.

The Second World War drew into it all the major countries and world powers of the time along with all their available resources and manpower and also that of their allies. On one side were the Axis nations of Nazi Germany, Italy and Japan, along with a number of countries which at some point aided and supported them such as Finland, Bulgaria, Romania and Hungary.

On the other side were the biggest Allied nations known as the 'Big Four', which consisted of the United States of America, the Soviet Union, China and Great Britain along with the countries of her Commonwealth and colonial possessions. These consisted of a staggering array of countries and islands all over the world from what was still considered the British Empire in one form or another such as Canada, South Africa, Australia, New Zealand, India, Ceylon (Sri Lanka), Kenya, Rhodesia, Nigeria, Uganda, Sierra Leone, Ghana, Gold Coast, Jamaica, Trinidad & Tobago, Barbados, Cyprus, Malta, Gibraltar, Mandate Palestine, Singapore, Hong Kong, Aden, Fiji, and many more, again reflecting the true global nature and scale of the conflict. Between them they provided a massive amount of manpower, material resources and very important bases from which the Allied powers operated in many theatres of war.

It should also be remembered that we were joined by the mixed nationalities of many occupied nations who continued the fight in many ways through active and organised resistance in their own countries, and additionally through and with the help of their countrymen who volunteered and served within every branch of our armed forces. These included the Polish, Czechs, Dutch, Danish, Norwegians,

Belgians, Greeks, Yugoslavians, French and those from the Baltic States of Estonia, Latvia and Lithuania and elsewhere.

Within this book these invaluable contributions are also rightly acknowledged and their veterans, some of whom settled in the UK after the war, are honoured alongside our own. This continues to show the diversity of those who served in what truly was a 'world war', who came from many different countries, cultures, religious and ethnic backgrounds (as the famous wartime poster shown below demonstrates), and served, worked, lived and in some cases died alongside British servicemen and women.

They were bonded and united by the absolute understanding of the need to come together to defeat the evil of the Axis countries and all that they stood for; as the stories within this book reflect, they did exactly that!

1

Army and the War on Land

Having looked at the bigger picture and the sheer scale of the war, the countries that took part and the diversity of those who served, we now feature each of the services, Army, Navy and Air Force, plus intelligence and the home front, in their own sections. We start with the Army, which has always existed in one form or another under the kings, queens and rulers of our isle but can quite legitimately trace its roots back to the first professional army in the field, Oliver Cromwell's 'New Model Army' in 1645 and a later standing army of King Charles ll in 1661. From then until the present day, the Army has served and defended the interests of Great Britain all over the world, and was responsible for policing the British Empire, which in its day covered a third of the Earth's surface.

During the Second World War, every branch of its services were at some point fully engaged on all fronts and in all terrains. This brought about the expansion of many varied types of existing units and the creation of new ones as a reaction to the challenges and complexities that arose.

This was reflected in the men being prepared, supplied and fitted out with the best the country could manage at any given time. This did, of course, vary quite considerably at various stages of the war and depended on many factors as the Army tried to provide for the massive variations in the regions in which it was engaged, from fighting in the desert to war in mountainous terrain to amphibious and jungle warfare, all of which required very different approaches, adaptations, tactics and kit.

Within this, as in all professional standing armies, were needed many varied units such as engineer, infantry, artillery, mechanised, signals, medical, intelligence, supply and logistics, catering and clerical, and amongst the many roles there were gunners, sappers, infantrymen, guardsmen, military police, tank crew, drivers, clerks, cooks, nurses, paratroopers and the newly formed special forces, complete with the essential command structure of officers and NCOs.

They made up every unit from company to divisional strength, came from every part of the United Kingdom and Empire, and served in well-known units such as the Lancashire Fusiliers, Yeomanry, Scots Guards, Welch Regiment, Irish Guards, and the Gurkha, Indian, Canadian, South African, New Zealand and Australian regiments, to name but a few, all with their own proud history and heritage. Legends were born through battle such as the famous Desert Rats, Chindits and the Long Range Desert Group. The veterans of some of these units are featured in this section and their stories make very interesting reading.

Sergeant John Clarke MBE

Served with: 6th Battalion, Black Watch & 1st Battalion, Argyll &
Sutherland Highlanders
Service number 2761256
Interviewed: Manchester, Lancashire, 10 July 2014

Service History and Personal Stories

- ❖ **Born:** 19 April 1924, Manchester, England, UK.
- ❖ As a soldier in the famous Black Watch, John saw fierce front-line action and service in many places, starting with Tunisia and Algeria in North Africa in 1943.
- ❖ John was at Monte Cassino, Italy, where he was involved in all phases of that difficult battle throughout 1944.
- ❖ Later on in Greece against ELAS Communist fighters 1944–45, he was involved in guerrilla-style warfare.
- ❖ Present as additional security during an attempt on the life of Winston Churchill in Athens, Greece, in December 1944.
- ❖ Served in Palestine, Middle East, with the 6th Airborne Division and was at the British HQ, King David Hotel in Jerusalem, when it was bombed on 22 July 1946.

❖ In 2004 John was awarded an MBE for many years of hard work with various
    veterans groups, including the Monte Cassino and Polish veterans associations.

In July 2014 I interviewed my first Second World War veteran, John Clarke. This
would be the start of many interviews all over the country that formed the basis of
my book, and what a great way to start, with a veteran who had experienced and
given so much for his country. As I looked and listened to him it was immediately
apparent to me that my choice to incorporate 'A Debt of Gratitude' into the
concept of the book was the right one, as it truly reflected my sentiments about our
veterans and what we owe them for what they have done for us. So to begin, here
is John's story, a superb introduction to the many incredibly interesting veterans'
stories that follow.

John's war started in 1939 while serving an engineering apprenticeship with
Metropolitan Vickers in Trafford Park, working on the Seascan naval radar
system. During that time he had the additional duties of a fire fighter on factory
fire watch putting out incendiary bombs during air raids in the Blitz. He enlisted
in 1941 in Manchester at 17 years of age in the Highland Regiment and at 18
was transferred to the 6th Battalion Black Watch. In 1942 he trained at Perth,
Dundee, and at Leigh-on-Sea and Southend on the Essex coast. He then served
in many places and in many varied terrains and kinds of battles, always at the
'sharp end' as John called the forefront of battle. This started in 1943 when he
was sent to Algeria and Tunisia to take part in the final phases of the North
African Campaign where he was in the 4th British Division, First Army. Then
in 1944 he was sent with the 4th British Division to fight in Italy as part of the
Eighth Army.

As the Italian Campaign raged on throughout 1944 John found himself in many
places including the famous battles of Monte Cassino, where he was involved in all
stages of the battles from start to finish. In late 1944 he was transferred to Greece
with the 4th British Division and ended up fighting in a very different kind of
guerrilla warfare situation against the communist ELAS fighters. This went on
until halfway through 1945 when his 6th Battalion (Territorial) was stood down
in Greece. John was then transferred to the 1st Battalion Argyll and Sutherland
Highlanders. He was sent with them as part of the 6th Airborne Division to carry
out policing duties in Palestine with the British forces that were tasked with
containing the growing Jewish resistance fighter groups such as the Irgun. It was
while serving there that on 22 July 1946 John was present at the British military
and administrative headquarters at the King David Hotel in Jerusalem when an
infamous bombing took place. Again John found himself at the heart of vicious
guerrilla-style warfare, and would do so for many more months to come. Once
back in England he was demobbed in York in May 1947, bringing to an end a
military career that had put him right at the frontline of many conflicts, from

the deserts of North Africa to the mountains of Italy and Greece to the streets of British Mandate Palestine.

We now return to the campaign in Italy where John was involved in many battles throughout the country. He was engaged in all phases of the particularly hard battles at Monte Cassino, where combat took place against elite German paratrooper units. Lots of the men who fought in Italy had already fought in North Africa and Sicily and in some cases had not been home for years. To many out there it seemed like theirs had become a forgotten campaign. John now shares various recollections from his time at Monte Cassino:

Ferocious Battles of Monte Cassino

Some of the stuff I remember about the Battles at Monte Cassino, well we had to deal with many things including the lack of reinforcements from the UK as most resources were being taken in preparation for D-Day, it felt like we had become a side show. What is still never really mentioned was that in Italy we were opposed by the cream of the German Army, German paratroopers, panzergrenadiers, Hermann Goering Division and Austrian Alpine troops, far superior to those defending the Normandy beaches. As a result of fighting such professional soldiers the battles were hard and nasty with a lot of vicious close quarter hand-to-hand fighting with small arms and bayonets against a tough and ruthless enemy in a very difficult terrain. This, of course, led to many casualties on both sides and the frequent bad weather didn't help. It significantly slowed down our advance, and I remember in some places there was phosphorus in the wet soil so when our troops dug slit trenches they would get this phosphorus on their uniforms, and at night this would illuminate them and made them easy targets for German snipers. We lost quite a few of our boys that way, too many.

Later that year, in December 1944, John found himself with the Black Watch in a different theatre of war in Greece. After being ordered to be additional security and help escort some VIPs in the centre of Athens he was witness to something quite unexpected:

An Assassination Attempt on Winston Churchill

There was stiff resistance from ELAS, many of whom were regular Greek soldiers, but civilians during daylight. On Boxing Day, we had received an order to join a party of VIPs who were gathering to hold a special meeting. I made contact near the town square. The party turned out to be headed by Winston Churchill and Anthony Eden along with the Archbishop of Greece with numerous MPs. As we walked along the business area, a shot rang out, a bullet flashed before my eyes, and I heard the familiar sound of a bullet hitting flesh. The lady behind me fell to the ground, dead; there was nothing I could do. Her name was Erula, an interpreter aged around forty. The

shot had been meant for Winston Churchill, he was lying on the ground, surrounded by his escort. Soon afterwards, the sniper was caught; it turned out to be a Bulgarian girl aged about nineteen. The Greek Campaign was the most brutal I had taken part in. Amazingly, the Atlee Government, in order not to offend the Russians after the war, did not issue a campaign medal to those who had taken part. Instead, they officially awarded the Italy Star, which all those who had been involved there had already won before being sent to Greece. This was not a medal for a campaign against the Germans, the Italy Star was!

Two years after first meeting and interviewing John in July 2014, I went back to spend time with him to hear more from this real front-line soldier, who now shares with us various accounts from his extensive experience of what it was really like:

To Be a Soldier at the Sharp End

The first battle I took part in was in Tunisia in 1943 and it was a nasty one, and when people say were you frightened going into your first battle, well you're

The King David Hotel, Jerusalem, after the terrible bombing of 22 July 1946 which left ninety-one dead. The hotel was being used as the headquarters of the British forces in Mandate Palestine, and the fatal attack was targetted at the very heart of their command structure. John was on guard duty at the hotel that day and, after being lucky enough to survive what was widely condemned as a terrorist attack, realised he was again engaged in guerrilla-style conflict.

not frightened, you're apprehensive. It's the second battle you're frightened of 'coz you know what to expect. With the Black Watch being of Scottish origin there were some traditions that were kept in battle. It is difficult to describe this but when you had a bayonet charge, which we did eventually at Cassino, the pipers played and it was walk, trot, charge and somehow or another you felt like a million dollars doing that. It was something unbelievable, the pipes seemed to fill you full of, well courage, I don't know. Strangely you were enjoying it in a way! I think I made four or five charges in my time and if you are charging the enemy who is dug in like on a machine gun you are above him, normally, and he gets frightened when he sees you coming. He doesn't know whether he's going to kill all of you or if you are going to get him kind of thing. It's like a desire to do what you are supposed to do, and not only that but you have got your lads there and you're all shouting. It's the heat of battle after all and in the end it's you or him.

Additional Information and Life After Service

❖ **Rank at end of service:** Sergeant.

❖ **Medals and honours:** 1939–45 Defence Medal, 1939–45 War Medal, 1939–45 Star, Africa Star, Italy Star, Palestine 1945–48 Medal, Polish Gold Cross of Merit, MBE.

❖ **Post-war years:** Returned to Metropolitan Vickers to finish the 'interrupted apprenticeship' and progressed to senior management, then moved on to Ruston Diesels in Newton-le-Willows and finished as a works superintendent. Later the company became part of BAE Systems. John married Olive, who was a Wren during the war. They were together for fifty-seven years from 1948 until 2005, and have two children, three grandchildren and two great-grandchildren.

❖ **Associations and organisations:** Co-founder of the Monte Cassino Veterans Association, which he served from 1968 to 2005, now the Monte Cassino Society. Also worked with various Polish veterans associations, after forming close friendships with Polish servicemen with whom he fought in Italy.

Lance Corporal Jozef Wojciechowski

Served with: 1st Polish Independent Parachute Brigade
Service number: 2530017
Interviewed: Bradford, West Yorkshire, 9 January 2015

Service History and Personal Stories

- ❖ **Born:** 28 September 1922, Mielnica Podolska, Poland.
- ❖ Jozef witnessed the Soviet Invasion of Poland in September 1939; in 1940 he was deported with his family to Stalin's dreaded Siberian work camps in Russia.
- ❖ Later he joined the Polish armed forces under British command and came halfway around the world to be trained in the UK and fight for the Allies.
- ❖ As a wireless operator he was in the 1st Polish Independent Parachute Brigade as part of the 1st Airborne Division, and was involved in Operation Market Garden in Arnhem, Netherlands, in September 1944.
- ❖ After the war he continued to serve as part of the British Army of the Rhine (BAOR) in Germany until 1947.
- ❖ Jozef settled in Great Britain after the war as a return to a communist-controlled Poland was not a realistic option throughout the Cold War period.

The story of how Jozef Wojciechowski ended up as a paratrooper in the 1st Polish Independent Parachute Brigade is one of great circucumstance and fate. It saw him deported from his hometown of Mielnicapodolska in eastern Poland after the Soviet invasion in 1939 to one of the infamous Siberian 'Gulags' in Russia in 1940 as forced labour. Then later in 1941, as a result of an agreement between Stalin and the Polish government-in-exile in London after the German invasion of Russia, he and many of his fellow countrymen were released and made an epic journey that in just over a year took them halfway around the world. They travelled from Siberia to Scotland, via Kazakhstan, Uzbekistan, Persia, Iraq, Palestine, Egypt, South Africa, Sierra Leone and finally on to the United Kingdom. At first receiving rehabilitation, then later a range of military training at British Army camps as they went along, Jozef called this his 'amazing journey to freedom'. This is the wartime story of one Polish man, one of the many who came to help us.

After his arrival in the UK in 1942, Jozef volunteered to be a paratrooper and received training at RAF Ringway, Manchester. He chose to specialise as a radio operator, for which he got further training at Lagerhouse near Fife, Scotland. Then, on 21 September 1944, he was dropped as part of the 1st Airborne Division into Driel near Arnhem, as part of Montgomery's Operation Market Garden to try to help relieve the beleaguered British airborne troops as things there began to go terribly wrong. These events brought him full circle back into Europe in the most dramatic way. After this operation he continued to serve in the armed forces and upon his return to England he was stationed at various bases such as Uffington near Stamford and Greyfield near Hull. He later served in Germany in 1945–47 as part of BAOR, stationed at Bersenbruck on the River Hase in Lower Saxony.

Jozef was demobbed in York in August 1947 and like so many other Poles stayed in the UK to make a new life for himself as a return to his beloved Poland was not a realistic option under communist rule. So he had his family in the safety of his adopted country, the United Kingdom, which by his efforts and service he helped keep free and safe for us all.

We now return to September 1944 when the 1st Polish Independent Parachute Brigade under the command of Major General Sosabowski was moved to Stamford in Lincolnshire in preparation for a very special mission. But before they undertook that mission, Jozef remembers there was a bad omen even at the planning stages:

The Ill-fated Operation Market Garden

As part of the 1st Polish Independent Parachute Brigade I was involved in operations in a town called Driel near Arnhem. But even before we went there was a bad omen regarding Operation Market Garden which we had heard about. This came from much higher up the chain of command and served as a warning of the bad things which were to come …

Before the operation there was a briefing of high-ranking officers and commanders of brigades in a big hall with maps on the wall, where they were pointing and saying we land here and go here, and go there, and Major General Sosabowski (pictured left) piped up saying, 'General, Germans. What about the Germans?' They could not believe that he had dared to speak up and address such high-ranking officers in such a manner, and that he had openly criticised many aspects of the operation! This caused bad feeling and led to him being very disliked by other generals, and later very wrongly and unfairly being used as a scapegoat for their failed operation. They ignored him and the intelligence reports about the German units around those areas, much to their peril. And the rest as they say is history, a hard history for many of the servicemen involved!

Jozef also recalls the chaos of the operation, saying amongst other things:

We were dropped over Arnhem on 21 September after two days' delay, due to bad weather. We were sent to help the British Forces trapped at Arnhem. It was a real mess; many things went wrong at every level from the very beginning, from radio equipment that did not work properly, to strong and well-organised German resistance. We had high casualties, having to retreat ourselves whilst trying to help the British paratroopers escape across the Rhine under heavy German fire after most of their division had been annihilated. It was all a real mess!

Polish Contribution to Allied Forces in the Second World War

This operation was just one example of the many contributions of the Polish forces to the Allied war effort. Poland and her people suffered terribly during the war with nearly 6 million killed. They were persecuted horrendously during the occupation of their country and as a result many became dispersed throughout the world, yet they chose to fight on when and where possible, many as part of the British armed forces. Having been the first to be attacked on 1 September 1939, Poland was involved with the war effort the longest of any Allied nation. Despite occupation, it continued to resist through ongoing sabotage and insurgencies such as the Warsaw Uprising in 1944, and by having a government-in-exile in London and servicemen in the British armed forces actively engaged in combat. Having a functioning intelligence service also meant its people resisted externally until the close of hostilities.

We now look closer to get a better idea of the extent of the Polish contribution. As part of the British forces Poles provided crucial help in many of the critical battles and theatres of the war in which Great Britain and the western Allies were involved, significantly in the Battle of Britain in 1940; the North African campaign, notably at the siege of Tobruk in 1941–42; and in the Italian campaign, where they had an important input at the battles of Monte Cassino and the final capture of the monastery in 1944 by General Anders' Polish II Corps. They were also involved in some of the major action after the invasion of France from 1944 onwards, such as the battle of the Falaise Pocket in Normandy, Operation Market Garden around Arnhem in Holland and later across the Rhine into Germany. It should also be remembered that there were significant Polish forces helping the Eastern ally, Russia, fighting with its troops all the way from Belarus and Ukraine on into the heart of Berlin.

Other notable contributions were from the Polish Navy, which operated twenty-seven vessels as part of the Royal Navy and fought in many engagements, including those against German battleship *Bismarck*. On the intelligence side vital pre-war and wartime work was done by Polish cryptologist Marian Rejewski and his team in helping to understand and reconstruct a German Enigma machine and helping break its codes. By the war's end the Polish armed forces in the West under British command numbered approximately 195,000; there were also sixteen main fighter and bomber squadrons in the RAF. These sacrifices have created strong and enduring bonds between the Polish and British people that last to this day. One person who understood this and held the Polish forces in high esteem was Winston Churchill, who said to General Sikorski, leader of Poland's government-in-exile: 'We are comrades in life and death. We shall conquer together, or we shall die together.'

Additional Information and Life After Service

❖ **Rank at end of service:** Lance corporal.

❖ **Medals and honours:** 1939–45 Star, 1939–45 Defence Medal, 1939–45 War Medal, France and Germany Star, Polish Army Service Medal, Polish Army 1939–45 Western Medal, Polish Cross of Merit, Polish–Siberian Cross, Polish Ex-Servicemen's Cross with Bar for sixty years' service to Polish Ex-Servicemen's Association, Arnhem Medal from the Dutch Government.

❖ **Post-war years:** Jozef, like so many other Polish ex-servicemen, felt he could not return home after the war and live under Soviet communist rule, as it was like continually living under occupation, similar they felt to that of the Nazis. So he decided to stay in Great Britain and make a life here, where he worked as a weaver at Salts Mill, Shipley in Yorkshire, from 1947 until 1977. Jozef was married to Emilia for sixty-four years and they have two children and two grandchildren.

❖ **Associations and organisations:** Served in the Polish Ex-Servicemen's Association for fifty-five years as treasurer and as a welfare officer for fifteen years, also treasurer of the Polish Parachute Association, Bradford branch, for fifty-seven years and the last surviving member of that association. He is an honorary member of the British Parachute Association, Bradford branch, and has been its president for ten years.

Regimental Sergeant Major Maurice Tinant

Served with: 13/18 Queen Mary's Own Hussars, 1st King's Dragoon
Guards, 2nd Royal Tank Regiment
Service number: 410623
Interviewed: Manchester, Lancashire, 19 November 2014

Service History and Personal Stories

❖ **Born:** 12 August 1921, Lambeth, London, England, UK.
❖ Maurice served for thirty-six years in the British Army, in three regiments, and experienced the transition from mounted cavalry to mechanised units.
❖ Posted to India before the war in one of the Army's last mounted cavalry regiments.
❖ Later he became one of Montgomery's famous Desert Rats, serving in armoured car reconnaissance as part of the 7th Armoured Division, Eighth Army, in North Africa.
❖ Served throughout the entire desert campaign from 1940–43, during which time he was involved in the siege of Tobruk and both battles of El Alamein.
❖ Went on to serve in Italy at Monte Cassino against the Germans, Greece against ELAS communist guerrillas, and in Palestine against Jewish resistance fighters.

❖   Maurice was mentioned in dispatches for his actions and bravery in Italy, and after
     the war was a part of BAOR (British Army of the Rhine) in Germany.

Maurice's story is one of a true 'lifelong soldier'. His career stretched an incredible
thirty-six years, spanning from the years before, during and after the war. He joined
and was part of a British Army that still had mounted cavalry when he served
in Risalpur, India, now Pakistan, near Rawalpindi. As a mounted cavalryman–
musician with the 13/18 Queen Mary's Own Hussars he saw its transition into a
mechanised unit during a time of historical change for the Army. Throughout his
military career Maurice served the crown in many places in what were also times
of huge worldwide historical change during which Great Britain slowly lost its
Empire and where the role of the Army was also constantly evolving and changing.

After his time in India Maurice became part of The King's Dragoon Guards and
with this mechanised regiment he went into battles in various theatres of war that
began in the deserts of North Africa, where he served from start to finish between
1940–43, and which included the siege of Tobruk, both El Alamein battles and the
final German defeat at Cape Bonn. Then it was on to Italy, where he fought from
the beach landings in Salerno to Monte Cassino and on to Naples and Rome. His
next posting saw him on policing and counter-insurgency operations in Greece,
where he fought against ELAS communist fighters while stationed in Kifissia,
amongst other places, from Christmas Day 1944 until May 1945. From then until
November 1947 he served in Palestine in Jerusalem, Haifa and Akko, where he
was up against Jewish resistance fighters. Also during that period he spent time
posted on similar types of armoured reconnaissance duties with the Dragoons up
in Tripoli and Beirut in Lebanon and Damascus, Syria.

Upon his return to the UK he was stationed at Catterick Garrison and Aldershot,
and also at Bovington at the Armoured Corps HQ dealing with ordnance recovery
on the firing ranges. In 1952 Maurice transferred to the 2nd Royal Tank Regiment
and went to Germany with BAOR based in Munster, Herford, and also at HQ
in Rheindalen. In 1952–73 his service would take him between BAOR and UK
postings with one exception, which was from 1959–61 when Maurice found himself
back in Libya on peace-keeping duties. He was also involved in the Chieftain tank
trials in Kirkcudbright, Scotland, and Bovington, Devon, from 1961–66, by which
time he was a tank instructor and troop leader who held an all-groups vehicle
licence, meaning he could instruct on anything mechanised. His last years in the
Army saw him return home to Manchester and work at the Army recruitment
office in Fountain Street in 1966–73, by which time he was a regimental sergeant
major. With such a long service history and vast array of military experiences to
choose from, it is not easy to select just a couple of stories, but I will take us back
to the famous Battle of El Alamein for the first one, as it is very rare to get such a
unique insight into a battle that marked the 'turning of the tide' during the war.

Emblem of the 7th Armoured
Division, the Desert Rats.

First, an historical overview of events in the Western Desert in October to November 1942. The war in North Africa raged from June 1940 until May 1943. It was fought right across most of North Africa, in the Egyptian, Libyan, Tunisian, Algerian and Moroccan deserts, giving it the name the Western Desert Campaign and the Desert War. This war moved up and down the coast of North Africa as the fortunes of the Allied and Axis forces changed during three years of hard-fought desert warfare. During that time legends would be born such as General, later Field Marshal, Erwin Rommel, the Desert Fox, who commanded the German forces known as the Afrika Korps, and Lieutenant General Bernard Montgomery who commanded the Eighth Army that included the 7th Armoured Division, the Desert Rats. It was also where the famous battles such as Tobruk and El Alamein were fought. It was at the second battle of El Alamein in Egypt from 23 October to 11 November 1942 where the British and Commonwealth forces had their first victory over the German Army in the field. Something that Churchill desperately and impatiently yearned for, needed and wanted was a truly British victory before the Americans became fully involved. It proved to be both a decisive victory and a turning point in the war, one of which Maurice Tinant was a part, and as one of the Desert Rats he recalls:

The Second Battle of El Alamein

I remember the vast number of troops that were everywhere waiting to start, British, Indians, Australians, New Zealanders, South Africans and French. As a reconnaissance unit we had to be careful on such a big battlefield not to get too far ahead of our own troops, and risk becoming victims of what they call today friendly fire, not a difficult thing to do in the heat and confusion of battle, and especially one as big as El Alamein. The opening barrage was a mighty one, I had never seen one like it before! A hell of a battle followed with a lot of damage and a lot of casualties on both sides. Our part of the line was not as bad as some but we still saw a lot of burned-out German armour and lorries and dead Germans and later a lot of POWs being brought back as we advanced. This battle was a turning point in the war and a major morale booster for both the British and Commonwealth troops and those at home, who as a result of that most important outcome could celebrate the first ever victory over the German Army in a full-on land battle during the war. And what a victory indeed, but when you think about it that took a long time to achieve, nearly three years! But we didn't falter and for that reason in the end we succeeded because every man did his best.

Every soldier must know, before he goes into battle, how the little battle he is to fight fits into the larger picture, and how the success of his fighting will influence the battle as a whole.

Field Marshal Bernard Law Montgomery

During the Battle of El Alamein, over 13,000 British and Commonwealth troops were killed, injured or missing. The 7th Armoured Division continued its distinguished service in campaigns that took it from the sands of North Africa to the gates of Berlin. They were immortalised in this moving tribute by the Prime Minister:

May your glory ever shine, may your laurels never fade, may the memory of this glorious pilgrimage of war you have made from Alamein, via the Baltic, to Berlin never die. It is a march unsurpassed through all the story of war. May the fathers long tell the children about this tale.

Winston Churchill, 7th Armoured Division 'Desert Rats' Tribute

Maurice was then posted to Italy, where he was mentioned in dispatches. When a soldier receives this honour it is to acknowledge a very brave action or actions he has undertaken in the line of duty, and comes from the Sovereign leader of the nation, in this case King George VI. It is further acknowledged by an oak leaf clasp being awarded to be worn on the ribbon of the campaign medal for the theatre of war where it was won. Maurice shares with us his memories of the occasion:

Mentioned in Dispatches

I think it was given for a number of tough actions that we were involved in as we made our way up Italy. There was stubborn German resistance and strong defences and we would be stopping, starting and getting held up all over the place. There was one action in particular that springs to mind and it was soon after that I was mentioned in dispatches. We were near the city of Perugia in 1944 when our troop came under attack and the leading armoured car took a direct hit from a German anti-tank gun which killed my corporal, and wounded me in the face. As the troop sergeant in charge I managed to get the troop safely to some buildings nearby where we could return fire and engage the enemy until reinforcements arrived, after which the Germans were 'persuaded to move on!'

Maurice finished by having this to say about his wartime experiences and time in the Army: 'I would do it all again if I had the chance, I loved every minute of it. I was lucky that I got through the war alive and to have survived all those things, unlike so many other poor sods that didn't. It's a queer old world, some make it and some very sadly don't.'

Additional Information and Life After Service

- ❖ **Rank at end of service:** Warrant officer first class – regimental sergeant major (WO1)
- ❖ **Medals and honours:** 1939–45 Star, 1939–45 Defence Medal, 1939–45 War Medal with oak leaf clasp for MID, Africa Star with Eighth Army Clasp, Italy Star, General Service Medal Palestine 1945–48, Long Service and Good Conduct Medal.
- ❖ **Post-war years:** 1973–86, worked at the Manchester Transport Training Group in the administration and finance office; 1986–88, worked in its HGV licensing admin office. Married to Sheila for sixty years and has four children, ten grandchildren, ten great-grandchildren.
- ❖ **Associations and organisations:** Member of the Royal British Legion, Middleton Branch; President of the Royal Tank Regiment Association, Manchester Branch.

Corporal Sucha Singh Grewal

Served with: 5th Indian Division, Royal Indian Army Service Corps
Service number: 208627
Interviewed: Nottingham, Nottinghamshire, 28 February 2015

Service History and Personal Stories

- ❖ **Born:** 14 December 1921, Kotegrewal, Gelunda, Punjab, India.
- ❖ Sucha served in the Royal Indian Army Service Corps as part of the British Army and in the Indian Army for nineteen years in supply and logistics.
- ❖ He fought in fierce battles in the jungles of Java, Sumatra and Burma.
- ❖ Mentioned in dispatches and honoured for his bravery in Burma.
- ❖ After the war, served throughout India during the turbulent period of the partition of the subcontinent.
- ❖ Stationed on the Indian–Pakistani border region of Kashmir a number of times and involved in many actions in the volatile mountain area.
- ❖ Later in 1959 came to England and started a new and very successful life.

Sucha's amazing story is one that starts from very humble beginnings in the small village of Kotegrewal in Punjab. After joining the Royal Indian Army Service Corps as part of the British Army at the age of 16, in 1940 he would be taken on a remarkable journey starting with the 5th Indian Division to the jungles of Burma, Java and Sumatra via Singapore, from where he was evacuated and narrowly avoided capture during the Japanese invasion in 1942. While involved in the Burma Campaign, Sucha was mentioned in dispatches for his bravery during intense jungle engagements against the Japanese, where he won the oak leaf clasp. Having lived through the diversity and adversity of war in 1940–44 he returned to India and was stationed in many places at a time of great change and upheaval during partition. Sucha continued to serve in India from 1944–59 and after it gained independence in 1947 he continued his service in the newly formed Indian Army, where he spent a lot of time stationed in the border region of Kashmir. Here he experienced much more action as the newly shaped and divided subcontinent came to terms with these major changes and contested the new borders.

We return now to the jungle battlefields of Burma for an overview of a very hard-fought and bloody campaign that took place in extremely unforgiving conditions against a very capable enemy who were experts in jungle warfare, in a theatre of war many out there called the 'Forgotten War'.

Burma – The Longest British and Commonwealth Land Campaign of the Second World War – 1941–45

The Burma Campaign in South-east Asia was a very complex and interesting theatre of war for many reasons. The difficulties of the terrain with its very limited infrastructure, which meant the movement and supply of troops and evacuation of the wounded was made extremely challenging, put the emphasis on military engineering and air supply to counter these immense logistical problems. Also the severe monsoons meant that effective campaigning could only realistically and effectively take place for just over half of the year, and tropical diseases seriously affected both sides. Additionally, within the Pacific theatre of war, this front was not the priority for the Allied forces, which after the defeat of Germany focused on island hopping towards Japan. This affected decisions in the use and allocation of vital equipment and manpower.

All these factors, combined with facing a determined, resourceful, tenacious and brutal enemy skilled in the art of jungle combat, led to hard drawn-out battles, which led to the longest continual British and Commonwealth land campaign of the war. Although it was known as the Burma Campaign it was fought in and over the borders of a few countries including Thailand, India and China. The campaign also had a fascinating and very varied array of forces pitted against each other. On the Allied side the British Empire forces consisted of troops from British India, British Burma, and East and West Africa. In addition to this the United States and

Republic of China fought against the Axis side, which consisted of the Empire of Japan, State of Burma (BIA–Burma Independence Army), Thailand and the Indian Nationalist forces (Azad Hind).

This conflict started with the initial Japanese attacks in December 1941 and finished with Allied victory in August 1945. The years in between were marked with fierce offensives and battles up and down the country that can be divided into four phases. First, there was the Japanese invasion, which led to the expulsion of the British, Indian and Chinese forces in 1942. Second, the failed and costly attempts by the Allies to mount offensives into Burma, from late 1942 to early 1944. Third, the Japanese invasion of India from early to late 1944, which ultimately failed after the battles of Imphal and Koima. Fourth, the very successful offensive by the Allies that reclaimed Burma from late 1944 until mid-1945.

Among all this, as part of the 5th Indian Division, was Sucha Singh Grewal, who recalls:

The Ferocious Nature of Jungle Warfare in Burma

We had a very bad time in thick, thick jungle, and one period that I will never forget we were without enough food and supplies for 29 days. Aeroplanes tried to drop water and other things but they got caught in the trees and you could not reach them to take them most of the time. The Japanese army, they were used to the jungle. Our army was not. Many times we could not see them until they attacked. They would shoot at us and attack close up and using their bayonets a lot, and most days the Japanese fighter planes would come and shoot and bomb us. Also, they would use the mortar, which was dangerous in the jungle because they had a 4in mortar and we had only a 3in mortar so they would be causing more destruction. All of these things happening daily made Burma the most and the worst fighting I experienced while I was in the British Army. Also, some Japanese spoke Hindi and tried to win us over by saying: 'We do not want to kill you, only kill the British', trying to make us come over to them! On top of this there was rain from above and the leeches from below, mosquitoes and terrible heat all around and the constant terror of jungle warfare, which was very challenging in every way, mentally, physically and emotionally, very hard and with casualties in all those different ways. It was very stressful for all the soldiers involved but we were strong in all those ways too; we had to be or we simply wouldn't have survived it. I did, so I can now share these things with you so that the efforts of the Indians and all others will not be forgotten.

It was while in Burma in the thick of this vicious close combat that Sucha was involved in actions in which he performed very bravely, and later his courage was honoured by being mentioned in dispatches for gallantry. Sucha tells us how it happened:

A Sikh soldier manning a Bren light machine gun on an anti-aircraft mounting in 1941 during the Desert Campaign in North Africa.

It was for my part in defending a bomb and ammunition storage that was being attacked by the Japanese. They surrounded us and were coming from everywhere, we managed to hold off the attackers until more ammunition and help could be sent to us from our headquarters. Very hard fighting, close combat, very nasty! And also I think for continuous actions whilst in the mountains keeping the supply lines open. It was during this time that I was also injured in the right thigh with shrapnel.

Sucha summed up his feelings about his time in Burma and in the war in general when he concluded by saying: 'They were very difficult times, I was very lucky to come back, I am very, very lucky still. Of the seventy-three of my original platoon who were sent out only six of us came back!'

Indian Servicemen's Contribution to the British and Commonwealth Forces

The contribution of all servicemen and women from what was then the British Empire, who came from countries all over the world and volunteered, risked their lives and in many cases died, should be acknowledged and remembered. The greatest number came from the Indian subcontinent and were a mixture of Sikhs,

Hindus and Muslims. From the First World War until the partition of India in 1947, approximately 2.5 million Indians served in the British and Commonwealth forces and approximately 112,000 died in action.

Additional Information and Life After Service

- ❖ **Rank at end of service:** Corporal or naik in the Indian Army.
- ❖ **Medals and honours:** 1939–45 Star, 1939–45 Defence Medal, 1939–45 War Medal, Burma Star with oak leaf clasp for MID, Indian Army Service Medal, George VI India Service Medal with Second World War Ribbon.
- ❖ **Post-war years:** In 1959 he retired from the Army and came to Nottingham to start a new life. From 1960 Sucha worked as a bus driver and as a conductor for Nottingham City Transport for twenty-six years, retiring in 1986. Working anything from sixty to seventy hours every week, he would support his family and, blessed with a good business head, he would then cleverly buy a house each year with hard-earned extra money as a property investment, eventually building a sizable property empire. He was married to his late wife, Resham Kaur, for sixty-five years. They have four children, nine grandchildren and six great-grandchildren.
- ❖ **Associations and organisations:** Not a member.

Sergeant Norman Prior

Served with: 1/5th Battalion Lancashire Fusiliers & 3rd The King's Own
   Hussars
Service number: 3451806
Interviewed: Manchester, Lancashire, 13 January 2016

Service History and Personal Stories

❖ **Born:** 25 February 1919, Wigan, Lancashire, England, UK.

❖ Worked at Bryn Hall Colliery, Wigan, as a fitter on the surface and underground of
   the coal mine from the age of 14 from 1933 until aged 20 in 1939.

❖ Joined the Lancashire Fusiliers in 1939 and in 1940 ended up with the British
   Expeditionary Force on the beaches of Dunkirk.

❖ In 1940–43 Norman was part of the UK coastal defence forces with the 108th Royal
   Armoured Corps at various places around Britain, including 'Hellfire Corner' in Dover.

❖ In 1943 he trained in Algeria, North Africa, then was sent to Italy where he joined
   and fought with The King's Own Hussars in 1943–45.

❖ From 1945–46 he went with the Hussars to Lebanon, Syria and Palestine where he
   was involved in policing actions during various uprisings.

I had been searching the country to find a Dunkirk veteran for the book when by chance I was reading the *Manchester Evening News* one day and lo and behold there was a big article on Norman Prior of Manchester. All this time I had been looking and unbeknown to me there he was right under my nose, only twenty minutes from where I lived! And so with the assistance of the *Manchester Evening News*, which has helped greatly with tracing a few veterans in the last couple of years, I was put in touch with this fabulous Lancashire Fusilier who is one of the few who holds the French Legion d'Honneur for being a veteran of Dunkirk.

In 1933, aged 14, Norman followed in the footsteps of his father and brothers and began work at Bryn Hall Colliery in Wigan as a fitter. He would service and fix the coal-cutting machines and conveyor belts on the surface or below ground when and where required. Work at the mine was hard and dangerous, as Norman found out when he was partially buried after a shot-firer shouted a belated warning and some explosive charges went off close to where he was working. He later recalled that it was experiences such as these that helped prepare him for what was to come in his service life during the Second World War, living with constant danger, explosions and casualties. These were things that were to become commonplace for Norman in the years ahead, especially on the beaches of Dunkirk in 1940 and elsewhere later on.

Norman's service career began on 16 October 1939 when, at the age of 20, he volunteered for the Lancashire Fusiliers. He underwent eight weeks' basic training at the LF Barracks in Bury, Lancashire, followed by a further six weeks at Lowercroft Mill near Bury, and then on to Rhyl in north Wales to train as a truck driver. After that he was sent down to Newbury Barracks in Berkshire to specialise as a gunner in Bren Carriers. By this time he was already in the 1st Regiment, 5th Battalion of the Lancashire Fusiliers, who were earmarked to go to France as part of the British Expeditionary Force (BEF) under General Viscount Gort, tasked to reinforce the French and Belgians against potential German aggression. Norman left England on 14 March 1940 and would soon find himself in the thick of it when the Germans began their invasion of Western Europe on 10 May. Not long after the invasion the Lancashire Fusiliers would find themselves fighting continuous rearguard and stalling actions against an overpowering enemy all the way from the Belgian border until their backs were against the sea at Dunkirk. From there Norman, along with the remnants of his Bren Carrier platoon and other Fusiliers, plus the soldiers of many other units, would be evacuated from an area in the northern part of the evacuation beaches at a place called the Bray Dunes.

This evacuation, code-named Operation Dynamo, would soon go down in history as one of the most daring actions of the war, where every conceivable marine vessel afloat was called into action to help save what was left of a shattered army that was once the BEF. The operation took place from 26 May until 4 June, and originally the British assumed they would rescue around 50,000 troops. However, in the end due to the bravery and persistence of those involved they managed to save approximately 340,000 British, French and Belgian troops in order that the British Army could, as it was said at the time, 'live to fight another day'. This was something Norman would certainly do; after his escape from the deluge and destruction of Dunkirk he returned to England, where for the next 2½ years from mid-1940 to early 1943 he would be moved around, first as part of the Lancashire Fusiliers and after 1941 as part of the 108th Royal Armoured Corps, to various coastal areas of England as part of the coastal defence forces that were mobilised in readiness for any potential German invasion. This included time down in Dover, Kent, in the notorious 'Hellfire Corner', so called because of the very intense and constant Luftwaffe bombings on the ports in those areas.

Once the threat of invasion had passed and Norman had completed various motor mechanic courses and transferred over to and trained on many types of tanks, in May 1943 he went to Algeria in North Africa. There he undertook further mechanised training on the new American Sherman tanks, following which he was sent to Italy and became part of 3rd The King's Royal Hussars. He then fought his way up Italy as a tank driver-gunner in many vicious tank battles from Monte Cassino to Florence and beyond with the Eighth Army. Then in February 1945 he was transferred with the Hussars to serve in Beirut, Lebanon, and in Homs and Damascus in Syria as part of the forces involved in internal security helping to put down civil unrest and uprisings. Later, under the command of the 6th Airborne Division, he carried out policing duties in Jerusalem and Tel Aviv in Palestine. In all those countries he was involved in heavy fighting against various underground and guerrilla factions. After all that incredible and varied service, Norman returned on a long journey back to England via Egypt, Malta, and France and was demobbed in Aldershot in May 1946.

Norman's service took him from the beaches of Dunkirk to the mountains of Italy and to the troubled capitals of the Middle East. When I interviewed Norman, I asked him to tell me more about the reality of Dunkirk, so now we return to focus on his unique experiences:

Evacuation From the War-Torn Beaches of Dunkirk

All the time the beach was under attack from German Artillery, bombers and fighter planes, there were men everywhere, equipment everywhere and there was so much of it going on that it was much the same all the time. The planes were coming over to bomb and machine gun; you would scatter and as soon as they were gone you would get back to doing whatever you were doing. And as attacks come in some are killed, some are wounded, and sometimes it was one or two, three or four, sometimes it was many more but you just sort of accept it as being part of the operation you know.

I asked Norman whether, as the Germans were getting closer, there was more of a feeling of desperation, and how he felt:

Thousands of men – remnants of the British Expeditionary Force – wait to be rescued from the beaches at Dunkirk.

I never had a feeling other than that I would get off safely in spite of everything that was going on, and that's what happened, eventually, on a minesweeper called HMS *Halcyon* on 31 May. I felt in my own mind a sense that I was going to be alright, and that's how I went all through the war and I used to say my prayers, of course, which I still do and I thank God that I got through it all right. I wasn't terrified, I sort of took it in my stride and thought we've got to do our best to do whatever has to be done, and that was the attitude I took. And there again, having worked in the pit we used to have explosives in the pits and people got killed you know and injured and so on, so you were almost battle hardened before you got in the Army.

The success of Operation Dynamo and the events that took place during the evacuations at Dunkirk led the new Prime Minister, Winston Churchill, to write one of his most rousing speeches, known as 'We shall fight on the beaches'. This was both a war cry and a speech to rally the nation during the dark days of 1940, the memorable main body of the speech being:

We shall go on to the end, we shall fight in France, we shall fight on the seas and oceans, we shall fight with growing confidence and growing strength in the air, we shall defend our island, whatever the cost may be, we shall fight on the beaches, we shall fight on the landing grounds, we shall fight in the fields and in the streets, we shall fight in the hills; we shall never surrender!

That is exactly what Norman did: he fought on and never surrendered, and has always carried with him what is known as 'the Dunkirk spirit'.

That spirit was shown again in the form of remembrance when on 10 May 2017 I was honoured and moved that 97-year-old Norman, one of the last veterans of Dunkirk, sent me an e-mail seventy-seven years to the day since the Germans began their Blitzkrieg in the West, which led to the famous evacuation of which he was a part. It read:

> Gary, 10th May 1940. The day the Germans started their offensive. Memories. Such a lot has happened since then, but those of us still around remember, I wonder how many are left? 26 days later and the evacuation started. Thanks to the efforts of all concerned, especially the Royal Navy, without them it could not have been achieved. I hope you are well Gary and busy with your write-ups. All is well here.

As Norman continued to honour the memory of his comrades so will I through having him in my book so that the story can continue to be told and the sacrifices will hopefully never be forgotten.

Additional Information and Life After Service

- ❖ **Rank at end of service:** Sergeant.
- ❖ **Medals and honours:** 1939–45 Star, 1939–45 Defence Medal, 1939–45 War Medal, Italy Star, General Service Medal Palestine 1945–48, Dover Hellfire Corner Commemorative Medal (Dover Municipality), Dunkirk Medal (Town of Dunkirk, France), King Albert Federation Medal (Belgium), Legion d'Honneur (French Government).
- ❖ **Post-war years:** Engineer and later senior manager at Hunt and Mosscrop Ltd, Middleton, Manchester. Thirty-eight years' service, which included the installing and commissioning of textile and paper finishing machines all over the world from 1946 until his retirement in 1984. Married to Elizabeth for sixty-nine years from 1942–2012, has one son, one daughter, two grandchildren, four great-grandchildren.
- ❖ **Associations and organisations:** Former secretary and president of the Manchester and District branch of the Dunkirk Veterans Association (1971–2005); Lancashire Fusiliers Association, which he joined on Minden Day, 1 August 1946, after returning from active service; Queen's Own Hussars Association (1946–2018).

Staff Sergeant Norbert Barrett

Served with: Royal Pioneer Corps and Royal Electrical and Mechanical Engineers
Service number: 16001311
Interviewed: Manchester, Lancashire, 24 June 2015

Service History and Personal Stories

- ❖ **Born:** 7 November 1921, Hockenheim, Germany.
- ❖ Grew up in Hockenheim, Germany, where he experienced the Nazis rise to power and persecution of his Jewish family and community.
- ❖ After six years of persecution, in 1933–39, he escaped to Great Britain in May 1939 as a refugee of Nazi oppression.
- ❖ Put into internment camps both in Great Britain and later in Australia as a potential threat to national security along with thousands of others of German and Austrian descent.
- ❖ After being cleared by the British Government, returned to the UK where he volunteered and served in the British Army in the Pioneer Corps and later in the 2 W/S Coy unit of the REME.

❖ He saw service in the United Kingdom and Egypt, then later settled in the UK after learning about the sad fate of most of his family in the Holocaust.

Horace Norbert Barrett was born Horst Norbert Baumgarten in November 1921 in the town of Hockenheim in the district of Baden in the Upper Rhine Valley, Germany, and it is here the remarkable story of this resilient and extraordinary gentleman begins. Norbert, as he became known, witnessed and experienced hard times at the hands of the Nazis, as he was from a Jewish family and lived in a Jewish community, making him and his people prime targets of anti-Semitic persecution. He lived through key moments of the Nazi rule in 1930s Germany, from Hitler coming to power in 1933 to the implementing and enacting of the Anti-Jewish Nuremberg Laws of 1935. He experienced the devastation of the 'Kristallnacht' (the Night of Broken Glass) in 1938, when Jewish businesses and synagogues were burned and Jewish citizens attacked, imprisoned, killed or in some cases simply disappeared. These included members of his own family, such as his father and brother who were interned in Dachau concentration camp for some time.

They were living through terrible times and it was very obvious to Norbert's family that the situation was only going to get worse, so he sought a way out of Germany as two of his sisters had successfully done some time before. His break came when he obtained a trade apprenticeship to continue his training as an engineer in Liverpool in May 1939. This was extremely lucky, as few Jewish citizens were being allowed out of Germany that late on and with war looming and with so many countries having turned their backs on Jewish refugees. So this really was almost like the last chance to escape to freedom, something the rest of his large family was not lucky enough to do and this sadly led to their fate being a very different one.

However, Norbert's troubles were far from over, as in 1940 the British Government reacted to the Nazi conquests of Norway, Holland, Belgium, Luxembourg and France by incarcerating thousands of people of German, Austrian and Italian descent in internment camps. This came as a great shock for someone who had already endured and then escaped from six years of the Nazi regime and who had entered the UK with the official status of 'Refugee of Nazi Aggression' stamped on his passport. He was first sent to a camp near Hyton in Liverpool and later shipped out with approximately 2,500 others to 'holding and internment' camps near Sydney, Australia, while the British Government determined whether or not they were a threat to national security.

This took more than twelve months and after they were deemed to be safe a British Army officer was sent to offer them the opportunity to return to the UK with full UK citizenship as long as they helped the war effort in some way. This Norbert did, and after returning to the UK in November 1941 he volunteered for the British Army and was enlisted into the Pioneer Corps (later Royal Pioneer Corps in recognition of its wartime contribution). He served with the Corps until April 1943 in various places in England and Wales doing storekeeping and finally in Scotland building huts and barracks. It was while there that he heard that other units were requesting tradesmen and he took the opportunity to apply for a transfer to the Royal Electrical and Mechanical Engineers (REME), for which he was accepted as he was a trained engineer. Along with Norbert's transfer came a new service number and he was asked to choose a new name so that if he were posted overseas and captured, his true identity, religion and nationality would be hidden from the enemy. This was when Private 13807029 Horst Norbert Baumgarten became Private 16001311 Horace Norbert Barrett.

For the next three and a half years Norbert served in the REME, first at Donnington Army depot in Shropshire until late 1945, doing all things mechanical from the servicing of artillery pieces to the overhaul of engines on all types of military vehicles. He was then posted to an Army base at El-Kabr near Ismailia in Egypt until late 1946, eventually becoming a staff sergeant. Norbert was demobbed in December 1946 in Aldershot but was kept on the Royal Army Reserve list for a further six years until 1952. In 1947, with the help of the British Red Cross, Norbert finally found out the heartbreaking news that all his remaining family in Germany had been liquidated in Auschwitz, and so feeling there was nothing to return home for he decided to make a new life for himself in Manchester, where one of his two remaining sisters lived. This he went on to do, having a family of his own and the much more peaceful life that he deserved in a country he had served for five years in active duty and six years as a reservist.

During my interviews with Norbert I asked him to tell me more about what he saw and experienced under the Nazi rule in Germany in the years running up to the war, as it was such a rare thing to speak to someone who saw the rise of Hitler and Nazi Germany and who later went on to serve in the war. He obligingly shared his memories:

Being Jewish in Nazi Germany in the 1930s

Jewish people suffered so much at the hands of the Nazis all over Germany and later the world, as did many other peoples. Even in our town of Hockenheim our situation was continually getting worse and I remember things such as the Nazis bringing in new laws against the Jews. We couldn't do this job, we couldn't do that job and Jewish shops were being taken over by those who were Nazis or simply destroyed by them. People began shouting abuses against Jews in the street, and even those non-Jews who associated with the Jewish, for example in shops, were themselves thrown out of the shops! As things got worse people even shot themselves; we witnessed the funerals of two of them. Jewish cemeteries were ruined, the stones broken, and during the Kristallnacht

A member of the SA (*Sturmabteilung* or Assault Division), also known as the Brownshirts, who helped to enforce anti-Jewish laws.

the Nazis set fire to our Synagogue. I looked out the window and saw the fire blazing like hell. I went out to look and I was told Horst, Horst go back they will kill you, because the Nazis, the Stormtroopers, were all full of alcohol and put petrol into houses and anything that set fire and poured it all over the place, and they broke into other houses and smashed things to smithereens. They damaged everything. This included people too, men, women, children, none were spared!

The Nazis were getting stronger all the time and we weaker and more helpless. They wanted to ruin anything and everything that was Jewish. Eventually my father and brother were arrested and spent a bad time in Dachau but returned home to us. Later, as I found out, my family and relations were not so lucky and it all ended for them in Auschwitz. Remember what history teaches: those who start by burning books finish by burning people. I was very lucky, God must have been good to me.

Having shared his pre-war memories of what he witnessed in Nazi Germany, we agreed that it was a frightening lesson from history that should never be forgotten.

We then went on to talk about his interesting circumstances, and the motivations and feelings that led to him to become a part of the British Army itself:

A German in the British Army in the Second World War

We saw the evil of Nazi Germany from the early days and it got worse and worse all the time, and what are you going to do, how are you going to fight them back? You can't, and if you stood up they would kill you there and then on the doorstep, and the way we were treated and the bad times we had to go through, we were complete enemies towards our own *volk* because we were not Germans any more, we were Jews. And how can you fight back unless you are a part of a big organisation that takes you in as one of theirs.

I asked if Norbert was contributing in his own way to help fight against the evil of Nazi Germany by joining our army. 'Exactly!' he replied. 'I became a German citizen in the British armed forces against Nazi Germany.' To conclude, from a man who stood up and did something came this reminder: 'The only thing necessary for the triumph of evil is that good men do nothing.'

Additional Information and Life After Service

- ❖ **Rank at end of service:** Staff sergeant.
- ❖ **Medals and honours:** 1939–45 Defence Medal, 1939–45 War Medal.
- ❖ **Post-war years:** From 1947 until 1958 Norbert worked at a measure metre and tyre metre company in Leicester Road, Manchester, making precise measuring equipment for the motor and engineering trade, then finally had his own business wholesaling clothes until the 1980s, when he retired. He was married to Hildergard from 1946 until 1983 and they have one daughter, four grandchildren and three great-grandchildren.
- ❖ **Associations and organisations:** Former chairman of the Association of Jewish Ex-Servicemen and Women (AJEX) and the Association of Jewish Refugees (AJR).

Lance Corporal Albert Cunningham

Served with: 2nd Canadian Road Construction Company, Royal
     Canadian Engineers
Service number: B134355
Interviewed: Normandy, Surrey, 11 February 2016

Service History and Personal Stories

❖ **Born:** 4 April 1923, Welland, Ontario, Canada.

❖ Volunteered for service in 1942 and as part of the 2nd Canadian Chemical Warfare Unit he undertook specialist chemical warfare training in late 1942–43.

❖ Later he trained in Aldershot in the UK in 1944, transferred to the 2nd Canadian Road Construction Company and became skilled in various engineer-related tasks such as bridge and runway building.

❖ Landed in Normandy on D+28 (twenty-eight days after D-Day) with heavy construction equipment and was involved in the rebuilding of roads around Caen and later on to projects in Neerpelt, Belgium, and Nijmegen, Netherlands.

❖ After the war, Al stayed on another year to serve as company medical orderly for the 2/6 Field Company Canadian Engineers as part of BAOR in Leer, Germany, until mid-1946, and later was discharged in Toronto.

❖ Al has continued to keep the memory of the Canadian contribution in the Second World War alive through his tireless work with the Canadian Veterans Association UK, of which, at time of interview, he was still the president, aged 93.

More than 1 million Canadian servicemen and women came forward to contribute to the Allied war effort as part of the Commonwealth forces under British command during the war. Of these some 20,000 stayed on in the United Kingdom to make new lives for themselves after the war, and of those fewer than 100 remained in 2016 when I interviewed one of the last of them, Albert Cunningham, national president and secretary of the Canadian Veterans Association UK. This former sapper of the Royal Canadian Engineers is also a Normandy veteran who interestingly has resided in the small and aptly named village of Normandy in Surrey for some years now. This is the story of a veteran who, like others in this book, left his country and came far from home to serve alongside our forces and help the Allied cause, another testament to those who stood by us.

Al, as he likes to be known, was born in Welland, Ontario, near Niagara Falls. He volunteered for service shortly after his eighteenth birthday in April 1942 and was sent to the Horse Palace in Toronto to be processed and kitted out. For his basic training he was then sent to Port Arthur, near the city of Fort William, later known as Thunder Bay, in the most northern part of the Great Lakes in Ontario. More advanced and specialist training followed when Al was affiliated to the 2nd Canadian Chemical Warfare Unit and sent to Suffield in Alberta, out on the Canadian prairies, where they were instructed in the use of poison gases with a view to calling them up to reform these specialist units if those kind of weapons were ever used. As Al was primarily a sapper he was also taught other engineer-related skills, including the use of munitions, bridge building and how to drive various vehicles from light to HGV. All the training in Canada took place in late 1942 to late 1943 and once completed he was sent on to Halifax, Nova Scotia, to await transport to the United Kingdom for the next phase. Others were dispersed to various other engineer units and sent directly into active service in the Italian Campaign. Al and other engineers arrived in Liverpool in the winter of 1943 and were then sent down to Aldershot, where they were billeted and formed into the 2nd Canadian Road Construction Company. They then went into further engineer-related training under British Army instruction in preparation for the intended invasion of Europe. Here they were schooled in many other engineer skills such as road and airfield repair, breaching obstacles and further bridge construction.

Then came the big deployment and time for active service in the war zones of Western Europe. On 4 July 1944, D+28, Al landed at Juno Beach in Normandy, France, as part of the 2nd Canadian Road Construction Company, with the 2nd Canadian Infantry Division, which joined the 2nd Canadian Corps as part of the British Second Army. They were allocated different construction projects as, when and where needed along the general route of the Allied advance as they moved up through France, Belgium and Holland between 1944 and 1945. This included the construction of a completely new road around Caen to aid the movement of military traffic after the city and its infrastructure were almost completely bombed out by the Allies, and later on road, runway and bridge projects in various places including Neerpelt, Belgium, and in the devastating aftermath of Operation Market Garden in Nijmegen, which is where the war finished for Al on 7 May 1945 and where he also served as company medical orderly for the 2nd Canadian Road Construction Company.

After the war Al and many other Canadian servicemen were given three choices regarding their next service move: they could either go back to Canada and get discharged, return to Canada and volunteer to continue on to the war in the Far East or continue in service as part of the forces of occupation in Germany for a year. Al chose to stay on for another year and serve in Leer, Germany, as he had just got engaged to his sweetheart, Averill. He became part of BAOR until mid-1946, where he continued his previous job as company medical orderly, this time for the 2/6 Field Company Canadian Engineers. When his service was finished he returned to Canada via England, and his discharge in Toronto meant he had come full circle in his military service. After spending a couple of months with family in Welland, Ontario, he returned to the UK to get married and to begin a new life.

The Canadian contribution during the war was a massive one in many ways, and here we look at its involvement in more detail. Canada entered the war on 10 September 1939 and it was engaged in many theatres and many operations from there on, starting early when it sent contingents that were meant to supplement the British Expeditionary Force in France but instead ended up helping with the defence of the British Isles. On the other side of the globe a small force of Canadians arrived in Hong Kong and fought alongside the British, Indian and Hong Kong forces against the Japanese until the surrender of the colony on Christmas Day 1941. Later, on 19 August 1942, the Canadian 2nd Division made up the bulk of the forces engaged in Operation Jubilee, the ill-fated raid on Dieppe, and suffered huge casualties as a result. Of the 5,000 who took part, nearly 1,000 lost their lives and a further 2,000 were taken prisoner.

Between 10 July and 6 August 1943 the Canadians were involved in the invasion of Sicily, in which the 1st Canadian Division and the 1st Canadian Army Tank Brigade took part. The Canadians were involved in the invasion of Italy from the

The Canadian recruitment poster 'Let's Go Canada!' that successfully encouraged many to flock to the colours and serve the Allied cause.

start on 3 September 1943 until its final engagements in February 1945. During the Italian Campaign, Canadian forces reached a peak strength of 76,000 combatants making up the 1st Canadian Corps. They were involved in many battles such as the Gulf of Taranto, Naples, Monte Cassino, the Liri Valley and the Hitler Line, the Foglia River and the Gothic Line, to name but a few. The next big involvement was in Western Europe with the landings in Normandy on D-Day on 6 June 1944 at Juno Beach made by the 3rd Canadian Infantry Division, part of what was later to become the bigger 2nd Canadian Corps. They fought with distinction in battles throughout Normandy at Caen, at the French seaports of the Pas-de-Calais and on through to Belgium and on to Holland via the Scheldt Estuary. Later on the Canadian First Army fought through the Reichswald Forest and across the Rhine into Germany.

At sea, the Royal Canadian Navy (RCN) contributed more than 100,000 personnel and 400 vessels, and it was involved in convoy escorts in the Atlantic and Mediterranean and the Arctic convoys to Russia. The Navy also hunted submarines and supported the landings in Sicily, Italy and Normandy. The contribution of the Royal Canadian Air Force (RCAF) was also a considerable one. During the war it enlisted 232,000 men and 17,000 women, and operated eighty-six squadrons, of which forty-eight were overseas in both Fighter and Bomber Commands. Its airmen also fought in the Battle of Britain, North Africa, Italy and the Normandy invasion and over Belgium, Holland and Germany. Also, Canada ran a massive programme to train British and Commonwealth aircrew known as the British Commonwealth Air Training Plan (BCATP), which turned out 3,000 trained aircrew a month.

The last words go to Albert Cunningham:

His Experiences as a Canadian Serviceman

I tried to join the Air Force because the girls liked the blue uniform better than the Khaki but when I told them I was a travelling salesman they didn't want to know and said you better go down the road and join the Army, so that was the end of that! Our training consisted of all sorts of things, munitions, road building, explosives, maintenance and several types of army bridges. The best was the Bailey Bridge and you just put it together like a jigsaw puzzle and pushed it across the river. Once we were in active service in Europe we worked behind our lines doing what we had to do. We were not fighting soldiers, but we saw a few things, in Caen total destruction when we came to build the roads, and in Nijmegen there were still bodies lying around when we entered the town. Years later I still feel keeping the spirit of remembrance alive is so important. Our guys came a long way to help during the war and many didn't return, so don't forget the Canadians.

Additional Information and Life After Service

* **Rank at end of service:** Lance corporal.
* **Medals and honours:** 1939–45 War Medal, 1939–45 Star, France–Germany Star.
* **Post-war years:** After returning to England Albert married Averill in September 1946. They lived in Cornwall and later moved to Normandy, Surrey, where they have lived for more than fifty years. Al worked in the early days for Warnes painting, decorating and building company. Later he owned a similar company of his own called A.J. Cunningham and Sons Ltd until his retirement in 1983. Albert and Averill have two sons, one daughter, and one grandchild.
* **Associations and Organisations:** National president and secretary of the Canadian Veterans Association UK and was chairman of Normandy Parish Council for twenty-five years.

Lieutenant Colonel John Humphreys OBE

Served with: Royal Engineers, 1st Airborne Division and SAS
Service number: 1877368
Interviewed: Royal Hospital Chelsea, London, 30 June 2015

Service History and Personal Stories

- ❖ **Born:** 14 January 1922, Gillingham, England, UK.
- ❖ John Humphreys gave an astounding forty-one years of army service for his country from 1936 until 1977. He was in the Royal Engineers, later airborne as a para-sapper and a commanding officer in the Special Air Service.
- ❖ Fought in North Africa and captured at Tobruk in 1942, later escaped from an Italian prisoner of war camp in Italy in 1943. Returned to England, retrained as a para-sapper in 1st Para Squadron RE.

❖ Dropped into Arnhem in Operation Market Garden as part of Colonel Frost's
    2nd Parachute Battalion, 1st Airborne Division, in September 1944. Captured at
    'the bridge too far' by the SS and escaped for the second time.

❖ Later went on to serve as an officer in the Special Air Service (SAS) in special
    operations in Cold War Europe and Northern Ireland. Won two oak leaf clasps for
    bravery and awarded a military OBE.

❖ Now very fittingly resides at the Royal Hospital Chelsea as a Chelsea pensioner.

There are few soldiers who have the military experience and the sheer number of
service years as John Humphreys; in fact it would be easy to write a complete book
just on his extraordinary exploits alone. So it was a great honour to interview John,
who is now one of the famous Chelsea pensioners, and to do so at the prestigious
Royal Hospital Chelsea in London. His story is that of another truly lifelong
soldier, one who gave more than four decades of his life in service to his country
and along the way was involved in some remarkable actions and escapes. Most of
these things he can and has spoken to me about and are shared here, but there are
still parts of his service that could not be divulged such as his time as a commanding
officer in the SAS, which is still strictly confidential under the Official Secrets Act.
Here is the rest of John's astounding story, which I think you will agree still makes
for some fascinating reading.

John's military life began at the age of fourteen when he enlisted as a boy
soldier in Changi, Singapore, in April 1936. This was a natural choice for him as
he came from a military family and was living out in Singapore because his father,
George, was stationed there with the Royal Engineers. He was then sent to the
Army Technical College in Chepstow, England, which he attended in 1936–39,
and he then joined the Royal Engineers. In 1940, aged 18 and with the war under
way, John was sent to North Africa as part of the 6th Field Company of the Royal
Engineers. He was involved in many actions and battles up and down the North
African coastline until his final capture in the Battle of Tobruk in June 1942. After
recovering from his injuries in a hospital in Benghazi in Libya he was then sent
to a prisoner of war camp near Ancona in Italy, and in October 1943, after nine
months in captivity, he and two others managed to escape. Dressed as civilians,
they walked from Ancona to Bari, approximately 288 miles, avoiding the enemy
until they finally reached the Bari area and linked up with Allied troops. John was
sent via Algiers back to the UK, after which a completely new phase in his career
would begin.

John joined a Royal Engineers Training Battalion at Clitheroe and then
volunteered for parachute duty. After training at Ringway, Manchester, John had
the combined skills of a para-sapper or airborne Royal Engineer. He was then
drafted into the 1st Parachute Squadron, Royal Engineers, B Troop, and for his
next mission, Operation Market Garden, this unit was part of the 2nd Parachute

Battalion under the leadership of Lieutenant Colonel John Frost, which overall was part of the 1st Airborne Division. It was tasked with taking the three bridges at Arnhem, the main road bridge in the town centre, a railway bridge out to the west on the lower Rhine, and a pontoon bridge that was discovered to have been dismantled on the eve of the operation. Below is an overview of that ill-fated mission.

Operation Market Garden – the Plan and the Outcome

The aim of Operation Market Garden under Field Marshal Bernard Montgomery was to capture the eight bridges that spanned the network of canals and rivers on the Dutch–German border, using as mentioned above the British 1st Airborne Division around Arnhem. In addition, the American 101st and 82nd Airborne Divisions were to capture strategically important bridges in other areas around Eindhoven, Sint-Oedenrode, Son, Grave and Nijmegen. These vital bridges spanned rivers such as the Rivers Aa and Maas and canals such as the Willems and Wilhelmina, which had to be secured and held by the airborne forces, who were the ('Market') part of the operation, until the land forces of the British XXX Corps could link up with and relieve them; this was the ('Garden') part of the operation. The greater aim was then to push on and become part of a much bigger offensive that potentially could have consisted of the British Second Army on its northern flank and the American First Army on its southern. This force, after having broken through the German defences, could later link up and push forward together. These Allied armies would then be able to advance much quicker and more directly into the German fatherland and eventually on to Berlin. They would hopefully achieve this by Christmas and essentially before the Russians got there, with the overall aim of shortening the war with a more favourable outcome for the Allies.

A very ambitious plan indeed, and one that sadly did not even succeed past its first goal of securing the bridges at and around Arnhem. A number of factors such as bad weather, insufficient equipment, hasty planning that ignored intelligence reports about German SS Panzer divisions in the area, and the loss of mechanised equipment during the early part of the operation, all combined to make it an ill-fated mission with very heavy casualties for the airborne troops; approximately 1,500 were killed and 6,500 missing or captured. In the end, the operation lasted from 17 to 25 September 1944 and resulted in a German victory that slowed up the Allies' advance considerably and hindered their overall plans to significantly shorten the war.

At the time of compiling this book there were few Arnhem veterans left. Even rarer was the chance to interview one who was in the thick of it at the main bridge in Arnhem itself. As such, it was incredible to hear recollections from a man who was involved:

The Arnhem Bridge, later renamed the Frost Bridge, as it is today.

In Action at the Legendary 'Bridge Too Far'

I parachuted into Arnhem from a Dakota on Sunday, 17 September and I was in B Troop who supported the 2nd Battalion Parachute Regiment that was commanded by Lt Colonel Frost. So we made our way to the bridge and as sappers took the explosives off the bridge, and after that we were told to make the school, this rather large building, ready for defence because Divisional HQ would come in and occupy it. So half my troop left to do it, the other half were missing somewhere. We made the school ready for defence. It dominated the north end of the bridge; nothing could come off the bridge or on the bridge without us letting them. That was Sunday evening. We fought from there until Wednesday the 20th, at times we shot them up like fish in a barrel, inflicting some heavy casualties, but by Wednesday afternoon there were only a few of us left, we had no ammunition and the school was on fire. We had to get out and I ended up looking up the barrel of an SP Gun, with the orders to come out or be blown out. We were fighting two SS Panzer divisions and the Germans kept attacking, again and again. The situation was impossible. We fought very difficult engagements and were taking ever increasing casualties. In the end there was nothing more we could do, it seemed that this was one battle that we hadn't won, and so I had become a prisoner of war once more.

John as a lieutenant colonel while in the SAS, 1969–72.

John escaped from his German captors at Emmerich after forty-eight hours, stole a boat and rowed down the Rhine to Nijmegen, where he joined the Allied forces once again. After the casualties of Arnhem the 1st Parachute Squadron was re-formed and sent to Norway near the end of the war to clear minefields, take explosives off the hydro-electrical plants and to help with other aspects of the German surrender. Then, in Oslo, he was transferred to the 9th Parachute Squadron ready for Japan.

After the war John's career continued to be so extensive that it has been summarised in the following way: 1945–48 – 9th Squadron, 5th Brigade, Ordnance search, Palestine. 1948–51 – 298 Field Company, Royal Engineers, WO2 permanent squadron instructor at Birkenhead. 1951–53 – 5th Field Squadron, 23rd Engineer Regiment, BAOR in Dortmund. 1953–56 – 24th Field Engineer Regiment, Head Quarters Land Forces (HQLF), Hong Kong. 1956–57 – 56th Squadron, WO2 on 9th Recruit Training, Aldershot. 1957–61 – 108th Welch Field Regiment, WO1 in Swansea. 1961–63 – WO1 at Junior Leaders Regiment, Dover. 1963 – Commissioned as lieutenant quartermaster, 131st Parachute Engineer Regiment. 1963–66 – 131st Parachute Engineer Regiment, Akrotiri in Cyprus, Radfan and Khormaksar in Aden, Yemen, for the Aden Emergency. 1966–69 – 9th Parachute Squadron, Nairobi in Kenya, Tobruk in Libya, Omagh in Northern Ireland. 1969–72 – 21st SAS Regiment, joined as a captain and left as a lieutenant colonel, served in Cold War Europe and Northern Ireland. No further operational information available regarding this part of his service, 1972–77 – 23rd Combat

Engineer Regiment, again as part of BAOR in Osnabruck, Germany. Retired on 14 January 1977 after forty-one years' loyal service.

To conclude, I feel it is true to say that John Humphreys' life as a career soldier can be summed up in the words of the SAS unit in which he was a commanding officer: 'Who dares wins'.

Additional Information and Life After Service

❖ **Rank at end of service:** Lieutenant colonel.
❖ **Medals and honours:** Military OBE, 1939–45 Defence Medal, 1939–45 War Medal with oak leaf clasp, 1939–45 Star, Africa Star with oak leaf clasp, France–Germany Star, General Service Medal with Palestine Clasp, Long Service and Good Conduct Medal, Commander of the Order of St John.
❖ **Post-war years:** 1977–86 Head of Local Government County Planning Emergency Office (CEPO) for West Glamorgan, in charge of nuclear contingency planning and regional emergency planning. Head of St John's Ambulance Brigade, West Glamorgan, all twenty-one divisions, voluntary role and position. Retired from civilian life in 1986. Married to Brenda for sixty-nine years; they have two daughters, two grandchildren and four great-grandchildren. Became a resident at the Royal Hospital Chelsea in 2013.
❖ **Associations and organisations:** Royal Engineers Association, Airborne Engineers Association, President of the Parachute and Airborne Association (Swansea).

Captain the Reverend Edward L. Phillips

Served with: Padre, Royal Army Chaplains' Department, 1st Airborne Division

Service number: 163854

Interviewed: Bristol, Somerset, 10 October 2015

Service History and Personal Stories

❖ **Born:** 6 July 1912, Bangalore, India.

❖ Volunteered for service as a padre in the Royal Army Chaplains' Department and received an emergency commission and the rank of captain in January 1941.

❖ Also volunteered for the airborne forces and trained as a paratrooper, and as an unarmed serviceman put himself in real danger in order to perform his duties and help his fellow servicemen in the front line of battle.

❖ Bill's active duty postings were with the 1st Airborne Division, firstly as padre to the 10th Parachute Battalion for Operation Slapstick in Taranto during the allied invasion of Italy in September 1943.

❖   A year later he served as padre to the 3rd Parachute Battalion in Operation Market Garden in September 1944 and was captured at Arnhem. He became a POW at Oflag 79 at Braunschweig until repatriated in April 1945.

❖   While serving as a Church of England vicar for thirty-two years in the UK, Bill was on the reserve list and later in the Territorial Army from 1946–67 before retiring in 1978.

There are many varied branches of the armed forces, some of which are represented in this book. I was very interested to find a different kind of veteran that is seldom written about in relation to the war and that is the military padre. I really wanted to have this spiritual angle represented here as it really is something so different. It fascinated me because the padres were ordained clergymen who volunteered to go as unarmed servicemen into the frontlines and battle zones of every theatre of war. There they performed their very special duties and administered spiritual help and comfort to servicemen and women during their most distressed times, and for many their last moments of life. This they did at great personal risk to themselves, driven and motivated to serve in a very different way by the strength attained by the belief in their faith; here in these most extreme circumstances they truly were putting faith into action.

They did not have to go as they were, and still are, given a rare exemption protected by British law that states words to the effect that no person of the cloth has to serve in the armed forces or in an active combat zone unless they by their personal choice volunteer to do so. Many did, and paid the ultimate price. They went to war equipped only with their standard chaplaincy kit consisting of a Bible, a copy of the Army prayer book, a small portable communion kit and some shell dressings. They were a shoulder to cry on, a confidant, someone to pray with and much more for those who wanted or needed such help. There is no doubt, though, that the comfort they brought to the brave young servicemen and women, especially those horrifically injured or passing out of this life, by their kind words, prayers, blessings, the tending of wounds, being a hand to hold and just being there at those critical moments is almost beyond words. They were a great consolation to the people they helped and also to their families, some of whom later found out that their loved ones were assisted while in great pain or had someone with them at the end, which is such an important thing.

One of those selfless individuals was the Reverend Edward Leigh Phillips, who was the last surviving padre of the war and an incredible 103 years old when I found and interviewed him in Bristol in October 2015.

Edward Phillips was born in Bangalore, India, on 6 July 1912. The son of Congregational mnisters, he returned to England aged 6. In his early years he was educated at Eltham College in Mottingham, London, where, among other things, he became an accomplished rugby player. After this he went on to Oxford University and the Church of England Wycliffe Hall theological college. After graduation and ministry training, and with the war raging, Bill felt moved to do his bit for his country in his own way and joined the Royal Army Chaplains' Department in January 1941. Upon doing so he was granted an emergency commission and the rank of captain. He volunteered for airborne forces and was trained at RAF Ringway, Manchester.

Captain the Reverend Edward Phillips, as he had now become, took up his first post as padre to the 10th Parachute Battalion in May 1943. He went into frontline active service on 9 September 1943 during the Allied invasion of Italy as part of the forces involved in Operation Slapstick, which landed at the heel of Italy with the main objective to capture the ports of Taranto and Brindisi. This they achieved and went on to advance a further 125 miles north to Foggia, then in late September they were withdrawn after two infantry divisions landed behind them to reinforce then take over from them. The 10th Parachute Battalion came under the command of the 4th Parachute Brigade, which overall was a part of the 1st Airborne Division. Bill remained with 10 Para after its return to the UK in November and, after further training in preparation for D-Day, he received a new posting.

However, Bill's next active service saw him being dropped into Arnhem on 17 September 1944 as padre to the 3rd Parachute Battalion, again as part of the 1st Airborne Division, in the ill-fated Operation Market Garden. Landing in Drop

Paratroopers being dropped during Operation Market Garden.

Zone X, 3 Para encountered very stiff German resistance from the beginning but by the evening had made it to the outskirts of Oosterbeek. While there, Rev. Phillips visited the wounded at the J.P. Heijestichting school. The next day they continued through Oosterbeek and got within 2km of the bridge at Arnhem and reached the environs of St Elisabeth Hospital, where the resistance increased significantly. Later they moved on to a house on the Utrechtseweg with Major General Urquhart and Brigadier Lathbury until the fighting became much fiercer and eventually German armour and troops drew closer. Rev. Phillips and Captain J. Rutherford, the battalion doctor, ended up retreating under heavy fire back to the hospital, and it was there whilst tending both British and German wounded that the hospital fell into German hands. So on 19 September Rev. Bill Phillips became a POW and ended up as prisoner No. 558 in Oflag 79 at Braunschweig in northern Germany. He remained there until his repatriation in April 1945, after which he returned to the UK and eventually finished his full-time service on 22 July 1946. Bill was placed on the Army Reserves List in July 1946 and later, while undertaking his regular civilian duties as a Church of England clergyman, he continued to serve as part of the Territorial Army and later Territorial Army Reserve of Officers until July 1967, by which time he had reached the upper age limit of 55. We now look more at the very interesting Royal Army Chaplains' Department.

During my interview with Reverend Phillips, some very special moments were shared, first because I received a blessing and was privileged to share a prayer with the last surviving British padre of Arnhem and the Second World War, and second because I heard a varied mix of memories from Bill, such as those described below:

To Be a Serving Padre During the Second World War

On the run-up to and at the beginning of the war I was pacifist, but as time went on and we saw what was happening with the Nazis I changed my mind. It was a long and arduous process but in the end I knew I had to do something so I volunteered for service. Balancing spiritual belief with the need to serve your country in a time of national crisis – not easy. Much later on, just before the Arnhem operation, I was talking to an officer from the brigade, a major, and he said that Brigade had been told by the GPO that the whole of the Arnhem operation had been heard over the public phone and didn't they think they ought to call it off! A huge compromise to the security of it all, not good! Once we were on the ground the Germans were very quick to react and to move their tanks and armoured guns against us.

Later on, as things got worse, Bill recalls:

As I discovered to my own amazement the following day, the signal system of the whole division just did not work! No one knew what was going on, the General, the Brigadier, nobody. We knew that the object was the bridge but we didn't get there, we ended up at the Elizabeth Hospital. There were a lot of wounded, British and German, who we talked to and tried to help. Later I saw a German on the door with a rifle and someone asked, 'Are you in the bag too Sir', then I realised that the hospital had been taken by the Germans, the war was over for us. We were marched off in a very shame-making way with our hands up on our head, passing through the square with a lot of our dead on the ground, very depressing. At that time as a POW you felt like the lowest form of life, like a complete failure.

To finish Bill tells us a little about life in a German POW Camp as prisoner No.558:

We were transported in cattle trucks and eventually ended up at Braunschweig, some of the prisoners had been there for years. We ended up staying for seven months or so, food was short but Red Cross parcels did get through at first. Things got worse when these stopped, there was even Allied bombing, some of which hit the camp, but thank God we survived it all and lived to tell the tale.

During the course of the war ninety-eight British and thirty-eight Commonwealth Army chaplains lost their lives. In remembrance of all the clergy who served is this, The Airborne Forces Collect:

May the defence of the Most High be above and beneath, around us and within us, in our going out and in our coming in, in our rising up and in our going down through all our days and all our nights, until the dawn when the Son of Righteousness shall arise with healing in his wings for the people of the world, through Jesus Christ, our Lord. Amen.

Additional Information and Life After Service

- ❖ **Rank at end of service:** Captain.
- ❖ **Medals and honours:** 1939–45 Defence Medal, 1939–45 War Medal, 1939–45 Star, Italy Star.
- ❖ **Post-war years:** Rev. Phillips served as a vicar for thirty-two years, at Ide Hill, 1946–49; Moulsecomb, 1949–52; Kingston, 1952–65; Lewes, 1965–75, and Kingston and Rodmell, 1975–78. During that time Bill's service to his country continued in the Territorial Army in 1946–67. He retired in 1978. Married to Nancy for fifty-six years, five Children, nine grandchildren, and four great-grandchildren.
- ❖ **Associations and organisations:** None.

Quartermaster Sergeant Jack P. King

Served with: 31st Battery, 7th Regiment, Coastal Artillery, Royal Artillery
Service number: 872096
Interviewed: Eastbourne, East Sussex, 2 September 2016

Service History and Personal Stories

❖ **Born:** 27 February 1922, Eastbourne, England, UK.

❖ Jack P. King was a twenty-five-year career soldier of the Royal Artillery. He joined as a boy soldier in 1937, serving extensively in the UK and overseas, and finished as a regimental quartermaster sergeant in 1962.

❖ He was serving in Singapore during the Japanese invasion in February 1942 and received serious shrapnel injuries from a mortar attack in the last hour of fighting, after which he was taken prisoner.

❖ For the next three and a half years Jack would be used as slave labour by the Japanese, and from October 1942 until September 1945 he would work on the 'Death Railway' and river bridges, made famous in *The Bridge on the River Kwai*.

❖ It was here at the hands of his ruthless and sadistic Japanese captors that he would personally experience and also witness unimaginable and dreadful suffering.

❖ Remarkably, after this he continued to serve in the British Army for another seventeen years, in the UK, in Hong Kong and as part of BAOR.

Some stories need to be told in order that the suffering and hardships endured and the terrible things experienced and witnessed are never forgotten or just consigned to history. One such story is that of Jack P. King, who while in the service of his country was taken prisoner on 15 February 1942 in what is considered one of the greatest defeats in the history of the British Army, the fall of Singapore. Jack was one of approximately 80,000 British and Commonwealth prisoners taken and later one of the unlucky prisoners of war put to work as slave labour on the 258-mile 'Death Railway' that stretched up through Thailand and into Burma. It was here that Jack and around 275,000 fellow prisoners went through hell and back at the hands of their cruel and heartless Japanese captors whilst building the railway line and its associated river bridges. This very significant piece of Jack's story is what we will be mainly focusing on but it is part of a much bigger twenty-five-year service history, all of which we will now look at in more detail. It is a story of great personal strength, courage and fortitude, harrowing in parts, but one that must be told in memory of all those who were victims of this brutality, those who returned, and for the 94,000 who never returned and still lie in the soil of a foreign country.

Jack joined the Army as a boy soldier at the age of 15 on 21 September 1937 as part of the Royal Artillery. Upon taking the oath and the King's Shilling, he was told by a captain: 'From now on until twelve years' time your souls are no longer your own.' This comment would prove to be largely fufilled in a very chilling way later on. Jack went on to be trained at the Grand Depot, Royal Artillery in Woolwich, London, as part of the 2nd Boys Battery RA, where he also trained as a trumpeter.

In 1939 he was posted to Singapore, where he learned the Malayan language. He remained in service until the war reached him in the most dramatic way with the Japanese invasion of Singapore on 8 February 1942. The invasion was no great surprise as the Japanese had been advancing down the Malay Peninsula since December 1941. As the battle for the capital port city of Singapore raged, Jack was seriously injured by two large pieces of shrapnel during a mortar attack within the last hour of hostilities on 15 February 1942, after which Lieutenant General Arthur Percival accepted the terms of surrender for all the British and Commonwealth forces on the island. This brought about what Churchill described as 'the worst disaster and largest capitulation in British military history'. After this the POWs were contained in holding camps in Changi while their fate was being decided by the Japanese victors. The fate awaiting Jack after time recovering from his injuries would be a very bad one.

From October 1942 until September 1945 Jack would become a slave labourer working on the aptly named 'Death Railway', which was being built from Ban Pong near Bangkok in southern Thailand up to Thanbyuzayat in Burma. During that time, ruthless treatment of POWs of many nationalities and enslaved civilian workers from South-east Asia took place at the hands of the brutal Japanese. They

One of the 'Bridges over the River Khwae', aka River Kwai, that inspired the well-known film.

wanted to build a rail link as a supply route for their forces engaged in campaigns in Burma and those planned for India. This line would mean cutting through dense jungle and sheer rock, and to build as many bridges as required, including one to get over the formidable obstacle of the Khwae Yai River, and they did not care how many lives of their expendable prisoners it would take to do it.

Jack shared with me many of the different tortuous things that he had to endure. Some of the memories were obviously still so painful even after seventy years that in parts of the interview there was silence, and for moments he was back there again amidst the horror of it all. I was deeply moved by what I heard:

A Slave Labourer Building the Death Railway

It is very hard to describe the true pain of it all, you can only truly know it if you have been through it. Every single day we were all made to suffer in so many, many ways, mentally, physically, emotionally and physiologically. We were seen as inferior and weak because we had surrendered and for this we were treated as the lowest form of life you can imagine because the Japanese had the warrior's code of honour called the Bushido. The Samurai use it in their teachings, and for them to become a prisoner of war was the ultimate dishonour and betrayal of their Emperor, better to die than suffer dishonour. This guided their actions in the Second World War but in a very wrong way. The torment came from everywhere, from the cruel and merciless Japanese and the constant uncertainty of life or death that hung over us all every minute of every day, to the regular vicious outbursts

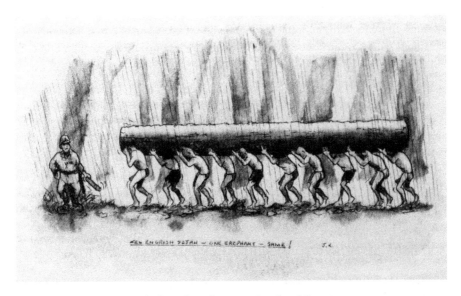

A painting by Jack depicting the bare-footed tree carrying slave labourers.

of violence that were commonplace, prisoners beaten with heavy bamboo sticks until the guards were too exhausted to carry on and also from the other enemy, the natural elements. We had to work in months of constant torrential monsoons; there were biting sand flies that would attack your whole body; rats infested our camps running over us as we slept and they brought diseases, as did the mosquitoes. During my time there I had malaria, dysentery, pellagra and hepatitis. In most cases you still had to work and you were beaten if too slow or if you did not understand a command. Some were beaten to death and if you were put on burial duty, as most of us were at one time or another, you could be burying comrades or your friends. If you got jungle ulcers this would lead to amputations, or if the infection spread it would be a death sentence.

I listened in complete dismay at what Jack had been through, and he went on to tell me:

We had to carry the back-breaking weight of the felled trees that were used to construct the bridges, and we built many over the River Khwae, and until you got or could make shoes of any kind you would be in bare feet on stony or rough jungle ground that would tear your feet to pieces until the skin grew that thick that you couldn't feel the pain as much. There were many times of real utter despair. The conditions were appalling. Men looked and moved like zombies, men drained of hope, men in the last stages of sickness, men who died and were buried naked in pathetic graveyards beside the railroad. This happened in all the camps along the Khwae. Some that I remember were Wampo, Tarsoa, Tamarkan, Hindok and Kanburi, where Allied air strikes blew up the bridge and killed POWs as well. There was one dead comrade for every sleeper of that accursed railway. Monsoons would wash unfelt over their graves, and mosquitoes would sing unheard above their heads, but their memory would live on, and I would always remember them as they were when young, with bright faces and hope in their hearts. Yet throughout this nightmare that you thought would never end I had never doubted that we would win. In the darkest times I never lost the conviction that we would end up victorious, and we did. I came through the hell that was the Death Railway but many, many others did not. The scars on my body healed, but those to my mind never will.

Additional Information and Life After Service

- ❖ **Rank at end of service:** Quartermaster sergeant major.
- ❖ **Medals and honours:** 1939–45 Defence Medal, 1939–45 War Medal, 1939–45 Star, Pacific Star, Long Service Good Conduct Medal (LSGC).
- ❖ **Post-war years:** After repatriation and a short leave Jack continued to serve his country with another seventeen years in the Army, finally reaching the NCO rank of quartermaster sergeant major. His post-war service from 1946 took him around the UK; he manned heavy guns on the Thames Estuary and was an instructor at a school for anti-aircraft artillery in South Wales. He was also posted out to Hong Kong and did his final five years of service in West Germany as part of BAOR before finally retiring from the Army in 1962. Jack found the transition into civilian life very hard as his life had been the Army since the age of 15. He returned to his native Eastbourne and had many jobs but could not settle and so emigrated with his family to Australia. There he worked for the North Queensland Regional Electricity Board as a design clerk and librarian in 1970–79. After returning to the UK once again he worked as an office manager for a cabinet-making company and as a company secretary for a transport firm until 1982. His war years returned to plague him once again when the last piece of shrapnel had to be removed and his seventh hip replacement left him on an Army invalid pension at the age of 57. Jack was married to Audrey from 1946 until 2010, and they have three sons, eight grandchildren and one great-grandchild. Jack has also had a prolific creative output over the last sixty years, having written and had published twenty-five books, including his autobiography about his wartime experiences called *A Magic Shadow Show*. He is a painter and has also written around 100 pieces of poetry, composed thirty pieces of music and scripted a pantomime – truly amazing achievements from a truly amazing man. To finish, I asked Jack his opinion about two films, *The Railway Man* – he said very factual – and *The Bridge on the River Kwai* – not so factual.
- ❖ **Associations and organisations:** No affiliations.

Captain Dalbir Limbu

Served with: British and Indian Armies, 4th Battalion 7th Gurkha Rifles
Service number: 471414
Interviewed: Ashford, Kent, 12 February 2016

Service History and Personal Stories

- ❖ **Born:** 17 December 1922, Haangum, Panchthar, Nepal.
- ❖ Dalbir Limbu served for twenty-six years in the 7th Gurkha Rifles, first as part of the Indian Army under British control before Indian independence and later directly in the British Army after independence.
- ❖ During the war he served from 1944 until 1945 training and instructing Nepalese troops to become the well-respected and feared Gurkhas at a camp in Palampur in north-west India.

❖ After the war he served in many conflicts in regions such as the Pakistan–Afghanistan border, the Indian–Burmese border, the Malayan Emergency in Borneo, Brunei and later at the Hong Kong–China border.

❖ He retired as a captain in 1969 and returned to Nepal. In 2012 he moved to the UK after the famous Joanna Lumley and Peter Carroll 'Gurkha Justice Campaign' won full pension and citizenship rights for ex-servicemen.

The 7th (Duke of Edinburgh's Own) Gurkha Rifles started as a rifle regiment of the Indian Army (under British colonial control), comprising Gurkha soldiers of Nepalese origin, before being transferred to the British Army following India's independence in 1947. During the six years of the war more than 137,000 Gurkhas directly served the British Crown, of which 23,000 were either killed, wounded or were missing in action. In early 2016 with the kind help of Peter Carroll, who was the driving force behind the Gurkha Justice Campaign, I was able to locate and get permission to interview Dalbir Limbu, thought to be one of only two Second World War Gurkha veterans in the United Kingdom at that time. The interview was truly unique, held in Ashford, Kent, with serving and retired Gurkhas of the British Army in attendance who were all part of the 'Gurkha Peace Foundation'. They acted as translators for Dalbir, whose generation of serving Gurkhas spoke little or no English, and they also advised and gave interesting information regarding various aspects of Gurkha military and culturally related matters; a great and very different kind of interview experience for me. This allowed me to piece together an incredible story of a man who for twenty-six years risked his life in the service of a country he had never even seen.

Dalbir's long service history began when he enlisted in the Indian Army in December 1943 in Darbhanga, Northern India. He was then sent to do his rigorous Gurkha training in Palampur, north-west India, where his instructors saw real potential in him. As a result of this he was eventually posted there as an instructor to teach all the various aspects of basic military training to the new recruits who were aspiring to become one of the much-respected and fierce-fighting Gurkhas. This included weapons training, hand-to-hand combat and constant drilling to make a good strong and well-disciplined soldier. Due to their Nepalese tradition they received extra training in the use of the Kukri, the traditional long, curved knife, which would sometimes be drawn in a charge and used in close-quarter combat, putting fear into an enemy and giving the Gurkhas their well-earned reputation as fierce and brave fighters.

This would be where Dalbir would see out all his war service until he finished in June 1945. During his time as an instructor he would turn out many fine soldiers that would be a part of the Gurkha regiments within the British Army and who would stand side-by-side with our troops as they fought bravely together throughout bloody battles and campaigns in Europe and Asia.

Gurkha veterans marching at the Cenotaph in London on Remembrance Day.

To understand the long and loyal service that the Gurkhas have given over the years we now look at the very proud history, association and affiliation they have with the British Army. From 1814 to 1816 a state of war existed between the British rulers in India and the city state of Gorkha in what is now western Nepal. The centre of this state was the village of Gorkha, the place from which the Gurkha takes his name. After two long and bloody campaigns of this Anglo-Nepalese war, a peace treaty was signed in Sugauli in 1816. During the course of these fierce battles a deep feeling of mutual admiration had developed between both sides and the British were very impressed by the fighting skills and other qualities of the Gurkha soldier. So much so that under the terms of the peace treaty large numbers of Gurkhas were permitted to volunteer for service in the British-run East India Company's army. They carried on volunteering later in the Indian Army of the British Colonial times through to the regiments of the Gurkha Brigade in the modern British Army of today. The Gurkhas are valued and respected as a great asset to our Army, proving to be the bravest and staunchest of allies, and Nepal is seen as the United Kingdom's oldest ally in Asia. They have been with us through all major conflicts from the Anglo-Nepalese war onwards, including: 1857–59, Indian Mutiny; 1900, Boxer Rebellion; 1914–18, First World War; 1939–45, Second World War; 1948–60, Malayan Emergency; 1962–66, Borneo Conflict; 1982, Falklands War; 1990s–2000s, Kosovo, Bosnia, East Timor, Sierra Leone; 2001–14, Afghanistan; 2003–11 Iraq.

After the Second World War Dalbir would serve and be actively engaged in many areas of conflict himself. This started immediately when his next posting took him with the Indian Army in 1945–46 to the very unsettled Northwest Frontier border region between what is modern day Pakistan and Afghanistan. Here he would be embroiled in fighting against the Patans. After this he was sent in 1946–48 as part of a peacekeeping force to help police in another sensitive area, this time on the Indian–Burmese border where tensions were high around the start of the Burmese Civil War. On 1 January 1948 Dalbir officially transferred from the Indian Army to the British Army. Next came the Malayan Emergency in Borneo, where he was deployed and fought as part of the British Army against communist rebels in serious jungle warfare. He was deployed there for eleven years from 1948 until 1959. Malaya gained independence in 1957 and became Malaysia in 1963. Then it was on to Hong Kong from 1959 to 1962 on policing duties before being put back into the thick of the action in Borneo again, this time when the Brunei emergency broke out. He was there between 1962 and 1965, and from their base in Sarawak the Gurkhas conducted long-range operations into dense jungle against Indonesian forces. Dalbir's final posting was back to Hong Kong from 1965 to 1969, where he was engaged in policing duties at the border town of Sha Tau Kok. This was during a time of high tensions in the Cold War period, which led to occasional clashes with communist forces around this Chinese border point. By this time Dalbir had reached the rank of captain and after twenty-six years' loyal service to the British Crown he retired and returned to a very different rural life in Nepal.

During the interview I asked Dalbir many questions about his life as a Gurkha and how it was to serve through so many conflicts from the Second World War onwards. He told me:

A Gurkha Serving in the Indian and British Armies

I did my basic training and more specialist training in jungle warfare both in India, and as Gurkhas it is the hard training and our energy and sheer determination that gives us that extra edge in the battlefield. Our loyalty to the British Crown is total, from the time we take the Oath of Allegiance we always completely stand by it

The famous Gurkha weapon, the kukri.

and you could say this is another strength that helps us in serving in the best way possible. As an instructor of troops during the Second World War I would teach them all the skills possible to equip them for the kind of terrain they would be fighting in. That would be from jungle to mountain terrain, everything and more! For any Gurkha in the battlefield, and I was in a few, it is a do or die mentality for every task you undertake, every battle you are in, to fight hard and stand by your comrade Gurkha or British and to the end if need be, and to proudly stand up for what you believe and in our case the countries we served.

The Gurkha is a soldier of high battle-skill, a world-famed fighting man and respected in every country where men fought alongside us in the last war.

Lieutenant General Sir Francis Tuker, While Memory Serves

It seems very fitting to end in praise for the generations of brave Nepalese Gurkhas who have served our country of which Dalbir Limbu is one, so I finish with true words of admiration from a British veteran I had previously interviewed who had gone into battle with them in Italy:

When you went into battle you were as safe as you could possibly be on a battlefield if you had the Gurkhas next to you, they were some of the best fighters I have ever seen, and I have seen many. They were loyal as friends and fierce, brave and unwavering as soldiers when engaged in combat, the best men you could possibly wish to have around you, and very luckily on your side!

Additional Information and Life After Service

❖ **Rank at end of service:** Captain.
❖ **Medals and honours:** 1939–45 War Medal, Good Service Medal with Malaya Clasp, Good Service Medal 1962 with Borneo Clasp, Malaya Peninsula Medal, Long Service and Good Conduct Medal.
❖ **Post-war years:** After finishing his service in 1969 Dalbir returned to Nepal and went back to his village of Haangum in the Panchthar district and to his family, his home and his land, where he went back to working in agriculture. In 2012 he and his wife, both in their nineties, chose to come and live in England once full pension and citizenship rights were granted by the government ruling of 21 May 2009 as a result of the famous 'Gurkha Justice Campaign'. He married Bishnukumar in 1943, they have been together seventy-two years and have ten children, thirteen grandchildren and thirteen great-grandchildren.
❖ **Associations and organisations:** Gurkha Peace Foundation.

Sergeant Cyril Tasker

Served with: 716 Company RASC, 9th Battalion, 6th Airborne Division
Service number: T/10696981
Interviewed: Lewes, East Sussex, 31 August 2016

Service History and Personal Stories

❖ **Born:** 25 April 1923, East Hoathley, England, UK.

❖ Cyril joined the Royal Army Service Corps (RASC) in April 1942 and after training as a driver he was posted to Northern Ireland, where he delivered supplies to many Army bases.

❖ In 1943 he returned to the UK, where he joined the 6th Airborne Division. He was trained in Horsa gliders for D-Day and dropped at Ranville.

❖ His unit, the 716 Company RASC, supplied forward units at Pegasus Bridge, the Merville battery and on throughout France, Belgium, Holland and eventually into Germany.

❖ As part of the 9th Battalion, 6th Airborne Division, in 1944–46 he was also involved at the Battle of the Bulge in the Ardennes, the link-up of Allied and Russian troops on the Baltic coast, and he later served in Gaza, Palestine.

❖ Cyril was chosen to escort Field Marshal Montgomery and Major General Gale to take soldiers' ashes to Ranville cemetery on 6 June 1954 for the tenth anniversary of D-Day.

Every man and woman who was involved in the war in any way whatsoever has a story to tell which is as unique and different as they are themselves. For each individual we get a very personal account of their own experiences, which helps capture many aspects of this global conflict. None more so than those in the services that were engaged in front-line action, where life and death situations were a daily occurrence. The story of Cyril Tasker is another great example of that, a serviceman who was involved in some of the most well-known events of the latter part of the war. He was at the heart of the action from the moment he landed in Normandy in his Horsa glider as part of the airborne assault on D-Day through to his involvement in the Battle of the Bulge in the Ardennes, to being present at the link-up of Allied and Russian troops on Germany's Baltic coast.

Cyril was driving and delivering supplies of one kind or another locally since he was 16 years old when he worked for the Allen West factory in Brighton that produced various commodities for the Army. Then, at 17 he was delivering goods to Army camps and depots all over the country. So it was no great surprise that he carried on with what he was already very good at and had a fair bit of experience in: logistics. He joined the Royal Army Service Corps (RASC) on 16 April 1942 aged 19 and was sent to Bulford Training Camp near Salisbury for his basic training, then to Hadrian's Camp near Carlisle for Army driver training. Then from September 1942 until September 1943 he was posted to Northern Ireland, where he delivered essential supplies to Army bases in Belfast, Antrim, County Londonderry and County Down.

The mythological emblem of the Second World War British Airborne Forces, Bellerophon riding the flying horse Pegasus.

When Cyril returned to Salisbury with his unit, the 716 Company RASC, the Allied preparations for D-Day were in full swing and he volunteered to become part of the airborne forces and joined the 6th Airborne Division. This choice would take him in a whole new direction and on a journey that would lead him to experience things he could never have imagined at that point. Cyril tried both parachute and glider training and chose to become part of an airborne glider troop, after which his training intensified in the months running up to D-Day.

On 6 June 1944 Cyril and his company were dropped around mid-afternoon into Ranville as part of the 19,000-strong force that would descend from the skies over Normandy in support of operations from the sea. He landed in a Horsa glider with two jeeps and two trailers loaded with petrol and supplies, and four men for each jeep. They were now attached to the 9th Battalion of the 6th Airborne Division, and once they had landed their remit was to try to keep the 9th and any other units they were ordered to help supplied at all costs in the areas where they were actively engaged, and wherever that front line was or moved to as they advanced. They were to continue supplying with the materials dropped from aircraft or brought up later after the beaches and ports were secured. This they successfully did from when they linked up with Major Howard and fellow 6th Airborne troops at Pegasus Bridge, through to getting essential materials to the 9th Battalion at the Merville gun battery. For three months they were based around the Pegasus Bridge area, where they had to make and guard their storage dumps and then deliver what was needed, wherever it was needed at the front line. Despite coming under close-range fire and being exposed to frequent shelling from the Germans during their supply runs, they stuck to their remit.

By mid-September 1944 the 9th Battalion had been sent home via the Mulberry Harbour at Arromanches to regroup after hard months in the line. Then on Christmas Eve 1944 the men got the immediate order to mobilise once again. There was a major emergency as the Germans had launched a massive offensive in the Ardennes and they were being sent to re-join the 6th Airborne to reinforce the line. By Boxing Day they were in Belgium and working to help supply the defensive line between Dinant and Namur. They also worked closely with the American First Army to supply beleaguered troops when and wherever needed during what was to become known as the Battle of the Bulge. In extreme winter conditions and under constant enemy fire they played their part in turning the tide and eventually thwarting the German offensive.

Once the panic was over, by mid-January 1945, the 9th Battalion, 6th Airborne, continued on into Holland, and in March 1945 was involved in Operation Varsity, the airborne operation over the Rhine. The 9th Battalion, of which Cyril's 716 company was a part, then continued through Germany, ending up in Wismar on the Baltic Sea where they historically joined up with Russian forces in May 1945. After the war in Europe was over, Cyril's service continued when he was again sent overseas as part of the 6th Airborne Division to the Middle East to help police the troubles in Palestine. Based in a big Army camp in Gaza, his unit experienced attacks from insurgents who, as Cyril recalls, would during some attacks randomly spray the Army tents with machine gun fire. Cyril was based there from September 1945 until December 1946, after which he returned home to Widdingdean near Brighton. He was eventually demobbed in May 1947 at the Kiwi Barracks, Bulford Camp, Salisbury, home of the 9th Parachute Battalion. However, Cyril's story does

Cyril with Montgomery and Gale, 6 June 1954, in Normandy.

not end there because ten years later, through his work with the Royal British Legion in Brighton, he was selected to accompany Field Marshal Montgomery and Major General Gale for the tenth anniversary commemorative service at Ranville cemetery on 6 June 1954. He carried soldiers' ashes at this very important event, which for him was also held at a place of great personal significance where a decade earlier to the day he had landed to play his part in the liberation of Europe.

During his time as a serviceman in the UK, Europe and the Middle East, Cyril experienced many things and has many stories, some of which he now shares with us:

Serving with the 6th Airborne Division in the Liberation of Europe

When we were driving into Ranville we came across General Gale. He said to me: 'You're lost, soldier.' I said: 'Yes, sir,' and whilst we were talking he suddenly pushed me into a ditch! A second later he was on top of me and behind us was a huge explosion, and when we got out he said: 'You haven't been in action before have you soldier?' I said: 'No, sir,' and he said: 'That was a mortar bomb that just landed where we were standing!' And so a general had saved my life that very morning. Ten years later when I went to Normandy with General Gale and Field Marshal Montgomery he remembered me and said: 'I had wondered if you survived the war, glad you did.' A lot of the time whilst in Normandy we were getting shelled and mortared and machine gunned, and the Germans used air burst shells that exploded over our heads. Many of our men died because of those. At Christmas when we were called to the Ardennes it was a very rough time, horrendous, severe cold, the German attacks were still strong, a huge loss of life, mainly American but we were taking some heavy casualties, too. It was all a huge shock from an enemy that we thought was nearly finished at that stage of the war, and even though we were the RASC we had Sten guns and found ourselves having to use them when we came across Germans. After the Battle of the Bulge we went up and through Holland over the Rhine and into Germany. Eventually we ended up in Wismar on the German Baltic coast, where we linked up with the Russians a few days before the war finished. When it was over we were dancing in the streets with the Russians. Throughout, we did our job and kept the supplies flowing from Normandy to the Baltic. We were a small part of a much bigger picture, each one of us proudly doing our bit to help win that long and hard-fought war, which we eventually did in the end.

Additional Information and Life After Service

* **Rank at end of service:** Sergeant.
* **Medals and honours:** Legion d'Honneur (French Government), 1939–45 Defence Medal, 1939–45 War Medal, 1939–45 Star, France–Germany Star, General Service Medal Palestine 1945–48.
* **Post-war years:** After the war Cyril returned to the Allen West factory in Brighton from 1947–67, then had one year as a farmhand in Billingshurst. In 1968 he returned to transport and worked for Sussex County Council at its Ringmar depot until his retirement in 1988. He married Jean in June 1947 and they have two children, five grandchildren and five great-grandchildren.
* **Associations and organisations:** Royal British Legion Lewes and Brighton, Blind Veterans UK.

Lance Corporal Vernon Parry

Served with: Royal Engineers, 188, 197 & 993 Transportation Stores
Companies
Service number: 14342411
Interviewed: Prestatyn, Wales, 14 September 2016

Service History and Personal Stories

❖ **Born:** 19 June 1924, Sarn Holywell, Wales, UK.

❖ Vernon joined the Royal Engineers in November 1942, did basic training at Heath camp in Cardiff, then his Royal Engineer training at Llandaff in Cardiff, and specialist railway training at Longmoor in Portsmouth as part of 188 Coy.

❖ Arrived in Normandy on D+17 on 23 June 1944 at the Mulberry Harbour at Arromanches. He was posted to the 197 Transportation Stores Company, Royal Engineers, carrying out important reconstruction work and logistics.

❖ From June 1944 until July 1945 he worked restoring the docks at Caen in France, on railway repairs at Halle in Belgium, Eindhoven in Holland, Osnabruck and Munster in Germany, and later on restoring the docks at Hamburg.

❖ From September 1945 until May 1947 Vernon was posted to various places in Italy with 993 Transportation Stores Company, including Naples, Bari, Trieste and Venice on reconstruction, and later as a batman at Company HQ.

❖ On 30 June 1946 Vernon and a friend were privileged to attend an audience with Pope Pius the XII in the Sistine Chapel at the Vatican in Rome.

Once I had interviewed Vernon 'Taffy' Parry I had managed to successfully complete interviews with veterans that represented a real spread of services and backgrounds, which I hope will embody and give the best balance possible from some of the last of our veterans in this country. This includes male and female veterans, those from the British backgrounds of England, Ireland, Scotland and now Wales, those from the Commonwealth and occupied countries who came to help our war effort such as Canada, India, Nepal, the Caribbean and Poland, and even one from Germany who fled Nazi persecution and served in the British Army. I feel it is so important to remember the true extent of the help we received during the war. When I interviewed Vernon he brought a Welsh perspective to things, in the same way that each of the other veterans brought their own viewpoint and outlook based on their personal backgrounds and experiences. He was one of the last and very important pieces of my jigsaw in completing the book.

As a Royal Engineer during the war, Vernon undertook some very important jobs rebuilding strategically vital areas that had been devastated by battle in order to get the essential transport hubs operational once again. They could then be used by the Allies to maintain the vital flow of supplies to the troops taking the war to the Germans as they advanced across Europe in 1944–45. Throughout his time in service he did this as part of the 188, 197 and 993 Transportation Stores Companies, RE.

Vernon's service began in November 1942 and after being called up he undertook his basic training at Heath Camp in Cardiff, Wales, during which time he did additional training to become a first class Bren Gunner, which as Vernon recalls, paid an extra three pence a day. Having chosen the Royal Engineers as his direction, his next more specialised training took place at the Royal Engineers Training School at Llandaff in Cardiff, where he learned many vital RE skills such as bridge building, explosives and munitions for demolition, also logistics and equipment loading and transportation. The training did not stop there, and it became even more specialised when he went to Longmoor Camp near Portsmouth to learn railway engineering skills such as line laying and maintenance and the special equipment for those tasks. While there he was involved in building part of the military railway on the Longmoor line out to Liss.

With the postings that were to follow came the chance to increase his experience when he was first sent to Faslane in Scotland, unloading ships and doing plumbing and engineering work from March until June 1943. Up until that point Vernon had been with the 188 Transportation Stores Company. However, his next posting from June 1943 until May 1944 would take him to a big railway maintenance yard in Melbourne near Derby, where he would become part of the 197 Transportation Stores Company. There he did various jobs: working with joiners, bricklayers, engineers and other tradesmen and adding to his knowledge to make an all-round, highly skilled Royal Engineer. After this he was equipped with a lot of the skills and experience that were required to undertake the jobs in infrastructure rebuilding that he would later undertake across Europe. Soon after his arrival via the Mulberry Harbour at Arromanches in Normandy on 23 June 1944 on D+17, those skills were put into action when, as Vernon recalls, he was based at a big RE depot doing logistics at a place called Saint-Martin-des-Éntrees. After the fall of Caen in July 1944 they began restoring the port and canal basin areas.

As the Allied advance continued, the 197 Company moved up behind the front line into areas where it was detailed to carry out much-needed infrastructure rebuilding between August 1944 and May 1945. The men undertook vital railway repairs in places such as Halle in Belgium, Eindhoven in Holland and the Osnabruck–Munster area in Germany, where the war finished for them. Then, in June 1945, the 197 Coy moved to Hamburg where it was involved in getting the docks up and running and during its time there they came across a German armoured train and made some interesting discoveries, which Vernon talks about later.

After a spell back at Longmoor in the UK another big adventure would start for Vernon in September 1945 when he was sent to Italy. He would now be part of 993 Port Company in Naples involved in logistics and the unloading of incoming supplies until November of that year. He was then posted to the Company HQ in Naples doing maintenance, and the same at Bari. From May until September 1946 he returned to Naples, where his many and varied skills were required for every kind of ongoing repair work at the HQ. Then, in September 1946, Vernon was sent to Venice and later Trieste, where his job changed and he was again in the officers' mess at the HQs but this time as a batman. This posting was his last as a serviceman in the British Army, as he returned to the UK in May 1947 and was demobbed in Aldershot. After his return to civilian life he was still on the Army Reserve list and in 1951 he was called up for active service once again, this time for the Korean War. He was sent to an Army camp at Midhurst, West Sussex, but luckily was not needed and was released from service. This would be the last time his country called upon this highly skilled veteran. During Vernon's time in active service he, like all veterans, experienced many interesting and diverse things in many places, and recalls:

Wartime Experiences Whilst Serving in the Royal Engineers

On 13 June, when we were doing map reading and camouflage training near Wickford, we saw the first V1 rocket come over on the way to London; that 'Doodlebug' went on past thankfully. In France, whilst working we had snipers

taking pot shots and our POWs trying to sabotage the work, which was hard
enough as it was, especially in badly damaged areas like Caen. We worked on all
sorts of projects repairing rail links, roads and anything that required engineering
skills. Later at the docks in Hamburg we found an abandoned German Military
Armoured Train and it had a flat wagon with a big gun. Around it was a kind of
fortified concrete wall and on it there were all these drawings of planes which
they had shot down, I suppose, and the names of the places underneath, like their
own little battle history. But all they had for Arnhem were pictures of lots of little
parachutes coming down and we found all sorts of British military equipment
such as binoculars and a parachute, which must have been from Arnhem judging
by the drawings and other things we saw. So I took it and kept half and gave the
other half to the lads.

I was very moved when Vernon gave me a piece of this authentic war history, after
which he went on to say:

I saw some important people along the way, as most of us did, such as Montgomery,
Eisenhower, Bradley, Churchill, Eden and King George VI, but something special
happened on 30 June 1946. Whilst on leave I was invited to go with some other
servicemen and join a private audience with Pope Pius XII at the Sistine Chapel
in the Vatican, Rome; a once-in-a-lifetime experience during my service years.

Pope Pius XII.

Vernon (right-hand side) and
friend at the Sistine Chapel.

Pope Pius XII was the wartime Pope who chose the outward stance of neutrality, which led to much controversy. In an impassioned speech in October 1939 shortly after the start of the war he warned, and most chillingly and correctly predicted: 'This is an Hour of Darkness, in which the spirit of violence and of discord brings indescribable suffering on mankind. The nations swept into the tragic whirlpool of war are perhaps as yet only at the beginnings of sorrows.'

Additional Information and Life After Service

❖ **Rank at end of service:** Lance corporal.
❖ **Medals and honours:** Legion d'Honneur (French Government), 1939–45 Defence Medal, 1939–45 War Medal, 1939–45 Star, France–Germany Star.
❖ **Post-war years:** In 1947 Vernon returned to his pre-war job at Vickers & Co. plumbers and builders until 1953. Then he was a freelance plumber at Rhyl Council until 1955, worked at Point of Ayr Colliery on coal trucks until 1957, then at Stubbs Engineering on government and civil contracts around the UK in areas such as Manchester, Coventry and Anglesey until 1970. Finally, he spent ten years at Rhyl Heating and Plumbing, retiring in 1980. Married to Yvonne 1955–2016, they have two daughters and three grandchildren.
❖ **Associations and organisations:** Normandy Veterans Association Rhyl Branch.

Lance Corporal Tommy Hopper

Served with: 1st Battalion, Lancashire Fusiliers, and Chindit
Service number: 3451462
Interviewed: Manchester, Lancashire, 10 October 2014

Service History and Personal Stories

- ❖ **Born:** 14 July 1918, Manchester, England, UK.
- ❖ Tommy Hopper joined the Lancashire Fusiliers in July 1939 at the age of 21, was trained at the Wellington Barracks in Bury, Lancashire, and served in the 1st Battalion, Lancashire Fusiliers.
- ❖ He was posted to the White Barracks at Quetta in the North West Frontier of India from 1940–43, then in Jhansi, where he trained in jungle warfare in 1943–44.
- ❖ Tommy was posted to Burma and became part of the Chindits under Major General Orde Wingate DSO. On 5 March 1944 he took part in Operation Thursday.
- ❖ After landing in a glider at an area code-named Broadway he was engaged throughout the whole jungle campaign in fierce combat against the Japanese as a machine gunner until August 1944.
- ❖ Tommy served with the Fusiliers until November 1946, when he was demobbed at the Ladysmith Barracks in Ashton, Lancashire.

Chindit Tommy Hopper was 96 years old when I interviewed him in October 2014 and at that time he was the oldest known veteran of the Lancashire Fusiliers. I first saw him in a *Manchester Evening News* article when he was reunited with fellow Chindit Ian Nivan in 2013 after nearly seventy years. Eventually I traced and interviewed both of them. In this book I have featured Tommy's story and in the next I am hoping to write I intend to feature Ian's story, giving a nice connection and continuity. As members of the 1st Battalion they both ended up in Burma under the command of Major General Orde Wingate, becoming a part of the special jungle force called the Chindits. They were engaged in fierce battles and savage jungle warfare against the Japanese in many areas and under extremely harsh conditions.

Tommy's service began in July 1939 as the spectre of the Second World War was looming. This Lancashire lad wanted to serve in a local regiment so he joined the Lancashire Fusiliers, and soon after he trained at the Wellington Barracks in the Fusiliers' home town of Bury, Lancashire. In early 1940 he was sent out with the 1st Battalion to Quetta on the North West Frontier of India (now in modern day Pakistan) to what was known as the White Barracks, where he stayed as part of the British Army presence until late 1943. After this, the 1st Battalion was earmarked to become part of special operations in Burma and was sent to the Chindits' training areas in Jhansi in India to undertake intense jungle exercises in preparation for this mission. Every bit of that training would be needed for the trials that lay ahead. On 5 March 1944 Tommy was dropped into the dense jungle of Burma in a glider, which arrived at a landing zone code-named Broadway as part of Operation Thursday. He was a machine gunner in the 20th column, 1st Battalion L.Fs, which was part of the 77th Brigade under the command of Brigadier 'Mad Mike' Calvert. For this offensive there was a specially put-together force of six brigades that were being deployed as Major General Orde Wingate's Chindits. They were tasked with undertaking long-range penetration jungle missions, to seek and destroy Japanese military targets in Burma and to disrupt and affect other operations that the enemy were planning or engaging in. To do this they employed large-scale guerrilla warfare-style tactics formulated by Wingate and Calvert and backed by Churchill.

There were two Chindit expeditions into Burma. The first, in February 1943, Operation Longcloth, consisted of a force of 3,000 men that marched more than 1,000 miles during the campaign. The second expedition, Operation Thursday, in which Tommy took part in March 1944, was on a much larger scale. It was the largest airborne invasion of the war up until that point, eventually second only to the later Normandy operations, and consisted of a force of around 20,000 British and Commonwealth soldiers from India, British Burma, Gambia, Gold Coast, Kenya, Mauritius, Nigeria, Rhodesia, Nyasaland and Uganda with air support from the RAF and the USAAF's 1st Air Commando and Tenth Air Force. Later

One of the most essential components to the Allied victory in Burma, the mule.

they were also joined by forces from the Republic of China. Other interesting and diverse forces that supported and were a part of the Chindits included the US Army 900th Field Unit (Engineers) and reconnaissance platoons made up of a British officer with Burma Rifles (Karen and Kachin native tribesmen), making it a truly combined international effort. They were up against the formidable forces of the Empire of Japan, who were skilled in the art of jungle warfare, and their allies, the Indian National Army. The fighting encountered there along the borders between Burma and India, especially in 1944, was known to be some of the most severe in the South-East Asian theatre during the war. There was a great deal of suffering to both man and beast, the mules being so important to the success of the operation that they too were dropped in with the men in glider operations. The casualty rate was high due to, among other things, enemy action, adverse weather conditions, disease and exhaustion. Battles such as Kohima and Imphal went down in military history and the campaign contributed significantly towards the eventual overall Allied victory against Japanese forces in Burma. The Chindits were finally disbanded in February 1945.

As a machine gunner, Tommy was involved in fierce fighting against the Japanese and engaged them in bitter struggles in the jungle. He now tells us about his experiences in more detail:

To Be a Chindit in Close Combat With the Japanese in the Jungles of Burma

Well, starting with a bit of a funny thing, the Japs were very good at camouflage and on one patrol when we were out they had several Japanese who could speak English, and I was out with Brigadier Calvert, they called him 'Mad Mike' and we could hear them saying: 'We know you're there Tommy, we know you're there Tommy.' Now, a Tommy is us, the Brits, and me, of course, so Calvert turns round to me and says: 'Christ Tommy, they know you. They know you're here. You're bloody famous!'

Anyway getting down to more serious stuff, we started a skirmish and we overpowered them, that was that. They were finished and we carried on and were always expecting another attack. That's how it was there: you didn't know when or where it was going to come from a lot of the time and when it did happen it was savage, bloody and mad.

I asked Tommy to tell me more about the jungle combat and he went on to say:

Calvert believed in saving ammunition because we very rarely got an airdrop in. The rifle was a soldier's best friend and the best friend a Gurkha had was his knife, the Kukri. We had knives and he used to say: 'Don't fire anything Tommy unless you really have to, get the Kukris out,' meaning our knives, 'and use those', and we did. When we were fighting it was all in, meaning anything went: knives, fists, elbows anything, it could be a pretty nasty business, real hand-to-hand stuff, no messing about. I also used a Vickers machine gun, it was water-cooled, belt-fed by a number two, and could fire 250 rounds a minute. When we used it we just gave short blasts most the time 'coz again the Japs were camouflaged and in a battle we just had to shoot at stuff when it moved in the jungle.

Things were very hard when we got there, the everyday conditions. The Burmese people helped us a lot and were kind with food and stuff. They understood and appreciated what we were trying to do there. We would see men fall in battle but the stretcher bearers took care of that. We just had to carry on, keep going, we couldn't stop for nothing, and we did this until we reached and captured Mogaung. After we were exhausted, not fit for active service, they sent us back to India for convalescence, but we did what we had to do, that's all that matters.

After recuperation and light duties in Teratun (more commonly Dehradun), northern India, Tommy returned to the UK in early 1946. Then he was posted to two Army camps to finish his service, Hunstanton in Norfolk and Hartford in Northumberland, before finally being demobbed at Ladysmith Barracks in Ashton, Lancashire, in November 1946. Tommy's safe return back to his home county had

The Chindit badge illustrates a Chinthe, the symbolic guardian of Burmese temples: a mythical beast, half lion, half flying griffin. It is from this creature that the Chindits take their name and insignia.

brought him full circle in his incredible journey. His service was over but he would always be a proud Lancashire Fusilier and Chindit who lived by the Chindit Special Forces motto 'The boldest measures are the safest'.

Sadly, Major General Wingate, leader of the 3rd Indian Division (Chindits), died in an air crash in Burma on 24 March 1944. He had issued an 'Order of the Day' on 13 March 1944 following the successful fly-ins that inserted his Chindits 'into the enemy's guts', as he put it. Below is part of that poignant message, which aptly sums up how all the veterans I have interviewed so far from all services and backgrounds seem to feel in general about having played their part in the war: 'This is a moment to live in history. It is an enterprise in which every man who takes part may feel proud one day to say "I was there".'

Additional Information and Life After Service

* ❖ **Rank at end of service:** Lance corporal.
* ❖ **Medals and honours:** 1939–45 Defence Medal, 1939–45 War Medal, 1939–45 Star, Burma Star.
* ❖ **Post-war years:** Tommy returned to his pre-war employer, Richard Johnson and Nephew Ltd in Manchester, where he worked another thirty-four years on the steel rod rolling belt producing wire for industry from 1946 until his retirement in 1980. He was married to Hilda from 1948 until 2009. They have two daughters, four grandchildren and four great-grandchildren.
* ❖ **Associations and organisations:** Burma Star Association.

PRIVATE RAYMOND SHUCK

Served with: 4th Air Landing Anti-Tank Battery, 13th Battalion,
   6th Airborne Division
Service Number: 4927330
Interviewed: Bolton, Lancashire, 26 June 2015
Additional Conversations: 2015–19

Service History and Personal Stories

- ❖ **Born:** 6 October 1923, Birmingham, England, UK.
- ❖ Joined the South Staffordshire Infantry Regiment at Worchester Barracks in 1941 at only 17 years of age. 1941–42 did basic Infantry training at Catterick Garrison in North Yorkshire, followed by more intense training at Whittington Barracks in Lichfield, Staffordshire which included the use of the 6-Pound Anti-Tank Gun.
- ❖ At the end of 1942 Ray volunteered to be in the Airborne forces and became part of the 6th Airborne Division, and throughout 1942–44 amongst other places was posted to Bulford Camp and Salisbury Plain, Wiltshire for Glider Training, and at RAF Ringway for Parachute Training with the 13th (Lancashire) Parachute Battalion with static line jumps over Tatton Park, Cheshire, all in preparation for the invasion of Europe.

❖ At 3.30 a.m. on 6 June 1944 Ray, now in the 4th Air Landing Anti-Tank Battery, 13th Battalion, 6th Airborne Division, was dropped in a Horsa Glider as part of the biggest Land, Sea and Air invasion in history, Operation Overlord.

❖ His Airborne mission (Operation Tonga) on what was to become known as D-Day was to help reinforce and secure areas around the captured key strategic Caen Canal Bridge at Benouville and the Orne River Bridge at Ranville (later renamed Pegasus and Horsa Bridges), to help repel Nazi counterattacks as and when they arose using his 6-Pound Anti-Tank Gun and personal small arms like his Bren Gun.

❖ Whilst in action around Ranville, Ray was shot in the head by a German sniper and by pure luck due to the deflection and angle of the bullet when it hit his helmet it passed in one side of his head, across the very top and out the other side.

❖ He was found by a young boy and taken to a makeshift medical station at Ranville Church, then medevaced to the UK, after plastic surgery to the head and convalescence in Cheltenham Ray was put on 'Light Duties' which included tending to returning malnourished POWs from the hellish Japanese prison camps in South-East Asia.

❖ Ray was demobbed in Aldershot in September 1946.

Dad, grandad, great-grandad, brother, friend to many, D-Day veteran, war hero, these are just some of the many different ways and words that we can use to describe this all round great man. A man that touched many lives in many good, positive and beautiful ways, he meant a lot, to a lot of people, and always will …

These were the opening words to the eulogy that I was honoured to write and deliver at the funeral of my good friend Ray Shuck at St John's Church in Farnworth, Bolton, on 1 February 2019. These carefully chosen words are an apt description of Ray and a very fitting tribute with which to describe the story of this remarkable and much loved veteran.

Ray now shares some of his incredible wartime experiences:

We did our Glider Training alongside some of the American 101st Airborne Division around Salisbury Plain and practiced glider drops with full equipment, like it would be for real when we went into battle, the only difference was there were no Germans shooting at us like there would be later! In our Horsa glider there were three men, including me, and two glider pilots a jeep and a gun, a 6-Pounder, I always remember in training we landed real heavy, we were shaken but not stirred! As the time got closer we knew that D-Day was coming because we were locked down in our camps to make sure no one talked and gave anything away, but as far as the training went we felt 100 per cent ready for anything and everything, we also had hours of briefings and felt like we almost knew France before we got there and we were motivated because we knew we were fighting for England, for our country and to liberate others!

So when it was for real, we crash landed our glider safely, and I remember before I got shot that we were fighting in Ranville and lots of Germans were giving themselves up. But there was still loads of vicious fighting with the Germans trying to take the bridges back because they knew by then if they didn't the troops landing on the beaches would get there, link with the Airborne troops and be able to secure those areas and that would be that!

You'd see a lot of your comrades dead and Germans dead, and the three of us from our Anti-Tank Battery who went into battle together didn't fare well at all, Private Les Atwell got his leg blown off below the knee and I got seriously wounded early on – a few days after arriving in Normandy when I was shot in the head. I don't know what happened to Sergeant Marriot, others I knew like Sammy Lines he was a Lieutenant he got killed and Bombardier Hill he got killed as well, very sad.

Horsa glider at Pegasus Bridge like the one Ray landed in nearby at Ranville on D-Day, 6 June 1944.

I was found by a young lad who I thought was French, it works out he was Russian. I had blood pouring from my head and in the heat of battle had been assumed dead, I ended up at a temporary medical station in the church at Ranville. Much later on I found out that Sergeant Atwell had shot the German Sniper out of a tree – the bugger had who got me! I don't remember much for a while after that because of my head injuries, but eventually I ended up back in Blighty, and after I had recovered in Cheltenham I was put on light duties like helping other convalescing soldiers who had been returned home from the Far East.

It was at this point when Ray was talking about the servicemen he had helped that I was very moved by his deep empathy and compassion towards them, especially after everything he had been through himself. He went on to say:

One of the jobs I had once I was on 'Light Duties' was helping feed up and get these poor half-dead prisoners of war well again, they'd been in POW camps around Asia and had been starved and beaten and used as slaves by the bloody Japs, who were as bad as the Nazis in how they treated people! We had to feed them like babies on liquids on what was like mashed food before they could take anything solid or they could die! Poor sods, I felt really sorry for them, they were in a very bad way. Just goes to show there are always people far worse off than yourself!

To conclude his profile, I finish with two things, first something humorous from Ray, as he was well known for his great sense of humour. With a big smile on his face, he recalled to me, 'In France there were always plenty of bullets flying around. I caught one of them, nutted it – when I look back I think it knocked some sense into me!'

The second on a more humbling and thankful note is this: the motto of the 13th Parachute Battalion, of which Ray was a part, was 'Win or Die', something he truly honoured. In service to his country, in combat Ray overcame near death to help the Allies win the Second World War. It is because of sacrifices such as these by Ray and many other veterans like him that we will always owe 'A Debt of Gratitude to the Last Heroes'.

To a great man, I know I speak for myself and many other people when I say it was an honour and a privilege to have known you and to be able to have had your magic in our lives.

No life is truly finished until all the lives it has touched and all the good it has done has passed away.

It is with these words in mind that I feel that Ray's legacy will be a long-lasting one indeed. 'Gone but Never Forgotten.' God bless you my friend. GBD.

Additional Information and Life After Service

- ❖ **Rank upon finish of service:** Private.
- ❖ **Medals and Honours:** 1939–45 Defence Medal, 1939–45 War Medal, 1939–45 Star, France-Germany Star, Legion D' Honneur.
- ❖ **Post War Years:** Between his demob in 1946 and his retirement in 1996 aged 70, Ray had a few jobs, including being a panel beater at Lomas's making Ambulances, whilst his wife Olwyn was a hairdresser. Later they set up Ray's Transport Cafe in Walkden, Manchester, then went into the camping and sports business that evolved into Tent Valeting Services (TVS), which was a family business. Ray married Olwyn in February 1944; they have one son, one daughter, four grandchildren and nine great-grandchildren.
- ❖ **Associations and Organisations:** Manchester Parachute Association (Manchester Branch), Blind Veterans UK.

2

Navy and the War at Sea

The United Kingdom being an island has meant that everything it has done and has been involved in as it pursued its outward ambitions militarily or when defending its own shores has been interwoven with the sea. As a result of this it has been essential throughout our history to have both a strong seagoing fighting and supply force to defend and serve our nation's interests both at home and overseas, and these are what became the Royal Navy and Merchant Navy fleets.

The Royal Navy, because it has the longest traceable military history, is known as the 'senior service'. It was officially created and established under that name following the restoration of Charles II in 1660; before that it was known as the English Navy with no defined moment of creation but over time it operated as an assortment of kings' or queens' ships and as a big and officially organised service in its own right. Yet throughout history, from the sea battles with the Spanish Armada in 1588 to the Battle of Trafalgar in 1805, the Battle of Jutland in 1916 and the numerous successful engagements of the Second World War, the Navy successfully answered the call to defend her country time and time again.

During the war the Royal Navy and Merchant Navy were involved from the first to the last day, and over the course of the conflict they were engaged in every theatre of that war in almost every sea, and participated in many famous engagements and sustained campaigns that helped successfully change the course of the war. These included the Battle of the Atlantic, which was the longest continuous military campaign of the war, and the dreaded Arctic convoys to Russia, where in both theatres the merchant fleet in particular suffered terribly at the hands of the German U-boats. Both the Royal and Merchant Navies also fought and were involved in fierce battles in the vitally strategic Mediterranean and the Far East areas, supporting and supplying other services engaged in operations, invasions and offensives in those parts of the world.

Among these were engagements that, for good or for bad, would become well known, such as the battles of the River Plate, Taranto, Cape Bon, Java Sea, Convoy PQ 17, and the hunting of *Bismarck*, *Scharnhorst* and *Tirpitz*. Both navies also made up a large and important part of the forces used for some of the biggest Allied invasions of the Second World War, such as Operation Torch in North Africa, Operation Husky in Sicily, Operations Avalanche, Baytown, Slapstick and Shingle in Italy, and, of course, Operation Neptune, the naval and amphibious part of the D-Day landings. The various branches of these navies such as the Royal Fleet Auxiliary, Royal and Merchant Navy Rescue Tug Services, Submarine Service, and the Royal Marines, along with the huge variation of seagoing vessels within them, again led to great diversity of roles for the servicemen and women within these branches, whose responsibility it was to take care of every aspect of seagoing operations during the war.

These roles included ships' captains, officers and other ratings such as able-seamen, engineers, stokers, gunners, torpedomen, signallers, radar and sonar operators, medical staff, Wrens, submariners, Marines, Navy frogmen, and pilots, based at naval training stations and other establishments in the UK and on vessels at sea throughout the world. In this section are the incredible stories of servicemen from some of these diverse branches of both the Royal and Merchant Navies.

Able Seaman Gunner Bernard Smith

Served with: Royal Navy Destroyer HMS *Venus*
Service number: JX419076
Interviewed: Salford, Lancashire, 2 October 2014

Service History and Personal Stories

- ❖ **Born:** 1 May 1925, Salford, England, UK.
- ❖ Trained and became an able-bodied seaman and anti-aircraft gunner (AAAB). He served on HMS *Venus* (R50) in various theatres of war and undertook many convoys and missions, such as escorting duties to Gibraltar and around the Mediterranean with the 17th Destroyer Flotilla.
- ❖ Completed nine Arctic convoys to Russia in 1943–44 with the 26th Destroyer Flotilla. Also assisted in the rescue of survivors from the torpedoed HMS *Hardy*, and later with sinking her hulk.
- ❖ Bernard was serving on HMS *Venus* on D-Day as part of Force 'J' assisting in Operation Neptune, supporting the Normandy landings at Juno Beach.
- ❖ Later, as part of the naval forces in the Pacific, he was directly involved in the action that sank the Japanese battleship *Haguro* in the Malacca Straights between Malaysia and Sumatra.

Bernard Smith, from Salford, worked labouring at the dry docks at Trafford Park before the war when it was a busy shipping hub and major port, so it was not too surprising that when he answered his country's call at the age of 17 in January 1943, he volunteered for and joined the Royal Navy. His love of the sea would take him to many places in the world during his active service and led to him seeing a lot of action along the way. He did his basic naval training at HMS *Raleigh* in Torpoint, Cornwall, and at HMS *Drake* in Plymouth, Devon. After this his complete seagoing service would be on one ship, the V-Class destroyer HMS *Venus* (R50), from August 1943 until December 1945. This is Bernard's story, about a brave young man who as a naval rating during the war experienced and was a part of some of the biggest and most well-known naval operations of that conflict.

He would first be on convoy-escorting duties to Gibraltar and around the Mediterranean as part of the 17th Destroyer Flotilla, then as part of the 26th Destroyer Flotilla on some of the hardest and most feared duties known, the Arctic convoys to Russia. He completed nine of these, from the end of 1943 to end of 1944, with the only 'break' in between when *Venus* was attached to 'J' Force to support the Normandy landings at Juno Beach on D-Day and other related operations that followed. During the Arctic convoys, HMS *Venus* was also involved in an action to pick up the survivors from the destroyer HMS *Hardy*, which was torpedoed by the German U-boat *U27b* on 30 January 1944. After this *Venus* destroyed the half-sunk hulk.

From February to June 1945 HMS *Venus* was sent as part of the 26th Destroyer Flotilla to a very different theatre of war in the Far East under the command of South East Asia Command (SEAC), where it would be involved in many kinds of operations and duties such as the sinking of Japanese merchant shipping, escorting and providing cover for convoys, and also intelligence gathering. This took place around various parts of South-east Asia such as Ceylon, Burma, Malaysia, Sumatra and Singapore, to name but a few. It was during this time that they also took part in a very special operation on 15 May 1945, the sinking of the Japanese heavy cruiser *Haguro*, one of their most famous battleships and equipped with formidable firepower. During this naval engagement, which was known as the Battle of the Malacca Strait, five destroyers of the 26th Destroyer Flotilla – HMS *Saumarez*, *Verulam*, *Venus*, *Vigilant* and *Virago* – engaged and sank *Haguro* using their guns and torpedoes in a hard-fought night-time battle. This turned out to be the last major surface gun and torpedo action of the war and is acknowledged as being one of the most professionally undertaken sinkings of a heavy ship by destroyers alone in a naval engagement during the conflict. Lord Louis Mountbatten, who was at the time the Supreme Allied Commander of SEAC and himself a distinguished destroyer captain, wrote in his report: 'The sinking of the *Haguro* is an outstanding example of a night attack by destroyers.' In the thick of all this action, dutifully

Bernard's ship, the V-class destroyer HMS *Venus* (R50).

manning his anti-aircraft guns on HMS *Venus*, was Bernard Smith, engaging different enemies and protecting his ship and the men on it in hard-fought battles as he had done all the way from the Mediterranean to the Baltic and finally in the Pacific. Bernard would return home with HMS *Venus* in December 1945 and would finish his days of service in the Navy in a far more peaceful role, working as a postmaster at HMS *Drake* and later at HMS *Demetrius* until he was demobbed in June 1946.

We now focus on two parts of Bernard's service: his experiences in the Arctic convoys and the sinking of *Haguro*, with excerpts from the conversations we had about both, starting with him speaking about his time in the Baltic:

Life on the Dreaded Arctic Convoys

Well the main thing that was memorable was to see so many other ships going down, merchant ships mainly. We took big convoys and we took small convoys out to Russia and we nearly always had attacks from the U-boats. We had a bad time of it getting attacked; there were many casualties and terrible things happened. Being on the convoys seeing other ships going up in flames one after another and having to drag in the survivors, there were lifeboats being found with all the men in them frozen to death and bodies in the water were a common sight. I remember once going over the side on the scrambling net and I pulled one of them in. He must have been a stoker because in his hand he had a spanner

The Japanese heavy cruiser *Haguro* that links two veterans' stories in this book. *Haguro*, shown here in action in 1943, was involved in the sinking of HMS *Exeter* during the Battle of Java Sea on 1 March 1942 with Geoff Stott on Board. Later, HMS *Venus*, with Bernard Smith on board, was involved in the sinking of *Haguro* on 15 May 1945 during the battle of the Malacca Strait.

that they used for tightening the wheels but he had died and it was frozen solid to him. I still think of it to this day.

The sinking of the *Haguro* was different. It was fought at night with I think five or six of our destroyers against two of their heavy cruisers. We were moving fast, maybe 30 knots, firing all the time, everything was go, go and although they had many guns I couldn't understand why she didn't do more? After the action there were survivors rolling about in boats and our skipper said we'll take some of them on board but they didn't want to come, they didn't want to be saved! So strange! But I would say that the Arctic convoys were the most horrifying of all actions because there were thousands of men died through that, and the memories are as chilling as the conditions were for us.

During his time serving on HMS *Venus* Bernard took part in all nine of the Arctic convoy runs that she did between 2 November 1943 and 12 April 1944, with a 'break' in between to participate in the Normandy landings and other assigned duties that came after. The Russian convoys that they escorted, in order, were: RA 054A, JW 054B, JW 056A, JW 056B, RA 056, JW 058, RA 058, JW 060, RA 060, and counting their returns in treacherous waters this made eighteen journeys in seas infested with German U–boats and which also contained enemy surface raiding vessels. This, along with the sub-zero temperatures and the rate at which shipping was being lost in the Arctic sea lanes, made it one of the most feared places for any seaman of either the Merchant or Royal Navy to see active service during the war.

Understandably so. From August 1941 to May 1945 a total of seventy-eight convoys numbering around 1,400 vessels made the perilous 2,500-mile journey from UK ports to those of Murmansk and Archangel in Russia, and in doing so they lost eighty-five merchant vessels, sixteen Royal Navy warships and around 3,000 seamen (sources vary). These convoys delivered a staggering 4.5 million metric tons of cargo, which included approximately 7,000 aircraft, 5,000 tanks and other vital materials such as medical supplies, fuel, cars, clothing, metals and various raw materials. These were especially needed in the earlier years of the German invasion of Russia for her immense struggle on the Eastern Front. These huge amounts of supplies were certainly a big contributory factor in helping Russia, as well as a very reassuring and much-appreciated gesture between the Allies of the time, one that is still valued to this very day, with the Russian government still rewarding former Arctic convoy veterans on a regular basis.

We will finish with the words of Bernard, who, despite all the hard things that happened, said in his understanding and forgiving way: 'I have a lot of time to think now, and I think after all that those Japanese and Germans, they had mothers and fathers too and they were only taking orders, like all of us.' Nearly all servicemen had loved ones at home whom they missed, thought about and couldn't wait to be with once again, and for Bernard this was his wife, whom he summed up in these few beautiful words: 'Everything I am I owe to my darling wife Grace, amazing Grace.'

After Bernard's passing in 2015 his son Neil, a good friend of mine, had this to say about his father when he delivered this very touching eulogy, which is a perfect way to conclude his story. It read:

Having volunteered under age to join the Royal Navy his desire was to protect his country for the benefit of all, fiercely proud of his fourteen decorations in recognition of his service to King and Country. Bernard was a man of honour who believed and placed trust in his fellow man, a man's man, a man of principle and compassion, who believed in commitment. His mantra was that maybe we are unable to achieve everything, however, we owe it to ourselves and others to try and achieve something for inner pride, for the good of all and to know that we did our best. Bernard is a true example on which Great Britain was built.

Additional Information and Life After Service

- ❖ **Rank at end of service:** Able-bodied seaman and anti-aircraft gunner (AAAB).
- ❖ **Medals and honours:** 1939–45 Defence Medal, 1939–45 War Medal, 1939–45 Star, Atlantic Star with Normandy Clasp, Arctic Star, Burma Star, Russian Arctic Commemorative Medals.
- ❖ **Post-war years:** After leaving the Royal Navy in 1946 things came full circle when Bernard joined the police and served from 1946–49, during which time he returned to the docks as part of the Salford City Dock Police Force to help control the widespread pillaging that was going on in post-war years. In 1949–59 he worked as a foundry worker for an engineering and foundry company, P.R. Jackson & David Browns Ltd, and then did the same job for another company, Benices Ltd, in 1959–79. After this his final working years were for Town and Country Frozen Foods as a cold storage manager. He was married to Grace for sixty-six years from 1944 until 2010 and they have two sons and two grandchildren.
- ❖ **Associations and organisations:** North Atlantic Association, shop steward for the Boilermakers Union for approximately thirty years.

Petty Officer Geoff Stott

Served with: Royal Navy heavy cruiser HMS *Exeter*
Service number: DJX170952
Interviewed: Salford, Lancashire, 11 July 2014

Service History and Personal Stories

* **Born:** 10 January 1924, Bolton, England, UK.
* Geoff volunteered for the Royal Navy in October 1939 at the age of 15 years and 10 months just after the outbreak of the war.
* After fourteen months' training at HMS *St George* and HMS *Drake* he served as an ordinary seaman and armourer in Y gun magazine on the heavy cruiser HMS *Exeter* (68) in the Far East.
* Survived the sinking of *Exeter* in the battle of Java Sea on 1 March 1942, after which he became a Japanese prisoner of war for the next three and a half years.
* Geoff was a POW on Koyagi Shima island in Nagasaki Bay, approximately 3 miles from Nagasaki, when the second A-bomb was dropped on 9 August 1945 and witnessed the start of the Atomic Age.
* After being repatriated back to the UK he went on to give a further eight years' service to the Royal Navy and later became a stores petty officer.

Among all the great veterans at Broughton House home for ex-servicemen in Salford was a gentleman by the name of Geoff Stott, one of the very few veterans who witnessed the start of the Atomic Age. I interviewed Geoff in 2014, 2015 and 2016, each time finding out more facts about his service, and I felt very privileged to be in the company of one of only a handful of servicemen left who were close to Nagasaki on that fateful day. Sometimes I had to pinch myself when I thought about what he had seen and survived. For Geoff, seeing what was such a cataclysmic event in world history was only part of his wartime experiences.

For him it all began after seeing the famous First World War poster 'Your Country Needs You' (presumably reused in some areas during the early part of the Second World War recruitment drive), Geoff joined the Royal Navy in Manchester in October 1939 just short of his 16th birthday. He was enlisted as a 'boy seaman', but life in the service of his country would, as it did with so many others, quickly make this boy into a man. A long period of training followed: fourteen months at HMS *St George* on the Isle of Man and later at HMS *Drake* in Devon, where he finished as an ordinary seaman (OS) and armourer. After this, on 10 March 1941, Geoff joined the heavy cruiser HMS *Exeter*, which had been repaired and refitted after the serious damage she sustained in the Battle of the River Plate. He was sent with the *Exeter* straight out on active duty to the Far East, where the ship showed the flag in many places on the way. Then, nearly a year later, he found himself in the thick of the action in a number of engagements in the Pacific from 27 February until 1 March 1942, where as an armourer in Lazy Y magazine he was involved in the Battle of Java Sea near Sumatra. During that engagement it was Geoff's job to feed the shells from the magazine below decks up to the ship's guns. He would be many decks down in the ship in the heat of intense battle.

The Imperial Japanese Navy achieved a significant victory at the battle of Java Sea on 1 March when it engaged the Allied naval forces with a number of battleships, including the heavy cruisers *Nachi*, *Haguro*, *Myoko* and *Ashigara*, along with their supporting destroyers; eight ships in total. They sank three Allied warships that day, the destroyers HMS *Encounter* and USS *Pope* and HMS *Exeter*. Geoff Stott was one of the lucky survivors.

In the heat of that battle, having been hit by shells and a torpedo, the *Exeter*'s captain, Oliver Gordon, sounded the one order that no sailor ever wants to hear – 'abandon ship' – and with shells exploding all around, fire coming from below and the ship listing, Geoff and other seamen managed to escape. However, fifty-four ratings, some friends of his, did not make it. As *Exeter* went down it was reported that a number of seamen adrift in the water gave her three last cheers as a sad salute.

Geoff and the survivors of the three ships were picked up by the Japanese Navy, starting what was to become three and a half years in captivity as a POW during which they would be on starvation rations, beaten and used as slave labour. Geoff

Geoff Stott's ship, heavy cruiser HMS *Exeter* (68).

was first sent to the port city of Makassar on eastern Indonesia's Sulawesi Island in the Dutch East Indies, where he spent six months clearing up bomb damage.

Then Geoff was sent to POW Camp Fukuoka 2, on the small island of Koyagi Shima in Nagasaki Bay only 3 miles from the city of Nagasaki. There he became prisoner 1096 and experienced a very long and terrible period of incarceration from 24 October 1942 until 12 September 1945. He was one of around 800 prisoners who were put to work repairing ships for the Imperial Japanese Navy in the Kanawami Bros. Dockyard, a subsidiary of Mitsubishi. Conditions were extremely harsh and 164 men died in this camp through illness, disease, malnutrition and mistreatment at the hands of their ruthless captors. On one occasion Geoff was beaten so badly by guards with bats that two discs in his back were put out. However, nothing could prepare him for what he would experience next. Here Geoff recalls being witness on 9 August 1945 to one of the most tumultuous events and biggest turning points in world history:

The Dropping of an A-Bomb and the Start of the Atomic Age

After six months 800 men were chosen to join a prisoner of war camp on a small island three and the half miles from Nagasaki in Japan, and we were treated like slaves for the next three years, forced to do manual labour and living conditions were cramped with 56 men sharing a room and only one toilet! In August 1945 things began to change, we saw strange flashes in the sky and an enormous mushroom cloud coming from Nagasaki. The Americans had arrived, bringing with them the second Atomic Bomb. We were witnessing the start of that Atomic Age.

As Geoff correctly remarked, he was observing the second type of A-Bomb being dropped, the first being on the city of Hiroshima on 6 August 1945, which was a uranium-based weapon code-named 'Little Boy'. The second type, which was dropped on Nagasaki, was a Plutonium-based bomb code-named 'Fat Man'. These two weapons helped to bring a swift end to the war but heralded the start of a terrifying new Atomic Age.

I asked Geoff how it felt to be a part of such a significant and pivotal moment in world history. He calmly replied:

> Things happen and things don't happen and there are things you come through that you just can't understand, but here you are and, as I say to people, you just keep going. You read it in the paper and think 'blimey, I was there'. It was only later that the real significance of it completely sank in, when we found out all about what we had witnessed; a bomb powerful enough to destroy a whole city at once, and it did!

After the bomb came the liberation and the return home, as Geoff further recalls:

> We were not quite sure what we were witnessing at the time because no one had ever seen anything like it before and we had purposely been starved of news by the Japanese, who didn't want us to know how the war was really going and that they were losing it. We occasionally got bits of news but nothing we could really verify, that was until they all disappeared after the A-Bomb had been dropped. Then the Americans began to appear, first dropping supplies to us by air and eventually their hospital ships came to take us on the long journey back home. Hard to believe we were really going home after three and half long, hard and tortuous years, but we were and that was great.

Repatriation to the UK followed and once he was reunited with his family and when his leave was over, Geoff had to return to the Navy only two months later in 1946 to continue with the remaining eight of the twelve years he had signed up for originally. With the future in mind, he retrained in stores work. Geoff then spent two and a half years in the Mediterranean fleet, and then postings at the Naval Air Stations in Warrington and Londonderry. He finished his service as a stores petty officer and was discharged in January 1954, returning to life as a civilian, which was something he had not known since he was 16. It was not an easy transition after all he had been through.

What Geoff had to endure all those years in captivity is almost beyond words, but throughout that and for the eight years that followed where he continued to serve his country, it is true to say that he lived by the motto of his ship HMS *Exeter*. *Semper fidelis* (Always faithful).

Additional Information and Life After Service

- ❖ **Rank at end of service:** Stores petty officer.
- ❖ **Medals and honours:** 1939–45 Defence Medal, 1939–45 War Medal, 1939–45 Star, Atlantic Star, Pacific Star with Burma Clasp.
- ❖ **Post-war years:** Civilian stores manager 1954–85 with Smith and Robinson Road Tankers Ltd, Trafford Park, Manchester. He married Doreen in 1951 and they were together for sixty-three years. They have two sons, one grandchild and two great-grandchildren. Geoff now lives at Broughton House retirement home for ex-servicemen in Salford. There is a brief history below.
- ❖ **Associations and organisations:** Member of the Manchester and District Branch of the Far East Prisoners of War Association (FEPOW).

Broughton House – Home for Ex-Servicemen and Women

This veterans' home in Higher Broughton, Salford, proudly celebrated its centenary with events in 2016–17 to mark its existence as one of the oldest purpose-built care facilities for veterans in the UK. It opened on 4 August 1916 when a First World War battlefield casualty named Robert Charles Fox of the Fourth King's Rifles was the first to be taken in. One century and approximately 8,000 men and women later they still do a great job serving the veteran community by caring for ex-forces personnel from all services and backgrounds, and the good long-term plans they have in place will hopefully ensure the same tradition will continue for the next 100 years as well. I am proud to be associated with Broughton House in a voluntary capacity and fully support the superb work they do there. You can support their great work by donating at: **www.justgiving.com/broughtonhousehome** and please quote 'The Last Heroes' in any donation.

Leading Seaman Gunner Kenneth Bell

Served with: Royal Navy battleship HMS *Royal Oak* and minesweeper
HMS *Bramble*
Service number: DSSX19019
Interviewed: Sale, Cheshire, 29 November 2015

Service History and Personal Stories

❖ **Born:** 9 March 1920, Sale, England, UK.

❖ Ken joined the Royal Navy in 1936 at the age of sixteen and served in many theatres of war. He had many 'close shaves' during his career.

❖ In 1937–39 he served on the battleship *Royal Oak* (08), which played an active part assisting in operations in the Spanish Civil War, including the evacuation of civilians from Barcelona.

❖ Soon after Ken left the *Royal Oak* she was sunk at Scapa Flow in September 1939 by Günther Prien's *U47*, with the loss of 833 men.

❖ On 20 February 1941 Ken was Mentioned in Dispatches for his bravery after shooting down a He 111 in the English Channel, and during the attack a bomb lodged itself in the side of HMS *Bramble*, near Ken, without exploding.

❖ In September 1941–December 1942, while on HMS *Bramble* (J11), Ken escorted a staggering thirteen Arctic convoys, with returns making it nineteen journeys in total, then left the ship. On her twentieth journey the *Bramble* was sunk in the Battle of the Barents Sea.

❖ He was also involved in the Atlantic convoys, operations in the Mediterranean, part of the landings in Salerno, Italy, in 1943, and was with support Force L on D-Day in 1944 at Gold Beach.

Leading Seaman Gunner Ken 'Daisy' Bell should have been nicknamed Ken 'Lucky' Bell after some of the incredibly close shaves and near misses he had during the war. Luck, fate or fortune certainly played a big part in Ken's life, as we will see as we recount his remarkable story. His very interesting and action-packed career began when he joined the Navy aged 16 in 1936, after which he trained at various naval establishments including HMS *Pembroke* in Chatham, Kent, HMS *Wildfire III* on the Isle of Sheppey, Kent, and HMS *Drake* near Plymouth, Devon. After this he was assigned to the battleship HMS *Royal Oak*, on which he served from 1937 until 1939. This ship had a proud history as she was part of the British Grand Fleet in the First World War and was in action in the most famous naval engagement of that conflict, the Battle of Jutland in 1916.

During his time on board *Royal Oak* it was actively involved in the Spanish Civil War, taking part in 'non-interventional patrols' around the Iberian Peninsula, although various actions did take place, as well as other operations that Ken recalls such as the evacuation of civilians from Barcelona. In June 1939 his time was up and he disembarked at HMS *Drake* in Plymouth, after which the *Royal Oak* took on a completely new crew and ended up being stationed with the Home Fleet at Scapa Flow in Orkney, Scotland. Then, on 14 October 1939, she was torpedoed by Günther Prien's *U47*. She exploded and sank in thirteen minutes after the second strike with the terrible loss of 833 men, including Rear-Admiral Henry Blagrove. Ken, by now serving on the Halcyon-class minesweeper HMS *Bramble*, was only a few hours' sailing time away in Loch Ewe when his previous ship went down, the first of a few chilling 'what ifs' he would encounter in the coming years.

The next one would earn him a mention in dispatches and the oak leaf clasp for his bravery when on 20 February 1941 HMS *Bramble* and other ships of the 1st Minesweeping Flotilla were attacked in the English Channel near Harwich. First Heinkel He 111 bombers riddled the ship with machine gun bullets, some of which hit the gun shield of Ken's anti-aircraft gun, which he was manning. Despite this he managed to shoot down one of the bombers, after which they were attacked by Messerschmitt Bf 110 fighter-bombers, which dropped bombs. One hit the ship and lodged itself in the starboard side not far from Ken but it did not explode. These actions led to the *Bramble*'s captain, M.H. Evelegh, recommending Ken and others for bravery awards. The captain's official report, which led to them being awarded, read:

I would like to mention particularly the names of Able Seaman James T Beale, D/JX.144283 AND Able Seaman Kenneth H Ball D/SSx.19019 who formed the 0.5" guns crew in *Bramble*. Their tenacity, coolness, courage and judgement were extremely good and I consider that these two ratings were chiefly responsible for the final destruction of one enemy machine and the possible 'winging' of the other, in spite of their gun shield being pierced by enemy machine gun bullets in three places.

After the damage was repaired, HMS *Bramble* went on to duties in home waters, minesweeping in the Atlantic approaches and convoy escort duties. Then, in October 1941, began a very long, hard and testing year on the Arctic convoys shipping supplies from Great Britain to the Russian port of Archangel. Ken's astounding luck continued to hold throughout his time on the Arctic runs, an example being that he served on convoys PQ 15 and PQ 16 but not on the following and tragic PQ 17 convoy that was decimated by the Germans in July 1942 with the loss of twenty-four of its thirty-five merchant ships. HMS *Bramble* came soon after and was ordered to pick up survivors from the Russian port of Polyarny. As *Bramble* made its way through the Kola Inlet it encountered, engaged and destroyed a U-boat and it also escorted surviving ships to Archangel.

HMS *Bramble* served on thirteen convoys from the UK to Russia between October 1941 until December 1942. Those prefixed with PQ were outward journeys and those with QP were additional return journeys. These totalled twenty, of which Ken Bell served on an incredible nineteen of them! These included: PQ 2, QP 2, PQ 3, QP 3, PQ 5, QP 4, QP 6, PQ 15, QP 12, PQ 16, QP 13, QP 14 and JW 51B.

Later that year, during his nineteenth convoy journey in December 1942 and while suffering from extreme fatigue and exhaustion, Ken fell asleep on his watch. His officer in charge knew it was time for him to be reassigned and so on 9 December 1942 he was sent back to the UK for leave, followed by shore-based duties and additional training at HMS *Osprey* and HMS *Drake*. Amazingly, as with his departure from the *Royal Oak*, this saved his life, because on 31 December 1942, while returning on its next and twentieth journey escorting convoy JW 51B, HMS *Bramble* was sunk by the German battleship *Admiral Hipper* and the destroyer *Friedrich Eckoldt* during the Battle of the Barents Sea. The crew of 113 men and Commander H.J. Rust went down with the ship, by all accounts with her 4in guns blazing, but she stood very little chance against the many more overpowering 8in guns of the *Admiral Hipper*.

On his later ships Ken would still be in the thick of it when he served on the corvette HMS *Nasturtium* from April 1943 to February 1944, and again on Atlantic convoys while the Battle of the Atlantic still raged. The *Nasturtium* also sailed into the Mediterranean, where Ken was involved in the landings at Solerno, Italy, in

Ken's first ship, the mighty HMS *Royal Oak*.

September 1943, and on duties in the Adriatic around Greece. Then he was posted back to HMS *Osprey* to be trained in the use of sonar anti-submarine detection equipment called Asdic. This added to Ken's training and skills, which had already led to him becoming a leading seaman and gunner.

Ken's next and last ship, the escort destroyer HMS *Avon Vale*, would see him involved in Operation Overlord, the biggest sea-based invasion in history on D-Day, 6 June 1944. She was part of Force L, the follow-up force to supply and reinforce the Sword, Juno and Gold beaches once the initial landings had taken place, and acted in this continuous support role until July. Then, in August, she was deployed as part of the 22nd Destroyer Flotilla in Alexandria, Egypt, and in September as part of that flotilla went to the eastern Mediterranean. For Ken 'Daisy' Bell that meant there was more action to come when HMS *Avondale* took part in a number of operations to occupy several islands after the surrender of Italy and was involved in engagements on 1 November 1944 that sank the German torpedo boat *TA-20* and the Corvettes *UJ202* and *UJ208* south of the island of Lussino. After this, Ken returned to the UK and completed his last period of active naval service, first at Harwich then at various land-based establishments such as HMS *Golden Hind* and HMS *Drake* until his demob in January 1946. He remained on the Royal Fleet Reserve, Davenport, until 1950, bringing to an end an outstanding period of wartime service with many close calls, and leaving almost 'as fresh as a daisy'.

I am honoured to be the first person to officially interview Ken since his service in the war and to capture his incredible story for posterity. Here Ken talks about Navy discipline and his lucky escapes:

Wartime Losses and Doing his Duty While Having a Few Close Shaves

The loss of any ship would hit you, especially after you had served on them for a long time. Many friends went down with them, but you soon learned to get over it because you were taught that way. You had to; you'd a job to do and you did it, and as long as you did your job you were alright. There was a war on and ships were going down all the time in those convoys, there was nothing you could do about it. You were taught strict discipline from being a boy, and if they turned round to me and said walk forward until your hat floats, I would have walked forward over the side until my hat floated. Always obey every last order; that was what we were trained to do from the very beginning. I was incredibly lucky, my number could have been up many times and it nearly was, what with missing the fate of the *Royal Oak* and the *Bramble*, and being attacked by the German planes and the bomb stuck in the side of the ship near me and not going off and in the same attack all around us and the shield of our AA Guns being riddled with bullets. Then, to top it off, not being on that terrible PQ 17 Convoy. I guess it just wasn't my time. I think someone up there has been looking out for me – good job, too, or I wouldn't be here to pass my story on to you.

Additional Information and Life After Service

❖ **Rank at end of service:** Leading seaman and anti-aircraft gunner (AAAB).

❖ **Medals and honours:** 1939–45 Defence Medal, 1939–45 Star with France and Germany Clasp, Atlantic Star, Arctic Star with oak leaf clasp, Italy Star, Russian Arctic Commemorative Medals, 1939–45 War Medal.

❖ **Post-war years:** Electrician for various private companies from 1946 until his retirement in the mid-1980s. Was an avid coarse and sea fisherman. Married Betty in December 1946 and they were together for twenty-nine years. They have two children, three grandchildren and three great-grandchildren.

❖ **Associations and organisations:** No military service-based affiliations, former president of the United Services Fishing Club.

Able Seaman Gunner John Dennett

Served with: Royal Navy, landing ship tank No.322
Service number: DJX347991
Interviewed: Liverpool, Merseyside, 3 December 2015

Service History and Personal Stories

❖ **Born:** 23 July 1924, Branham, England, UK.

❖ John served in a variety of vessels during his seagoing service, mainly on a large landing craft, landing ship tank (LST) *No. 322* as an anti-aircraft gunner.

❖ He took part in supply operations to North Africa and to the besieged island of Malta in 1943.

❖ John was then involved in most of the main sea-based amphibious invasions of the war: Sicily in 1943, Italy at Solerno in 1943 and Anzio in 1944, and D-Day in 1944.

❖ After this he served on the aircraft carrier HMS *Patroller* from mid-1944 to mid-1945, undertaking convoy escort duties in the Atlantic and also preparing for the invasion of Japan.

❖ His last and again very different vessel was the minesweeper HMS *Whitehaven*, which was tasked with mine clearance operations in the Western Approaches and the Irish Sea in 1945–46.

During the Second World War there were many amphibious operations and some full-scale amphibious lead invasions undertaken, the like of which had not been seen before and have not been seen since. The biggest of these were the Allied invasions of North Africa, Sicily, Italy and, of course, D-Day. If lucky, we might occasionally find a veteran who was involved in one of these operations, but to find one who was involved in nearly all of them is simply incredible. John Dennett is one of those very rare servicemen who did exactly that as an anti-aircraft gunner on *LST 322* as part of No.3 Flotilla for nearly two years. This is John's extraordinary story, one that leads us through most of the history of the Navy's supported seaborne landing operations of the Second World War.

John's military service started in March 1942 when he enlisted in Bristol at 18 years of age. Although he was actually 17½, he added six months to give himself the official age required to enlist for active service and hoped for the best. After being accepted into the Navy he went on to be trained at HMS *Raleigh* and HMS *Drake*. Once his basic and gunnery training was completed he was selected to be one of the anti-aircraft gunners on *LST 322*. This large landing craft was still being constructed when John and other members of the crew were on their way across the Atlantic from Scotland to the United States on the *Queen Elizabeth* to go and collect her.

Once in New York, John and many others were based at HMS *Astbury* until they collected the finished vessel *LST 322* from the US Navy shipyards in Philadelphia. This was to become his home for the next two years, during which time John and his fellow crewmates would experience more action than they could ever imagine. In January 1943, following sea trials, *LST 322* joined a big convoy with a mix of other ships that included oil tankers, freighters and troop carriers destined for Gibraltar but which had to go straight into Algiers and Oran in Algeria. After this they were involved in various operations to continually supply the Allies all the way along the North African coast for both the British Eighth Army, which was advancing from the east after its victory at El Alamein, and the American First Army, which was advancing from the west after its successful landings in Algeria and Morocco in Operation Torch.

From April 1943 *LST 322* continued to operate for some months along the Allied supply routes in the Mediterranean as part of No. 3 Flotilla, bringing vital supplies wherever needed in North Africa. During these operations they were also involved in the supply of the besieged island of Malta. After the Axis surrender in North Africa in May 1943 their efforts were directed to supplying the allied forces in the build-up for the invasion of Sicily. This would be the first full assault for *LST 322*.

Operation Husky, the Allied invasion of Sicily, took place on 9–10 July 1943, with the main amphibious assault on 10 July. This massive invasion force landed 150,000 troops on twenty-six beaches stretching across 105 miles of coastline. The operation involved 3,000 ships and 4,000 aircraft and it landed men on the southern and eastern coasts of the island between the town of Licata Torre di Gaffe and Mollarella beach in the west and Cassibile in the east, an invasion on a scale almost equal to that of D-Day. John and *LST 322* were again part of No.3 Flotilla and landed between Torre di Gaffe and Mollarella beach. By 17 August the Allies had taken Sicily and this led to the next two amphibious assaults in which John was to be involved, both in mainland Italy at Salerno and Anzio. These would not be easy.

On 9 September 1943 the Allies launched Operation Avalanche, the seaborne assault at Salerno, which was the start of the main Allied invasion of Italy. This met with fierce resistance from both land and air from a well-prepared and organised Axis force. *LST 322* took part in the transport of the British X Corps and the VI Corps of the 5th US Army, and contributed in the operation to land the 165,000-strong invasion force on the 20-mile beach area from which the Allies would advance. Despite a very strong German counter-attack, the Allies had gained a significant foothold in Italy by the end of the month south of Naples, but it was later thought that another landing was needed. This was to be in the Anzio area south of Rome and was called Operation Shingle. It took place on 22 January and initially met no resistance from the defending forces as an invasion so early in the year was very unexpected, but that would change later. On the first day *LST 322* was one of 238 landing craft in the operation to put 40,000 allied troops and 5,000 vehicles on to a 15-mile stretch of beaches between the towns of Anzio and Nettuno. During the 136 days of the operation, which ended with the liberation of Rome on 5 June 1944, six LSTs including No. 332 would travel from Naples to Anzio every day, bringing approximately 1,500 tonnes of supplies each. While doing their vital job they would, as in previous operations, be under continuous attacks from the air and from shelling. This was not to be the last such experience, as John and the crew of *LST 322* were being sent home in preparation for an even bigger undertaking, the largest amphibious assault in history, Operation Overlord.

On 6 June 1944, John and his landing craft tank set sail from Portsmouth to take part in the first stage of the amphibious assault on the Normandy beaches in Operation Neptune. It landed on Sword Beach around 10.30 a.m. and offloaded troops and vehicles of the British 3rd Division. After D-Day John made a further fifteen runs back to Sword beach from Portsmouth, Southampton and Tilbury between June and August, taking troops, fuel and heavy equipment to the beach and bringing back injured soldiers and prisoners of war. After this John was transferred to the escort carrier HMS *Patroller* (D07), where he was involved in convoy protection duties on the Atlantic crossing between August 1944 and August 1945. He was then posted to his next ship, the minesweeper HMS *Whitehaven* (J121), where he undertook minesweeping in the Irish Sea and Western Approaches. This he did until his demob in HMS *Straight* in Davenport, Plymouth, in May 1946.

When I spoke to John about his staggering service history, he had this to say:

Seeing Action in Almost Every Amphibious Landing of the War

When you were at 'Action Stations' and being attacked everything happened so quickly that you just concentrated on the job at hand. You didn't have time to think about it too much, as you were being strafed and bombed and you were running on adrenaline. Later, in quieter moments, you might reflect and say, 'do you remember this and that' or how bloody close something might have been. Salerno was bad but Anzio for us was the worst of the lot. It was a week of hell because the troops didn't move off the beaches to consolidate their landings, so the beaches were full of men and material and this meant that we couldn't get in to continue supplying and had to lay off shore waiting, and so came under constant heavy bombardment from the German 88s on land and dive bombing attacks from Stukas and various other aircraft from the air. It was so bad that every time you went back you knew and expected that something was going to happen to you. Believe it or not, for us the D-Day landings didn't seem that bad in comparison, but maybe that was because we had been in so many invasions and operations by then and seen so much action that we were used to it all. It was something you had to do and I am very proud I did it and thank my lucky stars that I came back OK.

LST's on D-Day similar to the one on which John served and undertook many amphibious operations during the Second World War.

Additional Information and Life After Service

❖ **Rank at end of service:** Able-seaman and anti-aircraft gunner (AA3).

❖ **Medals and honours:** 1939–45 War Medal, Defence Medal, 1939–45 Star, Italy Star, Atlantic Star with France–Germany Clasp, Legion d'Honneur (French Government), Malta George Cross Fiftieth Anniversary Medal (Maltese Government), Citizen of Honour Award (City of Liverpool).

❖ **Post-war years:** After the war John became a bricklayer and general contractor in Bath, Somerset, and in Wallasey, Liverpool. He worked for various firms over the years and had his own company called Drayton Contractors. He retired in 1995. John married Joyce in 1947; they were together forty-five years and had no children. He was very involved in local football from 1949 and managed his local club, Ashville FC, based in Wallasey, Liverpool. They won the Cheshire Amateurs Cup twice. He was awarded a special medal by the Football Association in recognition of fifty years' service to football.

❖ **Associations and organisations:** Landing Craft Association; Italy Star Association; Normandy Veteran Association; life president of Ashville Football Club; Liverpool Inner City Royal British Legion.

Able-Bodied Seaman Torpedoman Phil Wilcox

Served with: Merchant Navy, *Highland Monarch* and *Ocean Vintage*, Royal Navy, Submarine Service, HMS *Supreme*
Service number: CJX565797
Interviewed: Birmingham, West Midlands, 1 December 2014

Service History and Personal Stories

- ❖ **Born:** 8 January 1923, Newcastle upon Tyne, England, UK.
- ❖ Phil was a seaman in two of the naval services during the Second World War, the Merchant Navy and the Royal Navy, a rare veteran of both the civilian and military seagoing services.
- ❖ Joined the Merchant Navy at the age of 17 in 1940 and served on the *Highland Monarch* from August 1940–April 1942 when she was a civilian passenger ship and later a troop carrier from the UK to Egypt.
- ❖ His next vessel was the *Ocean Vintage* cargo ship, from July–October 1942. Phil was on board when she was torpedoed and sunk by Japanese submarine *I-27* in the Gulf of Oman on 22 October 1942.
- ❖ After this Phil was determined to get into the fight and joined the Royal Navy Submarine Service in 1943. He trained as a Torpedoman and was assigned to HMS *Supreme* from May 1944 until November 1945.

❖ His active service on HMS *Supreme* took him all over the world, including back to the Gulf of Oman and on to the Far East. There Phil and his crew sank many Japanese vessels, bringing his fight full circle.

When I was searching for a submariner for my book I was very lucky to meet Tony Parkinson while at the 11 November remembrance ceremony in Manchester. He was a veteran submariner from the Cold War period and also part of the Manchester branch of the Submariners Association. I told him about my book and he very kindly took me along to the monthly meeting to share this with the members. He also helped me with my search by putting my appeal for a veteran in their nationwide newsletter and on their website. Eventually news got back to me about a veteran in Birmingham by the name of Phil Wilcox who was willing to be interviewed and who had an extraordinary story. Phil was a veteran of both the Merchant and Royal Navies who survived the sinking of his ship by a Japanese submarine only to later become a submariner himself and go on to sink Japanese vessels in order to take the fight back to the enemy.

Phil joined the Merchant Navy at the age of 17 in 1940 and trained at the National Sea Training School in Sharpness in Gloucester called T.S. Vindicatrix. This was the main place where new recruits entering the Merchant Navy literally got 'shown the ropes'. Once he had successfully passed the training he went to sea on his first ship, *Highland Monarch*, from August 1940 until April 1942. She first left on trips from Cardiff to Buenos Aires, Argentina, during her last period as an 'official' passenger ship in 1940–41. She would take civilian passengers on the outward journeys and bring volunteer military recruits back on the homeward journey. Phil continued to serve on her between 1941–42, when she would be used purely as a troopship carrying service personnel from Glasgow round the Cape and up to Port Said in Egypt to deliver them for the desert war against Rommel in North Africa.

From July until October 1942 Phil would serve on his second ship, *Ocean Vintage*. His time on her would come to a dramatic end on the evening of 22 October 1942 when the armed but unescorted vessel was making the trip from New York to Bandar Shaphur in Iran to deliver 9,300 tons of cargo and was torpedoed near Masirah Island in the Gulf of Oman by the Japanese submarine *I-27* with Commander Kitamura at the helm. *Ocean Vintage*, a Ministry of War Transport-owned ship, was hit and sunk by one torpedo and her cargo of war supplies, which were intended for Russia, were lost. Luckily that was all that was lost and the crew survived despite the *I-27* attempting to ram the lifeboats before leaving the scene. The master of the vessel, Captain John Robinson, and his crew of forty-three seamen and six gunners were rescued, and an RAF crash launch towed their lifeboats into Ras al Hadd harbour in Oman.

After this traumatic experience in which Phil almost lost his brother, Dennis, the crew was returned to the UK as distressed British seamen (DBS) and put into the Merchant Navy reserve pool. However, the *Ocean Vintage* experience had a profound effect on Phil, who had decided that he wanted to be more involved and to really get in to the fight. The way in which he chose to do this was by applying to join the Royal Navy, and after being accepted in May 1943, he went into the submarine service as a torpedoman. This choice was his conscious or subconscious means of fighting back against an enemy in the same way it struck at him while he was on *Ocean Vintage*. Either way it was to prove a very successful tactic in the next year and a half. Phil's training as a submariner and torpedoman took place at HMS *Dolphin*, base of the Royal Navy Submarine School in Gosport, Hampshire, and after passing he became an able-bodied seaman torpedoman (ABST).

Phil's Royal Navy active service posting led to him becoming part of the first crew on the newly commissioned submarine HMS *Supreme* (P252) from May 1944, when she was taken from Cammell Laird shipyard in Liverpool, to the time of her sea trials in Holy Loch and Scapa Flow in Scotland in June and July 1944, and on through active service until November 1945. Phil served under Lieutenant Commander Thomas Erasmus Barlow, who proved to be resourceful and very successful. This was proven by the amount of enemy vessels engaged and sunk by HMS *Supreme* during this time, most in the Pacific Far East, namely

HMS *Supreme* where Phil served as an ABST (Able-Bodied Seaman Torpedoman).

thirteen Japanese sailing vessels, six Japanese coasters, a Japanese tug and a barge, and a small unidentified vessel. Phil's time in the submarine service finished when HMS *Supreme* docked in Portsmouth on 13 November 1945. Shortly after, on 8 December, she was paid off into reserve. Phil went home on paid leave and was eventually demobbed on 12 February 1946.

When I interviewed Phil we spoke at length about his wartime naval service, of which he had very clear recollections, including of the following:

The Sinking of the *Ocean Vintage*

When we were hit things seemed to happen quite quickly. It wasn't long before it became quite chaotic because it was night time and the attack and the explosion seemed to come from nowhere. As the ship started to go down and we had got the abandon ship order we were freeing and launching the lifeboat. It was during that time that my brother Dennis, whilst trying to lower a lifeboat, fell in the water. I was one of the people who helped save him. It wasn't normal procedure for brothers or as far as I know any family members to be serving on the same ship together for exactly this reason in case the vessel was lost and they went down together and were maybe lost together, which we nearly were! I always remember looking back and seeing the ship completely upright in the water under what I think was a full moon, and seeing her slip under the water as you see *Titanic* doing in the film. You can never forget something like that you know,

A haunting picture of a Japanese ship going down as seen through the periscope of an Allied submarine.

it stays with you forever. I found out some time later that we had been sunk by the Japanese submarine I-27.

After this I was determined to get more involved and take the war to the enemy in whatever way I could; I really wanted to get in to the fight. I later did this by applying for the Royal Navy and serving with the submarine service on HMS *Supreme*. I was on her from May 1944 until November 1945 and we saw a lot of action and we engaged and sank quite a few Japanese vessels of one kind or another. Funny how things go, there I was as a torpedoman helping sink Japanese ships after what they did to me on the *Ocean Vintage*. I guess what comes around goes around! During my time on her we went to loads of places such as Malta, Port Said, Aden, Trincomalee, Phuket, Penang, Langkawi, Andaman Islands, Sumatra, Malacca Straights and many more places as well. When we attacked enemy vessels, depending on the situation we either stayed submerged and used torpedoes or surfaced and used deck guns. Either way we caused considerable damage and had many successes. As an ABST I was down below in the torpedo room where we had six firing tubes. 1, 3, 5 were on the port or left-hand side and 2, 4, 6 were on the starboard or right-hand side of the sub. It was hard work down there. I wrote a poem about that, I'll let you hear it later, about the grinding work below decks. Hauly, hauly on the fish, we called the torpedoes fish and we had to haul them into place ready for firing.

Additional Information and Life After Service

- ❖ **Rank at end of service:** Able-seaman torpedoman.
- ❖ **Medals and honours:** 1939–45 Defence Medal, 1939–45 Star, Atlantic Star, Africa Star, Burma Star with Pacific Bar.
- ❖ **Post-war years:** Worked most of his post-war years for Land Rover as a quality controller until his retirement in 1989. Married Nelly in 1952. They were together for fifty-five years and have two sons.
- ❖ **Associations and organisations:** T.S. Vindicatrix Association; Submariners Association, Birmingham.

Leading Seaman Jim Radford

Served with: Merchant Navy, rescue tug *Empire Larch*, Royal Navy,
   admiral's dispatch vessel HMS *Surprise*
Service number: CSX815600
Interviewed: Honour Oak Park, London, 3 July 2015

Service History and Personal Stories

- ❖ **Born:** 1 October 1928, Hull, England, UK.
- ❖ Jim was a child evacuee from his home town of Hull from 1939–42. He later returned, and in 1944 joined the Merchant Navy at just 15 years of age.
- ❖ He became a galley hand on the deep sea rescue tug *Empire Larch* and on 6 June 1944 he was at Gold Beach where he helped pull into place the block ships and later the famous Mulberry Harbour.
- ❖ Aged just 15, Jim is thought to possibly be the youngest to have served at D-Day. At 18 he went on to serve in the Royal Navy from 1946–54.
- ❖ While in the Royal Navy he served on the frigate HMS *Surprise* (K346), which was the dispatch vessel for the Admiral of the Mediterranean Fleet.

❖   Since then Jim has been an active campaigner for many causes such as the homeless,
     the Campaign for Nuclear Disarmament (CND) and Veterans for Peace. He is also
     an accomplished folk and sea shanty singer, both in the UK and worldwide.

Jim Radford was one of the youngest, if not the youngest, to have taken part in
D-Day. At just 15 years of age while serving as a galley boy on the Merchant Navy
deep sea rescue tug *Empire Larch* at Gold Beach, Jim witnessed things no young
boy should see and very quickly came of age. These experiences are described
extremely well in his moving composition called *Shores of Normandy*, in which he
says: 'I little thought when I left home of the dreadful sights I'd see, But I came to
manhood on the first day that I saw Normandy!' This is a part of a much bigger
story, that of a boy who grew to be a man while in the service of his country in
both the Merchant and Royal Navies over a ten-year period.

Jim was a spritely 88 years of age when I recorded his incredible story in 2015.
It differs from the very beginning because Jim was so young when war broke out
that he was one of those sent as a child evacuee from the port city of Hull, which
would certainly be a key target for German Air Force bombing. He went to live
with a family in the relative safety of the country village of South Dalton in the
East Riding of Yorkshire from the age of 11 to 14 in 1939–42. He returned to
Hull and aged 15 finished his schooling at Hull College of Arts and Crafts at Easter
1944. He was so eager to take an active part in the war that despite his age he was
determined to find a way to do it, and that he did.

Jim was too young to sign up for any of the main branches of the armed forces
so for a young boy who came from a rich maritime family background the way
forward was obvious: he would enlist in the Merchant Navy. He went to the
office of the United Towing Company at Postern Gate in Hull and signed up.

This continued the seagoing tradition
within his family as his brother Fred had
already joined the Royal Navy Rescue
Tug Service in 1942, and sadly his other
brother Jack had been killed when the
ship he was serving on, SS *Cree*, was
torpedoed in the Atlantic in 1940. In
addition, his father Frederick, a First
World War Navy man, was working
on dredgers. Jim hoped that even at
his age he could at least get to sea as

Jim as a child evacuee.

a deckhand if he was lucky and that is exactly what happened. He was sent to a docking tug called *Bureaucrat*, where for the next month he learned the basics of seamanship in and around Hull docks. While he was working, there came an even greater opportunity for him when he was asked if he would like to join the crew of another tug called the *Empire Larch*, which needed a galley boy. Jim eagerly accepted and went to sign on at Albert Dock, Liverpool, because he knew that this was a deep sea tug and that meant he could really get out to sea, do his bit and get into the adventure that was the Second World War. Little did he know that eventually the reality would be quite different and would be an eventful, abrupt and dangerous transition from boyhood to manhood. As D-Day came ever closer and the build-up in all of the services continued, the *Empire Larch* would play her part in these preparations when she was sent to various ports around Britain such as Blythe, Sunderland, Shields and Oban on what was known as 'the Corncob Convoy' to help collect old merchant ships that would be used as block ships during the invasion. At that point the crew did not know they would be so directly involved in Operation Overlord. They soon found out when they reached Poole on 4–5 June that they would be playing a significant role that would put them right in the thick of it.

It is at this point we have a look at the role of the rescue tug during the war, because, as Jim said, they played such an important part in so many ways but now seem all but forgotten. The Rescue Tug Service essentially ran within two naval branches: the T124T, which was HM Rescue Tug Service and as part of the Royal Navy sailed under its red ensign or flag, and the Rescue Tug Service, which was part of the Merchant Navy and belonged to companies such as the Shipping Federation and the United Towing Company, sailing under the white ensign or flag. Although the Royal Navy requisitioned many merchant tugs and their crews, which then became uniformed and under RN discipline, other tugs and their crews continued to work as merchant vessels, such as Jim's tug *Empire Larch*. The rescue tugs made an important contribution in many ways through the varied tasks that they undertook, such as towing the block ships and artificial Mulberry Harbours into place while under enemy fire to create a vital supply line from the sea for the invasion forces on land, and also lugging out the massive drums of the Pluto fuel pipeline. Their work was at times very dangerous and their crews were made up of brave men who would also come to the aid of burning, stranded or damaged ships, often in atrocious weather conditions, and bring them back to safe waters and ports, just like an extended deep water lifeboat service. They were credited with saving the lives of thousands of servicemen and around 3 million tons of merchant shipping, many with their precious cargoes, and also 254 warships. Most of these ships had been hit and crippled by enemy action. Their towing and salvage expertise in a time of war were crucial skills that, as these facts show, served this country extremely well and therefore deserved to be remembered. However,

Empire Larch, later the *Masterman*, then *Smjeli*.

the price they paid was high: many brave sailors died and twenty rescue tugs were lost, some with all hands.

We now join Jim on board the *Empire Larch* to focus on one rescue tug, on one mission, which was one part of this bigger picture. It is the early hours of 6 June 1944, where in the murderous opening scenes of D-Day a 15-year-old boy is witnessing things almost beyond his comprehension. Jim now shares with us his accounts of this painfully historical day:

An Eyewitness to the Hellish Opening Hours of D-Day

I saw and experienced things that day that no man, never mind boy, should ever have to witness in their lifetime. We were pulling block ships into position near a place called Arromanches so they could be scuttled and detonated to form breakwaters for the artificial Mulberrys that would follow. Because of this we were positioned between the ships of the Royal Navy, who were behind us firing a non-stop barrage of flak, rockets, shells and tracers, and in front of us landing craft going into the beach and heavy incoming mortar, machine gun and artillery fire from the Germans directed our way and splashes from some of these landing near us in the water. Scenes of absolute carnage and hell unfolded before our eyes. There were landing craft on fire and bodies everywhere. They were bobbing all around us, laid out on the beach and caught on steel stakes in the shallows. I feel it now and remember them still, which is why I am a campaigner for peace! In the days, weeks and months that followed we assisted with many things including bringing over sections of the gigantic artificial floating Mulberry Harbours; these significantly helped the Allies achieve final victory. Years later when I returned to Normandy I openly wept as I saw young children playing on the same beaches where I had witnessed so many brave servicemen lose their lives for that freedom many years before. Seeing the beaches as they are now and remembering how they were then, very emotional. It was these feelings that led to me writing my first song as a tribute, called *Shores of Normandy*.

Once his service in the Merchant Navy was over, Jim joined the Royal Navy in 1946 and served his country for another eight years until 1954. During this time he became a leading seaman and served on the frigate HMS *Surprise* (K346), dispatch vessel for the Admiral of the Mediterranean Fleet, and on the cruiser HMS *Superb* (C25). Jim finished his distinguished service stationed at HMS *Harrier* Royal Naval Aircraft Direction Centre in South Wales, where he repaired radar equipment.

To conclude, Jim's story is a fitting tribute to his character and his service, echoed in these words, the motto of his former ship HMS *Surprise*: *Sola nobilitas virtus* (Valour is the only true nobility).

Additional Information and Life After Service

- ❖ **Rank at end of service:** Leading Seaman.
- ❖ **Medals and honours:** 1939–45 War Medal, 1939–45 Star, France–Germany Star, Legion d'Honneur.
- ❖ **Post-war years:** After leaving the Royal Navy and life on the sea in 1954, Jim devoted his life on the land to many good causes in which he believed passionately, and as a result has held jobs such as the Homeless Action's hostel advertising manager, director of Manchester Council for Voluntary Service, and director for the National Community Resource Unit. Jim has also been an active campaigner for peace organisations and, despite having officially retired in 1991, still actively supports many causes. He is a talented singer, songwriter and performer on the folk and sea shanty circuit in the UK and also performs around the world. Married to Jenny 1954–2006, they were together fifty-two years and have three sons, one daughter, five grandchildren and six great-grandchildren.
- ❖ **Associations and organisations:** Founder Member of the Deep Sea Rescue Tugs Association; Veterans for Peace UK; previously in the Normandy Veterans Association; CND.

Sergeant James Baker DSM

Served with: Royal Marines, 544 Assault Flotilla
Service number: PO/X105481
Interviewed: Blackpool, Lancashire, 11 July 2015

Service History and Personal Stories

❖ **Born:** 8 April 1923, Blackpool, England, UK.

❖ Jim Baker joined the Royal Marines just before his 18th birthday on 1 April 1941. After rigorous training he undertook U-boat hunting on a converted trawler in the Western Approaches.

❖ On D-Day he was a helmsman on a LCA (Landing Craft Assault vessel) on one of the first waves of the invasion to land on Juno Beach, after which he directly engaged the enemy and was injured.

❖ After being discharged from a field hospital he was later transferred to operations at Omaha Beach, working closely with the Americans, where he completed twenty-two troop drops to the beach.

- ❖ He won a Distinguished Service Medal for his valour, which was awarded at Buckingham Palace by King George VI in November 1944.
- ❖ After the war, Jim served as a captain in the Royal Marine Forces Volunteer Reserve (RMFVR) from 1946 to 1956.

In most cases, when we think of D–Day and the Normandy landings, we visualise the pictures, newsreel footage or a documentary that we may have seen, or think of the horrific scenes of a film such as *Saving Private Ryan*. That is probably as close as most of us will get to or be able to comprehend what it must have been like to be there in that most horrendous of situations on those beaches on that historical day. The only other way that you might get a real insight into what happened is if you are lucky enough to meet, talk to or interview a survivor. When I met former Royal Marine James Baker DSM at the seventy-first D–Day anniversary in Normandy in June 2015 and interviewed him at his home in Blackpool a month later, I felt that fate had picked me one of the finest examples of a veteran who was absolutely in the very thick of it right from the very beginning. He was part of one of the first assault landings on the morning of 6 June 1944 when, as one veteran put it, they 'stormed the gates of Hell'. This is the story of a serviceman who was trained in both amphibious and land warfare, who as a helmsman of a landing craft assault vessel (LCA) hit Juno Beach and went from his badly damaged craft straight into battle alongside his Canadian brothers in arms, showing the extreme bravery and leadership skills that earned him a Distinguished Service Medal for gallantry in the face of the enemy.

The Royal Marines is the United Kingdom's amphibious infantry force, forming part of the naval service along with the Royal Navy. The corps was formed in the reign of King Charles II on 28 October 1664 as a unit of seagoing soldiers, and in 1802 it was officially titled the Royal Marines by King George III. During its long and prestigious history it has been involved in more battles on land and sea around the world than any other branch of the British armed forces. So numerous are the corps battle honours that they are simply represented by the famous globe and single honour 'Gibraltar'. The Marines are also widely acknowledged to have some of the world's most elite commando forces; their dual combat role is echoed in their motto

Combined Forces emblem, representing each of the armed forces.

Per mare per terram, meaning 'By sea by land'. During the war some 80,000 men served in the Royal Marines, and they continued to operate at sea and in land formations, but 1942 saw the formation of the first Royal Marines Commandos. 5 RM Commandos was amongst the first unit to land on D-Day, and two-thirds of all the landing craft involved were crewed by Marines. Some 16,000 members of the corps took part in Operation Overlord in many roles, some even manning tanks. Jim Baker was a part of that proud tradition. He joined the Royal Marines on 1 April 1941 in Preston, Lancashire (All Fools Day, as Jim recalled with a wry smile), after which he was sent to do his intense basic training at the Commando Training Centre Royal Marines (CTC-RM) in Lympstone, Devon. This lasted six months, during which time he was also trained on Bren Carriers, and he was then attached to the 2nd Mobile RM Reconnaissance Unit. At that time at the end of 1941 the Royal Navy required more manpower to help in its war against the U-boats, so Jim volunteered and was transferred to HMS *York City*, a trawler that had been converted into an anti-submarine vessel and fitted with depth charges and other equipment.

He was based at Milford Haven in South Wales, from where he would set out on patrols in the Western Approaches. This would last until late 1942, after which Jim was attached to the 18th Battalion Royal Marines and sent up to Scotland for assault landing craft training. He was based at Inveraray and Port Glasgow, two of the many new Royal Marine and Commando camps that were set up for specialist training in Scotland. There he began training to be a coxswain or skipper in various types of landing craft, mainly the smaller LCAs that were used to deliver the first waves of infantry on to beaches during an invasion. He undertook continuous practice landing exercises, many under live fire conditions, mostly around the Isle of Arran. It was during this time that 'combined forces' training began to take shape, with joint exercises taking place incorporating Royal Marines, Royal Navy and infantry soldiers with the Royal Air Force in support. This would form the basis for the essential three services combined forces operations that would later be a key factor in making the Normandy landings a success. After Scotland, in early 1944, Jim was sent to Dartmoor in Devon for unarmed combat training, and finished with more intense combined training with Canadian troops of the French Canadian Regiment de la Chaudière doing LCA landings at Slapton Sands, Devon, where they narrowly missed being intercepted by German E-boats, and at Hayling Island, east of Portsmouth. Now they were as ready as they could be for the real thing, which would come soon enough.

Early on 6 June 1944, 21-year-old Jim Baker and his LCA full of Canadian troops from the Regiment de la Chaudière were lowered into the water from the landing ship infantry (large) SS *Monowai*, They formed part of the 544 Flotilla and were in the second assault wave as it hit the Nan sector of Juno Beach at around 8.30 a.m. These assault troops were helping to spearhead Operation Neptune,

Troops landing on the beaches of Normandy from a landing craft assault vessel similar to the one skippered by Jim.

the amphibious part of Operation Overlord. Jim now gives us a real insight into how things dramatically unfolded on that terrifying morning:

The Reality of Storming the Beaches of Normandy on D-Day

On D-Day I was part of 544 Flotilla that was landing in the Canadian Sector at Juno Beach which was under the 3rd Canadian Division. It was my job as the coxswain or skipper at the helm of an LCA to try and get my boys safely on to the beach. They were part of the Canadian Regiment de la Chaudière; some of our boys really were boys as young as seventeen, eighteen, nineteen! We were going in as part of the second wave with the 8th Brigade but this didn't mean we had it any easier than the first wave! Far from it, we were twelve LCAs, each with thirty-five fully equipped troops, three Marines, the skipper and two other crewmen. On the way in we lost ten LCAs to enemy gunfire and mines, that's a terrible loss of men, it was murderous! As we got within about 1,000 yards there was just my LCA and my dear pal Hooky Walker the coxswain on his LCA. We approached the beach side by side and as I looked across he gave me a bold thumbs up and a broad grin as if to say 'we've made it'. At that moment he hit some Teller mines and they just vaporised him, the infantry, the boat, everything; they were all gone in a split second. The blast blew us up in the air about 20ft and we landed on the 'Belgian Gates' defences. We were in the water and got to the beach but we were then held up by barbed wire coils. As we got through we were climbing over bodies that were already victims of sniper fire from the church tower and from mortars. I was injured but there was no time to hesitate,

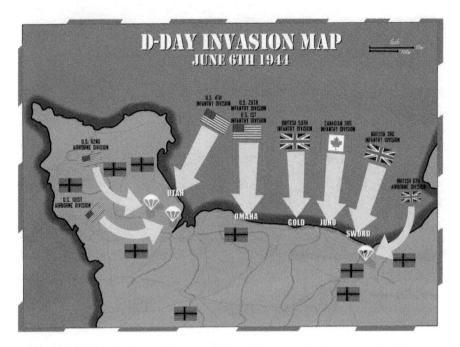

D-Day invasion map showing the forces involved and the Normandy beaches on which they landed during the biggest amphibious assault in history.

we were under fire, so I got together what infantry we had left to try and take out a German position that was causing us a lot of casualties. Me and a sergeant who had a flame thrower took care of them and we had to do it quickly because once we were on the beach proper we were in the killing zone of machine gun fire. I went forward just firing and praying! For that and other things along the way I won a DSM, but many others deserved it too. Everyone fought to the best of their ability and many good boys died that day. I still like to go back to Normandy when I can and pay my respects to those who I have always called my boys.

At the end of the interview Jim finished with these very kind and sincere words in memory of those servicemen who didn't come back, which moved me greatly. He said, 'Well for all the lads that can't be here to whom we owe a debt of gratitude, may I say a heartfelt thank you.'

Later on, Jim received more injuries, this time in Bernières from a six-barrelled mortar called a Nebelwerfer. After recovering from his injuries in a field station he was relocated to help the Americans at Omaha Beach, where he completed twenty-two LCA troop drops. Later he went back into the 2nd Mobile RM Reconnaissance Unit and was in an armoured Bren Carrier attached to the US 82nd Airborne Division. After returning to the UK in late 1944 to receive his DSM from King George VI and have time in hospital for plastic surgery, he was posted to Ceylon (now Sri Lanka) in 1945 as a platoon sergeant to train with the 544 Assault Flotilla for the Japanese invasion. He returned in 1946 and was demobbed in Portsmouth.

Additional Information and Life After Service

- ❖ **Rank at end of service:** Sergeant.
- ❖ **Medals and honours:** Distinguished Service Medal, Legion d'Honneur (French Government), 1939–45 Defence Medal, 1939–45 War Medal, 1939–45 Star, France & Germany Star, Various commutative medals.
- ❖ **Post-war years:** British Transport Police, Manchester, 1946–47; HGV driver for various companies, 1947–95; Courier driver with Baker Booth and Eastwood solicitors until retiring in 2005 at the age of 83. Married to May from 1949–2008; one son, one daughter, five grandchildren and five great-grandchildren.
- ❖ **Associations and organisations:** President of the Royal Marines Association, Blackpool; president of the Blackpool Ex-Servicemen's Association; member of the Mighty 82nd Airborne Association.

3

Air Force and the War in the Air

The Royal Air Force is the youngest of the three services and started its life during the First World War on 1 April 1918 when the Royal Flying Corps and the Royal Naval Air Service were amalgamated. It developed quickly out of necessity as this new dimension in warfare changed many things on the battlefield, along with the understanding that domination of the skies could not only give vital intelligence but also meant having a distinct advantage that might be enough to win a battle. In the late 1930s the RAF expanded rapidly as it was becoming evident that Nazi Germany was rearming even though it was still bound by the Treaty of Versailles, which had banned it from doing exactly that after the First World War.

When the existence of the Luftwaffe was announced by Germany in 1935, swift changes were implemented in the UK, when in 1936 the Air Council expanded the RAF and reorganised the air defence of Great Britain into four commands – Bomber Command, Fighter Command, Coastal Command and Training Command – and formed the RAF Volunteer Reserve. It planned for the increase in the number of squadrons within each of those commands and in 1938 Maintenance and Balloon Commands were formed as war drew closer.

By 1939 the RAF strength stood at 135 squadrons and the Royal Auxiliary Air Force had nineteen, and the Women's Auxiliary Air Force (WAAF) had been formed. These were backed up by ground crews, aircraft supply in the form of the civilian Air Transport Auxiliary (ATA), a network of radar stations and operation rooms, and all the essential personnel that were required to keep more than 200 RAF stations running. This included station commanders, fighter pilots, bomber crews, aircraft engineers, armourers, radio communication operators, radar operators, medical staff, fire crews, storemen, drivers, clerical and catering staff.

The RAF fought in every theatre of war in defensive and offensive operations and its roles were very diverse, from giving fighter cover and carrying out bombing missions over Europe and in the deserts of Africa, to defending the airspace over the UK during the critical Battle of Britain period. It also gave cover for convoys and hunted U-boats in the Atlantic, Baltic and Mediterranean, as well as dropping supplies in the jungles of Burma. During every major Allied invasion, including Salerno, Anzio and Normandy, the RAF provided the essential air cover that was required to make those operations successful.

The service's huge and varied role also involved and encompassed other types of operations, such as propaganda leaflet drops, scattering metal pieces of chaff called 'window' to distort enemy radar systems, and deploying specially adapted photographic aircraft for intelligence gathering. The RAF also covertly dropped SOE agents into Nazi-occupied Europe. The role of the Air Force also extended beyond that, as it was involved in the combined forces structure and had special beach units as a part of Allied invasion forces, as well as mobile intelligence units and the RAF Regiment. Coastal Command also carried out air-sea rescues.

Essentially the RAF was involved in every type of action on every front and in every place, and legends were born such as 'The Few' and 'The Dambusters', while heroes such as Johnny Johnson, Guy Gibson, Sailor Malan and Douglas Bader became household names. In this section, veterans who reflect many branches of the RAF during the war share with us their fascinating insights, memories and experiences.

Wing Commander Tom Neil DFC and BAR AFC AE

Served with: Royal Air Force, Fighter Command, Nos 249, 41 and 28
    Squadrons
Service number: 79168
Interviewed: Twaite St Mary, Norfolk, 17 February 2016

Service History and Personal Stories

- ❖ **Born:** 14 July 1920, Bootle, England, UK.
- ❖ Tom Neil served in the RAF for twenty-six years and had a very distinguished record with many great achievements. During his career he flew the Hurricane, Spitfire and American P-47, P-38 and P-51 fighters in combat.
- ❖ He is a Battle of Britain fighter pilot 'Ace' and one of 'The Few' who helped save Great Britain in the darkest period of her modern history during the summer of 1940.
- ❖ During his service over the skies of Britain and later in the siege of Malta in 1940–42 Tom shot down fourteen enemy aircraft. He later gave air support over Omaha Beach at D-Day in 1944 and flew in Burma in 1945.

❖   After the war he became a test pilot and flew 127 types of aircraft. He was later the officer commanding No. 28 Squadron in Egypt in 1952–56 up until the Suez crisis.

❖   Among his many awards is the Distinguished Flying Cross (DFC), later with bar added (meaning it was awarded twice). Tom finished his career in 1964 as a wing commander.

'Never in the field of human conflict has so much been owed by so many to so few.' These immortal words were used in a famous speech by Winston Churchill on 20 August 1940 in an address to the House of Commons when describing the brave young pilots of Fighter Command. It was the actions of these RAF pilots during the Battle of Britain in the summer of 1940 that changed the course of history and against immense odds saved Great Britain from the imminent threat of invasion from Nazi Germany. 'The Few', as they became known, were the last line of defence against an enemy that had to gain air superiority over our skies in order to launch Operation Sea Lion, the intended seaborne invasion of Britain. Had it succeeded it would have been the end for the United Kingdom and could have meant a very different outcome to the war. This is the story of Tom Neil, Battle of Britain fighter pilot ace.

His illustrious twenty-six-year career started when he joined the Royal Air Force Volunteer Reserve (RAFVR) in October 1938 at the age of 18. At the outbreak of war he was called up to full-time service and posted to No. 8 Flying Training Squadron (FTS) in Montrose, Scotland. After successful completion of his training, Tom was commissioned as a pilot officer and on 15 May 1940 joined No. 249 Squadron at its re-formation at RAF Church Fenton in North Yorkshire. During the Battle of Britain Tom flew 157 sorties from RAF North Weald in Essex and fought fierce air battles over the south of England during the long hard summer of 1940. This was a time when the fate of our country hung in the balance and the outcome depended to a large degree on the 3,000 or so brave pilots of RAF Fighter Command.

After the Battle of Britain Tom was promoted from pilot officer to flight lieutenant and received the DFC with bar. Aged 20, he was second in command of No. 249 Squadron when it was sent on the aircraft carriers *Furious* and then *Ark Royal* to help the besieged island of Malta. After arriving there, Tom once again found himself engaged in continuous actions and hard aerial combat between May and December 1941 as the island was under almost daily attack from the Luftwaffe. Once this tour of duty was finished, Tom returned home on a long journey via the Middle East, during which his first ship was torpedoed, then on to South Africa, West Africa, Canada and finally arriving at Liverpool in March 1942. In 1940–42 Tom had been credited with shooting down fourteen aircraft of various types, such as the German Messerschmitt Bf 109 and Bf 110, Heinkel He 111, Junkers Ju 87 and Ju 88, Dornier Do 17 and an Italian Macchi C.200.

After returning to the UK, Tom had various postings and held some very interesting positions between 1942 and 1944 with both the RAF and the United States Army Air Force (USAAF). These began in March 1942 at No. 81 RAF Group based at Avening Court in Gloucester, where he was tactics officer. Then in mid-June he went to 56 OTU in RAF Tealing in Scotland, and from September 1942 to July 1943 he became Officer Commanding No. 41 Squadron based at RAF Coningsby in Lincolnshire, from where various missions were flown over German-occupied Europe. In July 1943 he was posted to 53 OTU at RAF Heston in Middlesex as an instructor, and in December 1943 Tom became flying liaison officer to the American Ninth Air Force's 100th Fighter Wing and flew in an observational role, giving

Emblem and motto of 249 (Gold Coast) Squadron – *Pugnis et calcibus*, 'With fists and heels'.

top cover air support over Omaha Beach on D-Day. On 7 June 1944, D-Day +1, his P-51 Mustang gave close protection fighter escort for a C-47 Dakota that was taking some senior officers and an American general to a temporary airfield known as an advanced landing ground (ALG) that had been constructed in the Omaha Beach area. It was there that he landed what is thought to be the first Allied fighter on French soil during the invasion of Western Europe. This was, as Tom recalls, while fighting was still going on with the Germans at the far end of the airfield. Over the following months he went on to engage in further missions over Western Europe as the Allied forces advanced through France, Belgium, Holland and finally into Germany.

Tom's next posting in January 1945 took him to the School of Land/Air Warfare at RAF Old Sarum in Wiltshire as an instructor. This was a special place that was combining the training of land and air tactics and promoting Army and Air Force co-operation. His next posting took him out to Burma in March 1945 on special investigation/reconnaissance gathering, where he flew operational sorties with the No.1 Indian Wing, after which he returned once again to RAF Old Sarum in April 1945 until January 1946. Then he went on to another very different phase in his career, to train and become an RAF test pilot. For this he trained on a special course at the Empire Test Pilots School (ETPS) at Cranfield in Bedfordshire and, once qualified, he flew 127 different types of aircraft – from propeller-driven to those with jet engines – at Boscombe Down in Wiltshire until 1950. In the following years he continued to climb the ranks and while doing so maintained a very varied and interesting career. From 1950–51 he was a staff officer at Fighter Command at Bentley Priory in Herefordshire, then from 1951–52 he was at RAF Staff College at Bracknell in Berkshire. In 1952–56 Tom was the officer commanding No. 28 Squadron, which was part of the flying wing based in Egypt's

Canal Zone at RAF Abu Sueir near Port Said, and he left just before the Suez Crisis of 1956.

After this he returned to the UK and his next posting was instructing senior officers at RAF College Cranwell in Lincolnshire in 1956–57. Tom's last years of service took him to even higher levels when he became military secretary to Air Chief Marshal Sir George Mills and Admiral Denny at the British Embassy in Washington DC from 1957–62 as part of the British Joint Services Mission to Washington. The last posting of his career would bring him back to the UK once again, where he would serve in the corridors of power on this side of the ocean in the Ministry of Defence Planning Department in Whitehall from 1962–64. Tom Neil retired from the RAF in 1964 as a wing commander who had been decorated by both the UK and USA during his service, with the Distinguished Flying Cross and Bar, Air Force Cross, Air Efficiency Award, and American Bronze Star. He had flown many combat missions in both of the famous British wartime fighters, the Hurricane and the Spitfire, and also the American fighters the P-38 Lightning, P-47 Thunderbolt and P-51 Mustang among many others.

At the time of writing in 2017 there were fewer than twenty Battle of Britain pilots left in the UK from the original 3,000 of 1940, and from those Tom 'Ginger' Neil is one of the last 'aces' of that historical defence of our nation, so it was truly amazing to hear what he had to say:

Being One of 'The Few' in the Battle Of Britain

Well I flew in the Battle of Britain 157 times against the Luftwaffe and I am credited with 13½ or so victories and I survived. During the Battle of Britain, of course, there were 2,947 of us took part, mostly from Britain and a few

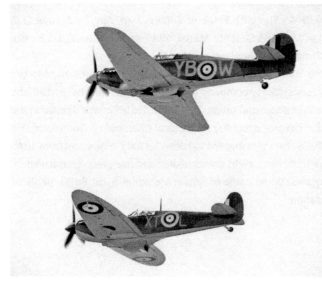

The Hurricane and the Spitfire, the main front-line fighters and backbone of Fighter Command during the Second World War. Tom flew both of these in combat with great success, becoming a high-scoring ace.

from Canada and New Zealand and South Africa and other members of the Commonwealth and elsewhere. They were all splendid people and we lost 550 killed and another 650 hideously wounded, burned and so on, and we lost 1,100 aircraft, Spitfires and Hurricanes. The Germans lost 1,800 aircraft, mostly bombers, and they lost around 3,000 airmen of one sort or another. On 15 September, which was the big day for us, we shot down sixty or so enemy aircraft. Actually it was claimed that we shot down 180 on that day but we didn't, and this was because most of the flying took place at 18–19,000ft and you couldn't properly claim an aircraft destroyed because by the time it hit the ground 20, 30, 40 miles away it was again attacked by four other squadrons on the way down who each claimed victories, so four times for the same aircraft! So as the Battle of Britain went on it didn't really finish on 31 October, it went on almost until Christmas and we had some severe fighting in November 1940. On 7 November I reputedly shot down three aircraft; I crash-landed once and I bailed out once all in the same day, so I achieved a certain notoriety for that reason. The Battle of Britain saved the world – few people sometimes change world history and that was one of those very important events where this happened.

In a later phone conversation Tom gave me some very good advice regarding being a writer and life in general. He said: 'Keep persevering and you will succeed,' just as this very fine and brave gentleman has done in so many ways.

Additional Information and Life After Service

- ❖ **Rank at end of service:** Wing commander.
- ❖ **Medals and honours:** Distinguished Flying Cross and Bar, Air Force Cross, Air Efficiency Award, 1939–45 Star with Battle of Britain Clasp, Aircrew Europe Star, Africa Star, Burma Star, 1939–45 Defence Medal, 1939–45 War Medal, US Bronze Star, Malta George Cross Fiftieth Anniversary Medal.
- ❖ **Post-war years:** Once Tom had retired from the RAF in 1964 he returned to the USA and led a British consultancy company in Boston, Massachusetts. In 1967 he returned to the United Kingdom and settled in Norfolk. He became a director in the shoe industry and also became secretary of his local Chamber of Commerce. He retired in the early 1980s. Tom was married to Eileen for sixty-nine years from 1945 until 2015. They have three sons, eight grandchildren and five great-grandchildren.
- ❖ **Associations and organisations:** Battle of Britain Memorial Trust; British Battle of Britain Fighter Association.

Leading Aircraftman Allan Wilmot

Served with: Royal Navy, minesweeper, HMS *Hauken*, Royal Air Force,
Coastal Command, Search and Rescue
Service number: 714553
Interviewed: Lambeth, London, 31 August 2015

Service History and Personal Stories

❖ **Born:** 24 August 1925, Kingston, Jamaica.

❖ Allan has a very rare service history indeed, having crossed over and been a serviceman in two of the three Armed Forces during the Second World War.

❖ Joined the Royal Navy in Kingston, Jamaica at the age of 16 in June 1941 and served on the minesweeper HMS *Hauken* on minesweeping and Atlantic convoy escort duties until late 1943.

❖ Aged 18, and with his service as a boy sailor over, Allan applied for the RAF, which was starting a new recruitment drive in Jamaica at that time. He was accepted into the RAF Air-Sea Rescue Service.

❖ Allan served as part of RAF Coastal Command at various stations around the United Kingdom from 1944 until 1946 as a leading aircraftsman on flying boats and as part of a motorboat rescue team.

I have been conducting interviews for my book since 2014, and I have, as mentioned before, been honoured to meet and record the varied and interesting stories of many of our great veterans. These are men and women from all sorts of backgrounds, nationalities and cultures who played very different roles within the services of which they were a part. With the war being truly global I am constantly amazed at the veterans I have found or who have come forward, their personal service histories and the incredible experiences they have shared with me. Allan Wilmot served in two completely different services during the war, something that is very rare indeed and until then not something I had come across.

It was probably no surprise that as soon as Allan was old enough he answered the Royal Navy's call and volunteered for service at sea, following in the footsteps of his father, Captain Charles Wilmot, who was already a 'master mariner' of many years' experience and who also served from 1939 to 1947 as chief officer of HM examination ship, MV *Western Explorer*. Allan was 16 when he enlisted as a boy sailor in late 1941 and for the next two years served as an ordinary seaman (OS) on board the British minesweeper HMS *Hauken* in the steward's department and as and when required helping out with other seagoing duties. Both his maritime and steward training was carried out on board the ship as ongoing on-the-job fast learning. During the time Allan served on board HMS *Hauken* the ship undertook many kinds of duties such as minesweeping patrols and escorting convoys of ships heading from the Atlantic to the Panama Canal. It operated in areas where attacks from German U-boats were common and where the sinking of British and Allied shipping such as oil tankers and cargo ships was a regular occurrence. In one such instance, on 25 May 1942, HMS *Hauken* rescued nine survivors from the unarmed merchant vessel SS *Empire Beatrice*, which had been torpedoed and sunk, and took them to Kingston, Jamaica.

Once Allan was 18 he had the choice to stay on in the Royal Navy or volunteer elsewhere. Ready for a new challenge, he saw an advertisement in the *Jamaica Gleaner* in late 1943 in which the RAF was recruiting Jamaican volunteers for ground crew. He applied and was accepted for the RAF Air-Sea Rescue Service, which was part of RAF Coastal Command, and after three months' intense training at Palisadoes Airport and Bishopbriggs, Up Park Camp, Kingston, he was transported to New York and put on the troopship SS *Cuba* bound for the UK, or the 'Mother Country' as it was affectionately known. Upon arrival at Liverpool docks the new recruits were welcomed by Air Vice Marshal Tedder with, as Allan recalls, the greeting: 'Thank you chaps for leaving your warm countries to help us in our hour of need. I wish I was going to your countries.'

During the war many West Indians came forward and volunteered for service from many parts of the Caribbean. Here we take a closer look at their very important input:

West Indian Servicemen's Contribution to the British and Commonwealth Forces

The Caribbean colonies of the British Commonwealth had a population of approximately 14 million at the outbreak of the Second World War. About 16,000 West Indians volunteered for service alongside the British and of these more than 100 were women who were posted overseas; eighty served in the Women's Auxiliary Air Force (WAAF) and about thirty in the Auxiliary Territorial Service (ATS). These volunteers came from many places such as Jamaica, Antigua, St Lucia, Bahamas, Trinidad and Tobago, Barbados, British Guiana and Bermuda.

Around 6,000 West Indians served with both the RAF and the Canadian Air Force in every role from fighter pilot to bomb aimer, air gunner and in air–sea rescue. They also served as ground staff, which varied from aircraft engineers to roles in medical and administration. At sea, thousands of West Indians served in the Merchant Navy; this dangerous service had a very high casualty rate with nearly a third of all its seamen killed during wartime service. On land, the Caribbean Regiment was formed from 1,000 volunteers and saw service in Egypt and Italy as part of the British Army. The Royal Engineers also had highly skilled West Indian technicians within its ranks. Overall they made a significant contribution to the Allied war effort.

Meanwhile, the service of one young man continued. In July 1944 Allan, at the grand old age of 18, was serving in a second branch of the armed forces. After further training at RAF Training Camp Filey, Yorkshire, his role in air-sea rescue would take him around the UK, serving at coastal stations such as RAF Calshot near Southampton. In February 1945 he went for more advanced training at No. 1 Marine Craft Training School, based at Corsewall House near Stranraer, Scotland. This was a part of the bigger RAF Corsewall/RAF Wig Bay Coastal Command flying boat facility. After finishing his course, Allan was promoted to leading aircraftsman (LAC).

He then went on to serve at various other RAF stations such as RAF Castle Archdale near Enniskillen, Northern Ireland, and RAF Benson, near Oxford, then to RAF Killadeas, again in Northern Ireland, where he remained until August 1945. Allan's final two bases were RAF Greenock near Glasgow and RAF Castle Archdale once again, where he finished in late 1946. He was on paid leave until officially discharged in February 1947, bringing to an end a fascinating service career.

Allan now shares with us some interesting wartime recollections, starting from the time when he was serving at RAF Calshot:

Rescuing Downed British and German Aircrews

As motorboat crew members we used to rescue Allied airmen who were shot down in the English Channel and were in danger of freezing to death in the water. Sometimes we even rescued German air crew as well. Once we rescued

Flags of the Royal Navy and the Royal Air Force, both of which Allan was a part during his unique service in the Second World War.

both German and British air crew during the same operation and it was quite funny on the journey back with the crews sat opposite each other just looking at each other in total silence, I guess the Germans were thinking it was better to be prisoners of war than die in the water!

I went on to ask Allan about the various duties he had to undertake whilst working on Coastal Command Air-Sea rescue:

I did many jobs during my various postings with the RAF. There was so much variety, no day was the same, we did everything from maintenance on the Sunderland and Catalina Flying Boats, to transporting air crews and maintenance crews to the planes, assisting the planes to their moorings, towing the planes to dry dock, reloading bombs, laying flare paths for the flying boats to land and take off at night. It was all very interesting, and I liked saving people. To me this was the kind of service I felt best doing.

I went on to ask about his special service record:

Well it is very different I guess to have served in both the Royal Navy and the Royal Air Force during World War II and I was proud to have done so. Any service anywhere is good when the cause you serve is a just one. I was one of many who came a long way to do what we felt was the right thing.

Additional Information and Life After Service

❖ **Rank at end of service:** Leading aircraftman (LAC).
❖ **Medals and honours:** 1939–45 Defence Medal, 1939–45 Star, 1939–45 War Medal, Atlantic Star.
❖ **Post-war years:** Allan's fascinating post-service life began in 1947–50, when he had many jobs including dish washing, work in a bookshop and as a postman; 1950–54, singer in the Ken Hunter Trio; 1954–74, singer in The Southlanders, where he worked

alongside and knew many celebrities, including Petula Clark, Cliff Richard and the Shadows, Shirley Bassey, Vera Lynn, Bob Hope, Tommy Steele, Marty Wilde, Spike Milligan, Frankie Vaughan, Joe Loss, David Frost and many more. He also co-wrote and performed the hit songs *Alone*, *Earth Angel* and *I Am a Mole and I Live in a Hole*. George Martin of Beatles fame was their recording manager and they recorded songs at the famous Abbey Road Studios in London. Along the way Allan also met Sammy Davis Jr, Walt Disney, Errol Flynn, The Queen and the Duke of Edinburgh, Prince Charles and Princess Diana. After this remarkable music career he finished his working years from 1974–90 with British Telecom as a telephone operator and later as acting supervisor at the Southbank Exchange in London. He married Joyce in 1967 and they have four daughters and eight grandchildren.

❖ **Associations and organisations:** The West Indian Association of Service Personnel (WASP), of which Allan is a former president and vice president.

Warrant Officer Jan Black-Stangryciuk

Served with: Royal Air Force, Bomber Command, Polish No. 300
    Squadron
Service number: 794829
Interviewed: Hammersmith, London, 4 April 2016

Service History and Personal Stories

- ❖ **Born:** 18 April 1922, Chelm, Poland.
- ❖ Jan joined the RAF in January 1942 and was a rear gunner in both Wellington and Lancaster bombers during the war.
- ❖ In October 1942 he was involved in a terrible crash while on a training exercise in a Wellington at RAF Bramcoat and was very badly burned.
- ❖ He was operated on by Archibald McIndoe using the new pioneering techniques of plastic surgery and became one of his famous Guinea Pigs.
- ❖ Incredibly, in 1944 Jan volunteered for active service and flew as a rear gunner in Lancaster bombers (wartime picture above, Jan on right-hand side) on eighteen bombing missions over Germany, which included raids on the Ruhr industrial area, Frankfurt, Dortmund and Kiel.

❖   After the war he continued to serve in the RAF from 1945 until 1948 as an air traffic
     controller at RAF Andover in Hampshire.

Jan Stangryciuk is a great example of someone who, like others in this book,
overcame great personal adversity to serve our country and the Allied cause. Jan
was born in Chelm, Poland, in 1922 and his family emigrated to Obera in Misiones
province, Argentina, in 1934 to to make a better life for themselves. This they did
as farmers with various agricultural holdings and plantations growing oranges,
grapes and bananas. They also had livestock that included cows, pigs and horses.
After seeing the plight of his native Poland and so many other countries under Nazi
occupation, Jan chose to help by volunteering for the RAF at the age of nineteen
in January 1942. He effectively went from a place of safety into the line of fire, such
was his true conviction to help at any cost.

    So in early 1942 Jan sailed from Buenos Aires to Belfast on the Royal Mail liner
Highland Monarch. After this he trained for six months at Blackpool Aerodrome
in Lancashire, and it was then on to the gunnery school at RAF Evernton in
Inverness, Scotland. This was a dramatic change from the culture and relative calm
of South America to that of wartime Britain, and it took some serious readjustment.
Later Jan was at RAF Bramcoat near Nottingham for further training as part of 18
Operational Training Unit (OTU), where in October 1942 he was involved in a
very serious crash in a Wellington bomber. He could have made good his escape
but instead he tried to save the life of the pilot from the blazing aircraft. While
trying to free the pilot he was shielding himself on the left side with his coat and
the right-hand side of his face and body sustained very serious burns. He got his
crew member out of the aircraft but very sadly he died afterwards.

    This incident left Jan with burns so severe that he ended up having to be
operated on more than twenty times in the coming years. Luckily for him the
new advances in the medical field of plastic surgery were just coming through
and at the forefront of these great innovations was an excellent surgeon called
Archibald McIndoe. Jan was first admitted to the burns unit at the hospital
at RAF Cosford for two weeks. He then went for five months of specialist
plastic surgery treatment at the Queen Victoria Hospital in East Grinstead, where
McIndoe and his team operated on him numerous times. After this he became
admitted to a very special club for severely burned airmen called the 'Guinea
Pig Club', a name that reflected the fact that they were first of their kind to be
recipients of this new cutting-edge treatment. It is a club that survives to this day,
a detailed overview of which accompanies the Guinea Pig anthem in the poetry
and songs section at the back of this book.

    Jan's operations and convalescence went on until mid-1943, and the medical
staff did such a good job on him that he was again deemed fit for duty, after
which he was posted back to RAF Evernton near Inverness in Scotland, this

300 DYWIZJON
BOMBOWY
ZIEMI MAZOWIECKIEJ

Crest of the Polish No. 300 Squadron.

time as a gunnery instructor. He stayed there until late 1944 but after a year had had enough of that role and wanted to do what he felt he was really trained for in Bomber Command: to be an aircraft gunner seeing real action. Incredibly, despite his terrible injuries, occasional referrals and ongoing treatment, this resolute and very brave young man volunteered and was accepted for frontline active service.

This led to him being posted to Heavy Conversion Units (HCUs) where he went from training on two- to four-engine bombers, first of all from Wellington to Halifax bombers at RAF Finningley in Yorkshire, then from Halifax to Lancaster bombers at RAF Blyton in Lincolnshire. After conversion training he went on to RAF Faldingworth in Lincolnshire, where Polish No. 300 Squadron was based. Jan flew on eighteen bombing missions over Germany between November 1944 and April 1945. Those took him to places such as Frankfurt, Kiel, Dortmund, Essen and targets in the Ruhr, Germany's industrial heartland. Then, in April 1945, Jan was recalled to hospital for further treatment and this saved his life, because while in hospital his Lancaster bomber was shot down and the crew lost.

After coming out of hospital in mid-1945 Jan was then transferred to RAF Andover in Hampshire where he would remain for the rest of his RAF career, serving a further three years until 1948. After new training he would take on a very different role, that of air traffic controller, until he was finally demobbed in December 1948 at the discharge centre at RAF Dunholme Lodge in Lincolnshire.

Bomber Command suffered some of the highest casualties of the war. Of the 120,000 who served, a staggering 55,573 were killed; that equates to an horrific casualty rate of around 45 per cent. So being one of these aircrew was extremely hazardous indeed and they had a potentially short life expectancy. We now hear from Jan about the experience of being in battle:

A Rear Gunner on Dangerous Bombing Missions Over Germany

When we eventually received new bombers, Lancasters, to continue our operational duty, I found for the first time what it is to be over German cities, over German sky, where they were still fighting fanatically. It was always a very unfriendly feeling because every time you never knew what could happen, but then I was young and I was brave enough to feel that what I decided to do would succeed in victory. My job was very difficult during the operational tours, because as a rear gunner I always had a big responsibility to keep looking in different directions for the dangers that were always coming so quickly. They were very long, demanding and tiring hours, but still by doing our duty we thought sooner or later we probably would gain our victory. What I was hoping was to return and to see my family again. In those days we were young and we knew the life was so short, because Bomber Command paid the highest casualties. When we returned sometimes we kissed that plane, touched him, because he had holes sometimes through the shrapnel, and we felt he brought us not from the German sky but from the German hell, and no matter what you expect or hoped, like many you might never return!

I went on to ask Jan more about being in the heat of battle and he recalled:

We were trained to recognise German aircraft. We spent hours in cinemas watching films showing them so we could recognise them for missions and against attacks, because when a German fighter was following you it could be at any second the end of your journey you see. I would shout to the pilot and he would turn the plane as much as possible so the German could not get you in his gun sights. If he did he would try and kill you off. Our pilot could not see anything that was happening behind, so the job of the rear gunner became

Rear gunner position at the back of a Lancaster bomber, the same as the one that Jan would operate.

even more important and he was sometimes acting like a second pilot. The rear gunner position was very confined, and you felt it on long missions. It was well known that a lot of rear gunners didn't make it if their plane went down because they were right at the back and getting out could be very difficult. When they came the attacks were very quick and we were moving everywhere, shooting and moving, a very frightening time indeed. And over the target much anti-aircraft fire and explosions close to you and all around you.

Additional Information and Life After Service

❖ **Rank at end of service:** Warrant officer.

❖ **Medals and honours:** 1939–45 Defence Medal, 1939–45 War Medal, 1939–45 Star, Air Crew Europe Star, Polish Air Force Medal, Bomber Command Commemorative Medal.

❖ **Post-war years:** After the war Jan worked for two companies in London, first as a supervisor at R. Wolf Rubber Factory until 1960, after which he moved on to work for Clark Electrical Company as a salesman until he retired at 65 in 1987. He has lived in the Ealing Common and later Acton areas of London. He married Evelyn in 1946 and they were together for fifty years and did not have any children. Jan is still very closely connected to various organisations such as the Polish Air Force Association based in Hammersmith, London, which deserves a special mention for the very good job it does caring for Polish veterans under Artur Bildziuk.

❖ **Associations and organisations:** Polish Air Force Association; Guinea Pig Club; Not Forgotten Association; Royal British Legion City Branch.

Squadron Leader George Johnson DFM MBE

Served with: Royal Air Force, Bomber Command, Nos 97 and 617
   Squadrons
Service number: 1199696
Interviewed: Bristol, Somerset, 8 October 2015

Service History and Personal Stories

❖ **Born:** 25 November 1921, Horncastle, England, UK.

❖ George 'Johnny' Johnson completed a staggering fifty missions as part of Bomber Command, thirty with No. 97 Squadron and a further twenty with No. 617 Squadron.

❖ During his huge amount of active service he flew on missions to various places such as Bremen, Hamburg, Berlin, Milan, Genoa, St Nazaire and the V1 missile sites.

❖ He flew in the Lancaster AJ-T for Tommy as part of No. 617 Squadron in Operation Chastise, the famous Dams raid on the night of 16–17 May 1943. His aircraft's bomb hit the Sorpe Dam and he became one of the legendary 'Dambusters'.

❖ George continued to serve in the RAF after the war, mainly as a trainer in Bomber and Coastal Command units in the UK and in Singapore. Retired in 1962 as a squadron leader.

On the night of 16–17 May 1943 Bomber Command launched Operation Chastise, a daring mission to destroy three dams in the Ruhr valley in Germany's industrial heartland, an area central to the country's wartime production. At the forefront of the mission was Wing Commander Guy Gibson, who led the specially selected 617 Squadron into the history books as a result of its endeavours that night, using the specially developed bouncing bomb designed by Barnes Wallis and code-named 'Upkeep'. This mission became the stuff of legends and the 'Dambusters', as they became known, would forever be immortalised because of it. Among all those brave men on that mission was young bomb aimer Sergeant George 'Johnny' Johnson in Lancaster AJ-T for 'Tommy', who in time has become the last British Dambuster. To spend time with Johnny and to interview one of our country's most well-known veterans from one of the most famous missions of the war was very special indeed, and again made me feel I was really connecting with an extraordinary part of our history.

George Leonard Johnson came from a very humble upbringing. He was the son of a farm manager; his mother died when he was 3 years old and he grew up with his father and five other siblings in a tied cottage in the rural East Lindsey district of Lincolnshire. He naturally followed his father's footsteps and planned to work in horticulture, studying at Lord Wandsworth Agricultural College in Long Sutton, Hampshire, and finishing in December 1939. The war had already started and this changed his path completely when in 1940 he joined the Royal Air Force Volunteer Reserve (RAFVR). His training began in earnest in June 1941 when he was sent to Florida, hoping to be selected as a pilot. Unfortunately he was not successful, but that did not put this young man off; he was determined to find a way to fly and serve in whatever capacity possible, and so he ended up training to become an air gunner in Canada instead. He was posted to No. 97 Squadron at RAF Woodhall Spa near Coningsby, Lincolnshire, on 27 July 1942. Along the way he also acquired the nickname of 'Johnny', taken from his surname Johnson, and a name he preferred to go by from then on.

Johnny flew first as an air gunner but in November 1942, when the opportunity came for him to train as a bomb aimer, he seized the chance and did the training required for this new role at RAF Fulbeck in Nottinghamshire. During his time in No. 97 Squadron he completed thirty operations with various crews in raids over France, Italy and Germany to areas such as St Nazaire, Milan, Genoa, Turin, Nuremberg, Karlsruhe, Bremen, Wismar, Hamburg, Munich, Duisburg, Berlin, Cologne, Wilhelmshaven, Osnabruck, Stuttgart and Essen. In December 1942 he transferred to the crew of Flight Lieutenant Joe McCarthy, and later that crew was personally selected by Wing Commander Guy Gibson to join the specially formed No. 617 Squadron. This they did on 25 March 1943 in preparation for a special mission called Operation Chastise, using Wallis' revolutionary bouncing bomb. There was a lot of training undertaken, much of it on the Upper Derwent

A modern-day flypast of a Lancaster from the Battle of Britain Memorial flight at the Derwent dam in 2014 as a salute to the Dambusters.

Valley dam in the Derbyshire Peak District, because of its similarity to the intended German targets. The goal was to attack the Mohne, Eder and Sorpe dams and to cause a breach in each of them, which in turn would potentially destroy a major water and power source that helped to supply the Ruhr industrial area in Germany's industrial heartland and hopefully create a major disruption to the Nazi war effort.

On the evening of 16/17 May 1943 three waves of aircraft took off from RAF Scampton in Lincolnshire and, using the visibility of a full moon, flew as low as 60ft when they reached their targets and used searchlights on their Lancasters to help them with pinpoint accurate bombing. Johnny was bomb aimer in AJ-T for Tommy, which on its tenth attempt managed to drop its 9,000lb bomb and hit its target. This caused significant structural damage but not a major breach; however, both the Mohne and Eder dams were completely breached and this caused the maximum anticipated disruption. The method of attack used on the Sorpe dam was a different one; due to its layout it required a side–on attack instead of a frontal one. The same kind of device was used but it had to be dropped inertly without any spin directly on the target from an incredible 30ft before the aircraft drew up very sharply to make good its escape.

The casualties were very high; of the nineteen aircraft that were engaged in the action, three turned back through various problems, eight were lost and eight

returned, meaning that they had 50 per cent
losses. From the 133 aircrew that took part there
were fifty-three dead and three POWs. Overall,
the attacks were successful and major German
resources and manpower had to be diverted to deal
with the aftermath.

Winston Churchill, who was in America at
the time, mentioned the raid in his address to the
US Congress and it was front-page news in both
Britain and the USA. After this operation No. 617
Squadron was given an emblem with the breached
dam in the centre and the apt motto *Après moi, le*
deluge, meaning 'After me, the flood'.

Thirty-four of the aircrew were decorated at Buckingham Palace soon after
their return, including Johnny who received the Distinguished Flying Medal
from Queen Elizabeth (The Queen Mother), wife of the then ruling monarch,
King George VI. Johnny went on to complete a further nineteen operations with
617 Squadron over San Polo d'Enza, Livorno, Bologna, V-1 sites, the Albert aircraft
factory, St Etienne, Woippy, Clermont Ferrand, Bergerac, Angouleme, Lyons and
Toulouse. He was commissioned in November 1943 and his last active duty
mission was to St Cyr on 10 April 1944, after which he finished on operational
duties and went on to serve the rest of the war as a bombing instructor on a
Heavy Conversion Unit back at RAF Scampton. Johnny decided to stay on and
make a career for himself in the RAF after the war. He received a permanent
commission and from 1945 until 1962 he served as an officer instructor in various
squadrons such as No. 100 Squadron at Hemswell with Avro Lincolns in Bomber
Command, with No. 120 Squadron at RAF Aldergrove with Avro Shackletons in
Coastal Command, and at No. 19 Group Coastal Command HQ, Mount Batten,
Plymouth. He then spent three years in Singapore as officer commanding at the
Maritime Operations Room at RAF Singapore in Changi before finally retiring
at RAF Hemswell as squadron leader after twenty-two years' service, bringing to
an end an illustrious career serving his country.

When I spoke to Johnny during the interview and in later phone conversations
we talked about his very varied career and, of course, we also discussed in great
detail the Dams raid:

The Last British Dambuster

I completed fifty missions on active service but the dams raid is the one most
people want to know about, and I have found the increased interest in the last few
years to be quite incredible. I think that just by the very unique and special nature
of the mission it is very interesting for many people. It wasn't an easy mission

and to achieve the results we needed meant having a number of factors exactly right on that night, which included bombing from as low as 30ft with only the moonlight and the special spotlights that were on our Lancaster, combined with excellent piloting and accurate navigation to guide us and make it all work. On the tenth attempt it all lined up correctly and I am proud to say that we got the result we all wanted when I hit the dam almost in the centre. One hundred and thirty-three men flew out that night, sadly just under half never came back and over time I am the last British Dambuster left!

I asked Johnny how he felt about that:

How do I feel? Well it is very important to say that when I do talks at various meetings and gatherings and for different associations that I don't do it to promote myself, it is to represent all those fine men from that special raid and all the brave men of 617 Squadron, so that they will never be forgotten.

Additional Information and Life After Service

- ❖ **Rank at end of service:** Squadron leader.
- ❖ **Medals and honours:** Distinguished Flying Medal, 1939–45 Defence Medal, 1939–45 General Service Medal with Malaya Clasp, 1939–45 War Medal, 1939–45 Star, Air Crew Europe Star, MBE (as part of the Queen's Birthday Honours List 2017), honorary doctorate awarded by the University of Lincoln (2017).
- ❖ **Post-war years:** After leaving the RAF in 1962 Johnny trained to be a teacher specialising in junior education. He then worked in junior and prep schools from 1964–70, after which he wanted to do something different and more challenging and taught general subjects and horticulture at Rampton Special Hospital from 1970–73. Later Johnny diversified again when he taught at Balderton Psychiatric Hospital from 1973–84, helping prepare patients for life in the community. He then retired in 1984 and moved with his wife to Torquay, where he was very involved with the Conservative Party. Johnny married Gwyneth Morgan in April 1943. They were together sixty-two years, and have an impressive three children, eight grandchildren and nineteen great-grandchildren. His autobiography, *George 'Johnny' Johnson, The Last British Dambuster*, was published in 2014.
- ❖ **Associations and organisations:** 617 Squadron Association; Lincolnshire International Bomber Command Centre honorary membership; honorary president of the Group 617 charity; Joint Services Association Bristol Branch; 41 Club honorary member; Bristol Savages Social Club honorary member.

Flight Lieutenant Kenneth French

Served with: Royal Air Force, Fighter Command, Nos 34 and 66
    Squadrons
Service number: 179034
Interviewed: Leigh-on-Sea, Essex, 25 January 2015

Service History and Personal Stories

❖ **Born:** 30 August 1920, Skiberdeen, County Cork, Republic of Ireland.

❖ Thought to be the last southern Irish volunteer fighter pilot of the war. First served in the Home Guard as a dispatch rider, 1940–41.

❖ Went on to serve in the RAF as a Spitfire pilot from 1941–46 with Nos 234 and 66 Squadrons on many types of operations over the UK and Europe.

❖ Gave close protection air cover for King George VI during his visit to Scapa Flow in May 1944 and later, along with other pilots, was thanked by the King in person.

❖ On D-Day he helped provide air cover for the American landings at Omaha Beach in Normandy.

❖ Ken took part in operations giving air cover to bombers on various missions to targets such as the U-boat pens at Brest and other operations throughout France,

Belgium, Holland and Germany, where he carried out low-level ground attacks on enemy positions and units.

As the work on my book progressed and interviews with the veterans continued, I was very fortunate to have had help from some very good people whose input both through their organisations and individually has been invaluable along the way. As a result of this I have been able to obtain access to amazing veterans whose contributions to my book have been both very special and invaluable. A fine example of this was when I was introduced to Ken 'Paddy' French, thought to be the last Republic of Ireland volunteer Spitfire pilot from the war. He came from the safety of what was a neutral country during that conflict and, driven by a strong sense of duty and overcoming personal challenges, he chose to put his life on the line to serve our country. Ken was one of approximately 50,000 volunteers who came from both Northern Ireland and the Republic to join every branch of the British armed services during the Second World War.

When I interviewed Ken his great Irish charm and storytelling abilities came shining through, starting from a very different time in Skiberdeen, County Cork, in the Ireland of the 1920s and 1930s. Then the troubles touched all corners of every community in some form or another during the time of Michael Collins, various uprisings and treaties, through to the turmoil of the Second World War. Ken had already come to Britain in July 1939, leaving behind the rural life of Ireland that he loved so much in order to obtain a much-needed job, and had joined his brother Phil in Leigh-on-Sea in Essex. It was there that he got the job as an underwriter for an insurance company called the North British and Mercantile Insurance Company and he worked for it until he joined the Royal Air Force in 1941. Along the way he would also play his part in our very own 'Dad's Army' when, after being relocated to Chalfont St Giles in Buckinghamshire for his work, Ken joined the Home Guard in late 1940, where among other jobs he was to be a dispatch rider when required.

However, nothing was going to stop this determined young man achieving his real and much bigger goal, which was now to be in the RAF and if possible to be a fighter pilot. There was, however, a potential problem, which was that he could not bend one knee fully and it had an operational scar on it.

During the medical, when told to bend both knees he cleverly did not bend the good one as far as it could go so as to give the impression that the other problem knee did not look as bad as it was. Amazingly, with the luck of the Irish, he passed the medical and obtained the required A1 grade. So after overcoming these problems the adventure really began, with his pilot training starting at Scarborough, the square bashing, classroom theory and tests and some assessment flights. He was then billeted at Heaton Park, Manchester, a big RAF training and billeting area during the war, after which he was sent on to Toronto, Canada, for the practical flight training on Tiger Moths, Harvards and Yales. He gained his wings at Dunnville on 1 November 1942 along with the rank of sergeant.

After returning from Canada on the famous liner the *Queen Elizabeth* Ken finally got trained on Spitfires at RAF Eshott, also known as Bockenfield Aerodrome, near Morpeth in Northumberland, which was home to No. 57 Operational Training Unit. Eventually, after passing all this training, in late 1943 he was posted for a short time up at RAF Skeabrae at Orkney in the Shetland Islands with No. 234 Squadron, which was providing air cover and protection against potential Luftwaffe air attacks on the British naval fleet based at Scapa Flow. After this he was assigned to No. 66 Squadron, with which he would serve for the rest

Crest of 66 Squadron with the Latin inscription *Cavete Praemonui*, meaning 'You have been warned'.

of his RAF career, and both the places he served and the operations he was involved in were many and varied. He served at RAF stations such as RAF Perranporth, Ford, Tangmere, Kenley, Southend and Hornchurch on operations that provided air cover for convoys in the English Channel and Irish Sea. He also flew on bomber escort missions with both the British and American air forces into France to targets such as the U-boat pens at Brest and V1 missile sites near Dieppe, as well as others in Belgium, Holland and Germany. Ken was also chosen for special high-security air cover operations for VIPs and flew from other operational bases such as RAF Castletown in Caithness, Scotland, to give close protection air cover for the visit of King George VI to Scapa Flow in May 1944, after which he and other pilots were thanked personally by the King at the port in Thurso. Later, in June 1944, Ken would also be part of another special fighter escort, this time bringing General Eisenhower and Air Chief Marshal Tedder from France back to the UK.

In preparation for the Allied invasion of Europe No. 66 Squadron became part of 132 Norwegian Wing, which was part of the Second Tactical Air Force, and on 6 June 1944 Ken flew from RAF Bognor to take part in Operation Overlord and contribute towards the Allied air cover for the American landings at Omaha Beach. Later he took part in ground attack operations in many places such as around Caen and at the battle of the Falaise Pocket, where eventually most of German Army Group B was destroyed. In November 1944, after a year on active flying duties, Ken was 'rested up' and given the lighter duties of being an operations officer, assisting the wing commander in operations rooms at airfields in the forward positions where No. 66 Squadron was assisting with air support as the Allies moved forward through France, Belgium and Holland. This too had its dangerous moments due to its proximity to front-line activity. On one occasion Ken recalls being at an airfield in Belgium that came under German air attack during the Battle of the Bulge. Ken's war ended at another airfield near a town on the border between Holland and Germany called Twente on 30 April 1945 when his group captain announced the squadron was being stood down. His return journey home on VE Day was via the port of Blankenberg, which was having an all-night party as most of Europe was doing on 8 May 1945. The next day they boarded ship, sore heads and all, and returned home to England, arriving at Tilbury docks in London.

From May 1945 Ken had a few postings in the UK doing controlled flying exercises with his beloved Spitfires and working closely with radar units at RAF Manston near Margate, RAF Rudloe Manor and RAF Colerne near Bath before finally being demobbed in Walsall in the Midlands in July 1946.

From D-Day onwards, Ken and No. 66 Squadron were involved in a lot of ground attack missions of various kinds on enemy targets. Here Ken tells us about them in his own words:

Using the Spitfire for Dive Bombing and Strafing Attacks

People don't realise that Spitfires were also used as dive bombers; they put a 500lb bomb under our fuselage where we would normally have our drop tank for extra fuel. Our method of attacking was rather strange; you would fly over and would find your target and wait until it appeared behind the wing and then you would turn the plane completely upside down and would dive straight down aiming at the target. When you reached about 2,000ft or so you would slowly pull back

Ken and Spitfire at Grimbergen, Belgium, in 1944.

on the stick and count I think it was five seconds, then released your bomb. After this you would pull back hard on your stick and you would shoot away up and I would always become unconscious at that point. I blacked out always but it didn't matter because the plane kept on going and then you would wake up and you were alright. It was a very dangerous method and we encountered lots of flak and the like but later we tried other methods that worked much better.

We then went on to talk about the ground strafing and Ken told me:

We did a lot of dive bomber missions but it was more usual that we were attacking things on the ground. When the Army was advancing up from Normandy every day they used to give us a line on the map and say: 'That's our line and anything beyond that you attack!' So we would fly up ahead of the army and if the enemy came out in the open, bang we would go down on them and within no time at all the roads would be full of burning vehicles of every kind. The Germans soon learned they could not move in the daytime.

To finish I enclose this lovely Irish toast, passed on to me from Ken and one that is filled with beautiful Irish sentiment and always reminds me of this wonderful gentleman: 'May the saddest days of your future be no worse than the happiest days of your past.'

Additional Information and Life After Service

- ❖ **Rank at end of service:** Flight lieutenant.
- ❖ **Medals and honours:** 1939–45 Defence Medal, 1939–45 War Medal, 1939–45 Star, Air Crew Europe Star with France & Germany Bar, Legion d'Honneur (French Government).
- ❖ **Post-war years:** After the war Ken moved back to Leigh-on-Sea, where he eventually became an insurance underwriter until he retired in 1980. For some years Ken still managed to maintain the excitement of flying as he was put on the reservist list from 1946 until 1953 and actively kept up his flying skills by flying Chipmunks from the nearby airfield of RAF Hornchurch. He married Joan in 1947 and they were together sixty-one years. They have two sons, two daughters and three grandchildren.
- ❖ **Associations and organisations:** RAF Association and the Spitfire Society.

Air Commodore Charles Clarke OBE

Served with: Royal Air Force, Bomber Command, No. 619 Squadron
Service number: 138404
Interviewed: Richmond, Surrey, 1 September 2015

Service History and Personal Stories

- ❖ **Born:** 25 November 1923, City of London, England, UK.
- ❖ Charles Clarke joined the RAF in 1941 at only 17 years of age. After training he was posted to No. 619 Squadron, where he flew nineteen missions as a bomb aimer.
- ❖ On 24 February 1944 Charles was shot down by a German night fighter while on a raid over Germany. Only four of the seven-man crew from his Lancaster survived.
- ❖ Soon after he was captured and sent to Stalag Luft III prison camp, and in March 1944 he was a 'watcher' for one of the most audacious POW escapes of the war, later famously known as 'the Great Escape'.
- ❖ From January to May 1945 he and the other prisoners were forced to walk vast distances from Poland to Germany on the 'Long March'; many POWs died.

❖   After the war Charles continued to serve in the RAF in areas such as Palestine,
    Cyprus and Aden, finishing a very successful thirty-seven year career as an Air
    Commodore and continuing to work tirelessly for RAF associations since.

Charles Clarke OBE had an RAF career that spanned an incredible thirty-seven
years from 1941 to 1978, one that was filled with remarkable experiences and
extraordinary stories, and he was a part of some particularly well-known events
of the war such as the 'Great Escape' and the 'Long March'. After the war his
remarkable career continued as he worked his way up the ranks until he was made
an Air Commodore. He held many interesting and varied positions and postings
along the way, serving in places such as Palestine, Cyprus, Malta and Aden and with
the MoD in the United Kingdom.

   It all started when Charles Henry Clarke joined the RAF in October 1941 in
Oxford. From then until mid-1943 he was trained in a number of places such as
Scarborough, Carlisle, Heaton Park in Manchester, RAF Dumfries in Scotland,
RAF North Luffenham in the East Midlands and RAF Swinderby in Lincolnshire.
He was commissioned in January 1943 and became a pilot officer, later joining
No. 619 Squadron in July of that year at RAF Woodhall Spa in Lincolnshire,
from where he flew nineteen missions as a bomb aimer to targets in Europe such
as Leipzig, Stuttgart, Frankfurt and Berlin. On his nineteenth operation on the
fateful night of 24 February 1944 he and the crew of Lancaster bomber PG-N for
'November' were shot down over Germany. Charles and three crewmen, navigator
George Knight, radio operator Peter Smith and engineer Jimmy Trail, all managed
to safely parachute out of their burning aircraft, but sadly the rest of the crew, pilot
Keith Williams, mid-upper gunner 'Snake' Glazebrook and rear gunner Bill Welch
all died. These were three brave men of the 55,573 from Bomber Command who
were killed during the war, which is more than those who serve in the entire Royal
Air Force today. The statistics are staggering: on average, of every 100 men who
joined Bomber Command, forty-five were killed, six seriously wounded, eight

The original prisoner ID tags of Charles
Clarke from Oflag/Stalag Luft III camp
of the 'Great Escape'.

The seven-man crew of Lancaster Bomber PG-N for November, of which three did not make it home. Charles is on the back row, second right.

became prisoners of war and only forty-one escaped unscathed, physically at least. All this happened while they were serving and living according to the Bomber Command motto, 'Strike hard, strike sure'.

After being captured, Charles ended up in the German Air Force prisoner of war camp Stalag-Oflag Luft III in Poland as prisoner 3567, in a camp that would very soon go down in history as the place of 'the Great Escape'. Flight Lieutenant Clarke, although not an escapee himself, would still play his small yet important part in that history. As a 'watcher' he and others would look out for any approaching Germans who might be suspicious of their activities, acting as the eyes, ears and if required the early warning system for the men digging the three escape tunnels, Tom, Dick and Harry. This audacious plan began in the spring of 1943 under the direction of Squadron Leader Roger Bushell, AKA Big 'X', and the date for the escape was finally set for the evening of 24 March 1944, coincidentally one month to the day since Charles was shot down. Although it was originally planned for 200 POWs to get away, in the end seventy-six men escaped from Stalag Luft III. Of these three managed to reach safety, fifty were later executed by the Germans, seventeen were returned to the camp, four were sent to Sachsenhausen Concentration Camp and two were sent to Colditz Castle.

Much greater hardships lay ahead when at 2 a.m. on 28 January 1945 all the prisoners were woken up and ordered to ready themselves to leave. The camp was being evacuated from the advancing Russians, who were less than 20 miles away. This was the start of the 'Long March' and was one of the 'Death Marches' that would claim the lives of many POWs along their deadly routes. This particular march in sub-zero temperatures was from Poland to Germany, starting at Stalag Luft III in Sagan, where they were forced to walk around 60 miles to Spremburg. After that they were put on to cattle trucks and transported for four days, during which time they came under Allied air attack. Eventually they arrived at Tomstadt and were then sent to a camp called Marlag Nord. They were marched on and on until they crossed the River Elbe and finally reached a farm, where

The badge of 619 Squadron with their motto *Ad Altiora*, meaning 'To even higher'.

they made camp on the outskirts of Lubeck. It is here that their hellish three-month ordeal finished in May 1945 when a scout vehicle from the British 21st Army group turned up at their camp after the Germans had apparently cleared off over night. For the lucky survivors, the Long March was over and repatriation could begin.

We now get an interesting and revealing insight into these two historical events as Charles tells us about some of his experiences:

The Great Escape and the Long March

I arrived only a few weeks before the Great Escape took place and as a result only played a minor part as a watcher, not as a tunneller or an escapee, but still a small part of what would later become something very well known, equally and sadly for the loss of the airmen involved, 50 of whom were shot by the Germans. As for the escape itself, we would look out for any German activity that might get a bit too close to the tunnels and give a signal of them coming by putting out a cigarette in a certain way, if I remember correctly. This signal would get passed on and evasive action would be taken by those tunnelling. It was the Long March that I was completely involved in. It was a difficult ordeal that tested you in many ways. One of the worst things was the uncertainty, after the Great Escape we felt the Germans were capable of anything and even thought that we might be marched off to be executed. The conditions were very difficult, it was minus 30C and we only had what we stood up in. Thousands of us were forced to march continuously, some didn't survive, but I try to honour their memory and that of the March itself by taking part in 'Exercise Long March' where we walk part of that original route with RAF personnel each year in Poland. It's important to remember.

Charles was instrumental in, among other things, the successful campaign for a Bomber Command Memorial in London. He now shares some thoughts about Bomber Command and the importance of remembrance:

> It is about time there was some memorial for Bomber Command. The opprobrium heaped on them, and on Sir Arthur Harris, is unjustifiable. I know that politicians have difficult decisions to make, but it's regrettable that Churchill should have distanced himself from the bombing and left Harris to carry the can. Right up to the eleventh hour he was praising us, then sadly it all changed. Now there's a permanent tribute to the 55,573 who died – rightly so!

After the war Charles' RAF career led him in the following fascinating direction: 1945–46, the liaison officer for the Ministry of Aircraft Production; 1947–49, staff officer, RAF HQ in Jerusalem, Palestine and Nicosia, Cyprus; 1950–52, staff officer, RAF Andover; 1952–55, staff officer, RAF Flying College, RAF Manby; 1955–57, staff officer, Air Ministry, London; 1957–58, squadron leader, Senior Officer Training School, RAF Staff College, Bracknell; 1958–60, staff officer, RAF HQ, Valetta, Malta; 1960–62, wing commander, RAF Bassingbourn; 1962–66, wing commander, Air Force Planning, MoD London; 1967–68, staff officer, Aden, RAF HQ; 1968–69, commanding officer, RAF Stafford; 1969–70, group captain, RAF Hampshire; 1970–71, Senior Officers War Course, Royal Naval College, Greenwich; and 1972–78, Air Commodore, Director of Systems co-ordination, Ministry of Defence, London. Charles retired from the RAF in 1978.

To finish, a quote that was given to me and I believe very aptly sums up all that the bomber boys did for our country and fits in well with what this book is all about: 'The young men of Bomber Command faced dangers we can barely imagine, all in defence of our freedom. Their sacrifice and extraordinary courage should never be forgotten.'

Additional Information and Life After Service

- ❖ **Rank at end of service:** Air Commodore.
- ❖ **Medals and honours:** 1939–45 Defence Medal, 1939–45 War Medal, 1939–45 Star, Air Crew Europe Star with Bomber Command Bar, Palestine Medal, Aden Medal, OBE.
- ❖ **Post-war years:** After the RAF he had a successful career in business development from 1978–98. He married Eileen in 1946. They were together sixty-six years until 2012. They have one daughter, two grandchildren and two great-grandchildren. In 2012 he received an award for 'Outstanding Achievements' by the Soldiering on Through Life Trust and he continues to work hard for RAF associations that he represents.
- ❖ **Associations and organisations:** President of the Royal Air Force's Ex-Prisoner of War Association; chairman of the Bomber Command Association; vice president of the Caterpillar Club.

Warrant Officer Frank Tolley BEM

Served with: Royal Air Force, Bomber Command, No. 625 Squadron
Service number: 1152777
Interviewed: Sale, Cheshire, 18 October 2014

Service History and Personal Stories

- ❖ **Born:** 20 July 1921, Tipton, England, UK.
- ❖ Frank joined the Royal Air Force Volunteer Reserve (RAFVR) in July 1940 and was trained as a ground gunner at RAF Bramcote near Nuneaton.
- ❖ While on leave he passed through the shattered remains of Coventry, which made a deep impression on him. By 1942 he was one of the first to serve in the newly formed RAF Regiment protecting UK airfields.
- ❖ Still motivated to get involved in a more direct way and strike a blow against Nazi Germany, he volunteered for Bomber Command in 1943, and after training in Canada and the UK he was posted to No. 625 Squadron.
- ❖ As a bomb aimer on Lancasters he took part in twenty-two missions over Germany to places such as Dortmund, Nuremburg, Hanover, Hamburg, and in the well-known and controversial raid on Dresden on 13 February 1945.

❖ Frank also took part in four humanitarian food drops to help the starving people of Holland in April and May 1945 called Operation Manna.

Whilst on leave in November 1940, RAFVR ground gunner Frank Tolley passed through what was left of Coventry just after the German bombing, which had reduced the city to almost nothing. As he walked around streets filled with smouldering rubble, bewildered people and lines of bodies with blankets over them, he was deeply moved by what he saw, and during those moments the things he was experiencing made him realise at first-hand that the United Kingdom was dealing with a very dangerous enemy that was hell-bent on the total destruction or conquest of the country that he loved so much. The things he saw that day filled him with a deep conviction and motivation to do much more to engage and stop Nazi Germany in any way possible. He carried this resolve with him while serving in the RAF Regiment and later the way in which he chose to take the fight back to the enemy was to volunteer for aircrew in Bomber Command. In time he fulfilled this conviction and this led to him taking part in twenty-two successful missions, mostly over Germany, as a bomb aimer in Lancasters as part of No. 625 Squadron. Frank's long journey took him from the streets of Coventry to the skies over Dresden in the service of his country doing what he could to contribute in the war against the evil of the Nazi regime.

Frank's wartime service began in July 1940 when he joined the RAFVR, where he was trained as a gunner on Lewis and Vickers-Armstrong guns. Then, shortly after its formation in February 1942, Frank was one of the first recruits into the new RAF Regiment, whose job it was to be the ground fighting force of the RAF and to protect RAF stations, airfields and other interests throughout the United Kingdom and elsewhere. He was based at RAF Bramcote near Nuneaton as part of No. 2735 Royal Auxiliary Air Force Regiment, and eventually he fulfilled the promise he had made to himself earlier in the war after what he had witnessed in Coventry and volunteered for Bomber Command as aircrew in March 1943.

Emblem of the RAF Regiment with the motto *Per Ardua*, which is part of the RAF motto *Per ardua ad astra*, and means 'Through struggle or adversity'.

After an interview in St John's Wood, London, he was accepted for the pilot/navigator/bomb aimer (PNB) training programme. This began in Scarborough, Yorkshire, where he did his basic training, then on to RAF Longtown near Carlisle where he undertook some flying in Tiger Moths and gained twelve hours of flying time. After that he was sent to Heaton Park, Manchester, for the selection process that would decide what job he would do and where he would go next, which took him all the way to Canada under the British Commonwealth Air Training Plan. Frank made the transatlantic crossing on the famous liner the *Mauritania*. Once in Canada with the International Training Wing No. 4 Squadron, he completed his training at the No. 1 Air Observer School in Malton, Ontario, and with No. 4 Bomber and Gunnery School at RCAF Station Fingal, near Ontario, using Anson aircraft. This was finished by April 1944, after which Frank returned to the UK for further training at No. 3 Advanced Flying Unit at RAF South Cerney in Gloucestershire and the water dinghy and parachute course at RAF Moreton-in-Marsh in Gloucestershire with 21 Operational

The 625 Squadron emblem with the motto 'We Avenge'.

Training Unit, by which time he had moved on to Wellington bombers. These courses were completed by October 1944, after which Frank began the next part of his extensive training, which was with 1667 Heavy Bomber Conversion Unit at RAF Sandtoft in Lincolnshire. There he converted on to the Lancaster, and so with his training successfully completed by December 1944 Frank was now a fully qualified and skilled bomb aimer and was ready to go into active service.

In January 1945 he was posted to No. 625 Squadron as part of No. 1 Group RAF Bomber Command at RAF Kelstern in Lincolnshire, and by February 1945 he had started on bombing missions. Despite being quite a late arrival into front-line bomber service in the war, Frank notched up a very impressive twenty-two operations from that base from February until April 1945. These included targets such as the cities of Mannheim, Chemnitz, Dortmund, Nuremburg, Bremen, Hanover, Hamburg, and soon after his arrival the contentious mission to Dresden. He was also involved in various other kinds of bombing missions, including Army support at Cologne and attacks on aircraft factories at Dessau and Kassel and oil refineries at Misburg. After the relocating of No. 625 Squadron to RAF Scampton in Lincolnshire in April 1945 he took part in humanitarian food drops at the Hague and Rotterdam in Holland, and later he was involved in repatriation missions to bring back British troops from Positano near Naples in Italy. This continued until the squadron was disbanded on 7 October 1945 and he undertook most of these operations in his beloved Lancaster CF-Y for 'York II'. After the squadron was disbanded Frank, who by that time was a warrant officer, moved to a number of postings for shorter periods of time including RAF Cardington in Bedfordshire, and he was finally demobbed at the Oval cricket ground in May 1946.

We now look at two well-known missions in which Frank took part. They were the controversial bombing of Dresden on 13 February 1945, which was part of the scaled down Operation Thunderclap, and the humanitarian food drops into the Rotterdam and Hague areas of the Netherlands, of which he did four, on 29 and 30 April and 3 and 5 May 1945, called Operation Manna. These were two missions that were a world apart in their aims, objectives and outcomes:

The Bombing of Dresden and the Food Drops in Holland

Dresden was supposed to be about us heavily bombing the German Forces retreating from the Eastern Front in support of our then allies the Russians. In fact, as we now know, that was not the case as it was mostly civilians that suffered as a result of it, over 50,000 casualties, terrible. Some people who were there can't talk about it, but I think I have to talk, glad to talk about it to draw attention to the futility of war. But what we were doing we believed was for the greater good because we were trying to defeat a regime and an ideology of real evil that could not be allowed to win no matter what, and we were still proud to serve our country and we all put our lives on the line every time, every mission whilst doing it. Although Dresden is controversial, as with all other missions we were not asked if we would like to do it, we were told that is where we were going and that this is your target for tonight. We were ordered to carry out the operation and that was that. We had a job to do and we did it. Like all other raids, you trusted that these were legitimate targets based on good intelligence information and that's why they were sending you, to undertake an operation that was strategically important in some way. On that night I was in the 2nd or 3rd wave of bombers and when we got there everywhere was just a mass of flames, a sea of red, and there was just no point in continuing to bomb, so our Master Bomber told us to drop past our main targets and that is what we did. But in this particular case we did have our doubts about the whole thing.

Many years on these doubts led Frank to write a moving piece of poetry called 'Until Much Later', which is included as part of the poetry and songs section at the back of this book. We move forward now to a completely different kind of mission that Frank undertook called Operation Manna, which involved dropping food to the starving people of the Netherlands right near the end of the war. This humanitarian mission was the kind that suited Frank much better and was where, during a unique truce with the occupying German forces, they truly delivered 'Manna from Heaven', as Frank described:

Even on my first bombing mission when I had released the bombs and as I watched them fall I found myself repeating 'I am breaking the sixth commandment' (Thou shall not kill). Later, during Operation Manna, we were being told to drop food, not bombs and that was absolutely superb. That felt really good and something I was much more comfortable about doing.

Some time ago I spoke to a Bomber Command veteran who told me: 'We were ordinary people doing an ordinary job in a time of war.' I believe they were extraordinary people doing an extraordinary job, which greatly helped us win that war.

Additional Information and Life After Service

- ❖ **Rank at end of service:** Warrant officer.
- ❖ **Medals and honours:** 1939–45 Defence Medal, 1939–45 War Medal, 1939–45 Star with Bomber Command Bar, France–Germany Star, British Empire Medal, Operation Manna Dutch Medal.
- ❖ **Post-war years:** After his service in the RAF, Frank worked as a cost clerk for Accles and Pollock, which was a tube manipulation company in the Midlands, and later for one of its subsidiaries as an estimator and salesman. He was then employed by a company called Press Parts Limited in Greater Manchester, where he became sales director until his retirement in 1990 at 69 years of age. He married Betty in September 1945 and they were together sixty-two years until 2007. They have two sons, six grandchildren and five great-grandchildren. In 2013 Frank received the British Empire Medal, which is awarded for meritorious civil or military service worthy of recognition by the Crown. In his case this was for his services as a volunteer to the Imperial War Museum North and to the community.
- ❖ **Associations and organisations:** President of the Sale branch of the Royal Air Force Association; member of the Manchester Aircrew Association.

Warrant Officer Edmund Creegan

Served with: Royal Air Force, Fighter Command, No. 243 Squadron
Service number: 1388579
Interviewed: Bournemouth, Dorset, 10 October 2015

Service History and Personal Stories

- **Born:** 31 May 1922, Colchester, Essex, England, UK.
- Edmund joined the RAF in 1941 and his story is quite remarkable right from the very beginning. He was trained in the UK, Canada and Hollywood, California, where he met many stars of the day.
- In active duty he served as a Spitfire pilot in North Africa and Malta, also during the invasions of Sicily and of Italy at Salerno and in Aleppo, Syria, and Corsica, all with No. 243 Squadron.
- He was shot down twice and on both occasions managed to land his Spitfire safely. The second time he became a POW and was sent to Munich, where he was interrogated by the Gestapo.

❖   After this he was sent to Stalag Luft VII POW camp in eastern Germany. He
     escaped in 1945 and made his way towards the advancing Russians, to whom he
     surrendered. He was later repatriated via Odessa in the Black Sea.

The service career highlights of Spitfire pilot Edmund Creegan listed above give
you a very good indication of the extraordinary story that we are about to look
at in more detail. His war experiences are quite incredible and during his time as
a fighter pilot with No. 243 Squadron he was involved in active duty and aerial
combat in the skies above many different countries in a great variety of situations
and theatres of war. He is the first fighter pilot I have interviewed who was involved
in the North African Campaign and in air operations in the desert, and who went
on to support some of the biggest invasions in the Mediterranean. He also ended
up giving air support in the Middle East and as a very skilled pilot managed to land
his badly damaged Spitfires on two occasions in the heat of battle. There is much
more to this story both before and after these events, showing once again as with
the other incredible veterans in this book the astounding depth and diversity of
what they went through during the war. We can always remember, learn from and
be enriched by what our brave veterans did for us through narratives such as this
one, the story of one man who served with Fighter Command.

Edmund was 19 years old when he volunteered for the Royal Air Force in
October 1941 at Lord's Cricket Ground in St John's Wood in London. This
facility was being used by the RAF as an aircrew receiving centre because it
had the capacity to deal with the ever-growing numbers of new recruits that
were being absorbed during the massive ongoing recruitment process. After the
initial selection, Edmund was sent to RAF Oxford for 'trying out' to see if he
was suitable to continue on to further training as a fighter pilot. There he was
taken up in a Miles Magister to see how he reacted in the air and also did some
parachute training. He passed selection and was sent from Liverpool to Halifax,
Nova Scotia, Canada, in late 1941, where he was put in a holding camp in a place
called Mumpton until his training camp was allocated.

Edmund could not believe his luck when he was sent to down to a US base
called War Eagle field in Lancaster near Hollywood, California. There he recalls
receiving exceptional training at the Polaris Flight Academy. One of his instructors,
Mr Bowman, had been a stunt pilot before the war and taught him many useful
things, some of which would help keep him alive later in the war in real combat
situations. British airmen, even those in training, were treated as heroes over there
and as a result he and other trainee pilots met many famous actors of that period
during their time in Hollywood. This included Roddy McDowall, with whom
Edmund remembers autographing war bonds in Perishing Square in downtown
Los Angeles. They were also invited to Warner Brothers parties at weekends and
spent time with stars such as Errol Flynn, Carmen Miranda, Ronald Coleman,

George Burns, Gene Autry, Monty Woolley, Basil Rathbone, Nigel Bruce, Alan Hale and Mickey Rooney. They were really having the time of their lives and living in what seemed like another world. But, of course, back in the real world there was a war on and they were there on serious business too. During the week Edmund undertook intense flight training on various American aircraft such as the Stearman, Vultee and Harvard, and this continued until Edmund gained his wings in June 1942.

243 Squadron insignia with the motto 'Swift in Pursuit'.

After this he returned to the UK on the cruise liner *Queen Mary* and undertook conversion training from American to British aircraft at RAF Calveley in Cheshire with the No. 5 Pilot Advanced Flying Unit on the British Miles Master advanced trainer. He completed his training with 52 Operational Training Unit at RAF Aston Down in Gloucestershire on his final aircraft, the Spitfire, and became a fully trained fighter pilot by February 1943. Flight Sergeant Creegan joined No. 243 Squadron in April 1943 to take part in the closing stages of the North African Campaign, where he also did some training on Hurricanes. He flew from RAF bases such as Blida near Algiers, Algeria, and Souk el Khemis near Tunis, Tunisia, and after the Allied victory in May he then went on to Hal Far in Malta the following month. During those postings he took part in various operations such as destroyer and convoy patrols, bomber protection, ground and troop support and emergency scrambles. In North Africa No. 243 Squadron was part of the 324 Wing of the Desert Air Force. Later in other operations it became part of 322 Wing, all under Mediterranean Air Command.

Edmund, third from the right, during his pilot training near Hollywood, here with actress Brenda Marshall who starred opposite Errol Flynn and James Cagney.

Next Edmund participated and gave air cover in two big Allied invasions in the Mediterranean, the first being Operation Husky in Sicily in July, where he operated out of Malta and later was based at Comiso and Pachino in Sicily. The second was Operation Avalanche at Salerno in September 1943, where he operated out of the Sicilian bases. He was later stationed at Tusciano near Salerno and as the Allies moved up the Italian coast he moved to Capodichino, Naples. Then, in December, came a totally different posting to the Middle East when Edmund was sent to Aleppo in Syria with other pilots from No. 243 Squadron to help maintain an Allied presence in the area amid fears of the uncertain position of the neighbouring power of Turkey.

Once this mission was completed they were sent to Ramat David air base in Palestine, where they stayed until February 1944. This was followed by a return to operations over Italy, where Edmund would be flying out of Poretta, Corsica, from April until June 1944 using long-range fuel tanks attached to his Spitfire to reach his targets in the north of the country. In May Edmund was shot up by a Messerschmitt Bf 109 during aerial combat but managed to get his damaged Spitfire safely back to Corsica. The second time he was hit, in June over Cecina near Florence, he was not so lucky. He again skilfully landed his aircraft but was captured by the Germans. Thus began another incredible part of his story, this time as a POW.

Edmund's incarceration began when he was held by the Luftwaffe in Verona. In July he was transferred to Munich for interrogation by the feared Gestapo. After his captors realised they could not get any useful information from him he was sent to Stalag Luft VII prisoner of war camp in Bankau in the province of Silesia in eastern Germany, now Poland. He stayed until January 1945, when he took an opportunity to escape before the Germans could make him take part in the forced march that would bring about the death of so many POWs. Edmund made the very dangerous

Edmund (top row, third left) with No. 243 Sqn in Sicily in 1943.

choice of heading east towards the front lines of the advancing Russians where he was taken prisoner once again, this time by allies. When they had confirmed his identity, they eventually repatriated him back to the United Kingdom in February 1945 via the Black Sea port of Odessa and Alexandria, Egypt, on a voyage of about a month. After his safe return to Great Britain in late March 1945 he then recovered at RAF Squires Gate, also known as RAF Blackpool, followed by a period of leave until he was finally demobbed there in May 1945.

Edmund now recalls various parts of his very interesting war service:

A Spitfire Pilot and Later Prisoner of War

The day I was shot down and captured was supposed to be my day off! It was the 14th June 1944 and I was approached by my C/O, who asked me to fly instead of him. I wasn't too keen on the idea but then he offered me his brand new Spitfire: how could I refuse? Anyway I wish I had because both me and the Spitfire didn't come back from that op, I wonder what he made of that? After my capture I eventually reached Munich, where I was interrogated by the Gestapo for a number of weeks. I must have been quite lucky because I didn't receive terrible physical torture, just mental, but in my cell at night you could hear the screams of some poor buggers who were not so lucky. I guess they were trying to get whatever information they could from me regarding anything I knew about Allied plans and intentions anywhere, especially as D-Day had begun shortly before my capture and they just tried to find out whatever bits they could. In the end they realised I was no good to them and sent me on my way to my next accommodation, Stalag Luft VII POW camp, which I managed to escape from in January 1945 as the Germans were forming up all the POWs to go on what was known as the Long March. I didn't fancy that so I got away and thought I would head towards the Russians. It was frightening but once again luck was on my side as it had been all the way through my days as a fighter pilot. That's what you need to survive, determination and luck.

Additional Information and Life After Service

- ❖ **Rank at end of service:** Warrant officer (made up to that rank in his absence while a POW).
- ❖ **Medals and honours:** 1939–45 Defence Medal, 1939–45 War Medal, 1939–45 Star, Italy and North Africa Star.
- ❖ **Post-war years:** From 1946 until his retirement in 1984 Edmund worked in sales for companies such as Standard Brands, Jays and Maritz Inc., where he worked his way up from trainee to sales director. He also played guitar professionally at the Royal Exeter Hotel in Bournemouth for six years. He married Nancy in 1947 and they were together until 2010.
- ❖ **Associations and organisations:** Probus – the association for retired businessmen.

Corporal Sam King MBE

Served with: Royal Air Force, Bomber Command, ground crew
Service number: 715839
Interviewed: Brixton, London, 21 March 2015

Service History and Personal Stories

❖ **Born:** 26 February 1926, Portland, Jamaica.

❖ Sam served in the Royal Air Force in Bomber Command as a ground crew engineer and finisher at various bases around the UK from 1944–47.

❖ After the war he returned to England as one of the 492 West Indians on the SS *Empire Windrush*, as part of the first post-war immigration into the UK.

❖ Upon returning he continued to serve the country by re-joining the RAF for another five years from 1948–52.

❖ Some of his many later achievements included being instrumental in setting up the first West Indian Carnival in 1959, later the Notting Hill Carnival, and he became the first black mayor of Southwark in 1983–84.

❖ Sam received an MBE in 1998 for his tireless community work. He was also honoured
    by the people of Southwark, Lambeth and Brixton in 2009 with an historic blue
    plaque mounted on his former home in Southwark. He was awarded the Freedom
    of Southwark in May 2016.

Sam volunteered and joined the RAF in Kingston, Jamaica, in September 1944 when
he was only 18 years old to go and help the Mother Country's fight against the evil
of Nazi Germany. He had no idea what great adventures and achievements lay ahead
in service and in his life in general. Indeed, very different experiences and a totally
new way of life were what followed, taking him from a quiet farming community in
Portland, on the beautiful Caribbean Island of Jamaica, to many places throughout
the UK during his service in Bomber Command as a ground crew engineer and
finisher. He started with his basic training in Filey, Yorkshire, and trade training at
RAF Hawkinge near Folkestone, before being based at approximately ten other
RAF stations during his two periods of service in the RAF, 1944 to 1947 and 1948
to 1952, finishing up at RAF Kinloss in Scotland. He eventually ended up in London,
where he settled in the country that he came thousands of miles to defend. There
is much more to Sam's incredible story, which we will now look at in more detail.

In between his two periods of service Sam returned to Jamaica but found little
in the way of good work opportunities there. When he returned to England on
22 June 1948 he did so on the SS *Empire Windrush*. Sam was once again sailing into
history, this time because it was on the ship that started all the official post-war
immigration to the UK. In fact, it was so controversial at the time that even while
the ship was in transit it was being debated in the Houses of Parliament whether
the immigrants should be allowed into the country. A major consideration and a big
factor that swung it in favour of the 'Windrush Generation', as they later became
known, was the fact that many on board were recent ex-servicemen who had been
part of the British and Commonwealth forces during the war. Sam was one of only
half a dozen surviving Windrush veterans when I interviewed him in March 2015.

Later he also achieved many more commendable and notable things along the
way in a life of many 'firsts' for the Black/West Indian community in the UK.
We go back to the start of that journey and look at what brought Sam a long
way from home to do his bit for Great Britain during the war:

Serving the 'Mother Country' in Her Time of Need

Well we were aware that the Germans were doing bad things. When I was fourteen
at school they were teaching us to read the newspapers and telling us about some of
the things the Germans were doing, and when I was eighteen and able to I joined
the Royal Air Force. I arrived in England on 9th November 1944 and served in
different areas. I was glad to be British and to be helping and doing things because
once there was England alone fighting Nazi Germany. I remember I had signed

to go and work in America on a farm and that was real money in 1944 and I also passed the academic test to join the Royal Air Force, and my Mother said: 'Son, the Mother Country is at war, go and help and if you live it will be a good thing.' She was right! On the way over, about a week out of Kingston on our ship, we heard on the loudspeaker, 'Now hear this, take your life jacket,' and when you took your life jacket you went to your position on deck. There were depth charges going off around and about, because submarines were about and I was scared! But I always felt that even if I was torpedoed that by God's grace I would survive and I am here today after everything to say I have survived. Not only that but we served on the side of good, and good always wins over evil in the end.

I went on to ask Sam about his training with the RAF and his experience of life in wartime Britain:

Things were very bad in Britain. Food was rationed, you couldn't just go and get it, and overall people worked together to win the war; that is what we came to help with. It was sad but about 20 per cent of Britain was destroyed by enemy action, and so later we came back to help rebuild it. In the RAF I repaired aircraft from Lancasters to Spitfires but my favourite was the Dakota because it was simple like a Ford car. I was at RAF Hawkinge near Folkestone to RAF Kinloss in Scotland and in between at about ten other RAF stations during my times of service for the country.

To gauge the attitudes of the people in the UK towards overseas and especially black serviceman, I asked Sam what his personal experiences of this both with the general public and within the RAF was like during his years of service:

The vast majority were very helpful because they realised that we were working together and that we volunteered and they appreciated that. Especially when we were in uniform.

The iconic Spitfire, one of the many aircraft that Sam serviced as an LAC (Leading Aircraftman) during his service on RAF bases throughout the United Kingdom.

From Australians to the people of Norway and the Sudan and us, we all pulled together because Germany was doing a lot of bad things. We had to defeat Nazism and by the Grace of God we did. In the RAF we were all treated reasonably well and fair because we were all pulling together, and I got a fair crack of the whip when I was in the RAF. The people we worked with and under were respectful and that is the most important thing.

Additional Information and Life After Service

* ❖ **Rank at end of service:** Corporal.
* ❖ **Medals and honours:** 1939–45 Defence Medal, Battle for Britain Medal and Royal Air Force Bar, MBE.
* ❖ **Post-war years:** The service career of Sam King finally came to an end when he was demobbed at RAF Kinloss on the Moray Firth in northern Scotland in 1952. He then worked for the Post Office for thirty-four years from 1952 to 1987, first as a postman, then as a sorter and later as assistant inspector of post based at Borough High Street in Southwark, London. During that time he was also busy serving the interests of the West Indian community in London, and he was the driving and creative force behind the first black newspaper in the UK, *The West Indian Gazette*, in 1956. Along with Claudia Jones he was one of the key organisers and founders of the first West Indian Carnival in 1959, later known as the Notting Hill Carnival. Sam met and served tea to another famous King in 1964, Martin Luther King Jr, when he stopped off in London at the *Gazette* offices on his way to Oslo to collect his Nobel Peace Prize. In 1982 he was elected and served as councillor for Bellenden in the Borough of Peckham, south London. Soon after he was elected and served as Lord Mayor of Southwark, south London, from 1983–84. He was the first black mayor in London and the only one of a West Indian background serving in London at that time.

    In 1995 he jointly set up the Windrush Foundation with Arthur Torrington to honour and remember the Windrush Pioneers and to establish multicultural community projects around London. In 1998 his autobiography, *Climbing up the Rough Side of the Mountain*, was published. In that same year he was awarded an MBE for all those contributions and more, and in 2009 Sam was honoured by the people of Southwark, Lambeth and Brixton for lifetime community achievements with a blue plaque at his former home in Southwark. This was followed by being given the freedom of the Borough of Southwark in May 2016. Sam was married to his first wife, Mavis, for thirty years until she passed away and has been with his second wife, Myrtle, for nearly thirty years. He has three children, three grandchildren and three great-grandchildren. As Sam said and truly proved in his life: 'If you do good, good will follow you.'
* ❖ **Associations and organisations:** Co-founder and member of the West Indian Association of Service Personnel; member of the RAF Ex-Servicemen's Association, London; member of Lambeth Road Baptist Church, Brixton.

Warrant Officer Jim Latimer

Served with: Royal Air Force, Bomber Command, Nos 102 and 462
    Squadrons
Service number: 1551478
Interviewed: Manchester, Lancashire, 11 October 2014

Service History and Personal Stories

- ❖ **Born:** 21 December 1923, Edinburgh, Scotland, UK.
- ❖ Jim joined the RAF in mid-1942 and was trained with the RAF around Ontario in Canada until late 1943. After returning to the UK he continued further training on Wellington bombers with No. 102 Squadron.
- ❖ After completing conversion training on to Halifaxes he was later transferred to No. 462 Squadron. He undertook a staggering forty-six operations as a bomb aimer between July 1944 and March 1945.
- ❖ These dangerous missions took place over France, Holland and Germany. They included giving air support to ground troops during the hard fighting in Villers-Bocage in Normandy in July 1944.

❖   Later he was involved in an operation to bomb airfields in Eindhoven, the Netherlands, and many military targets in Germany such as Bonn, Hamburg, Koblenz, Essen, Hanover, Dortmund and the U-boat pens at Kiel.

❖   Jim also undertook day and night missions as part of the famous 1,000 bomber raids, and later finished his RAF service as a warrant officer.

It is amazing sometimes in life who is around or near you at certain times and how you can know so little about them until you have a particular reason or cause to do so. I have been a parishioner at St Paul's Church on Moor Lane, Salford, since 2003, where I have been attending that lovely church on and off between my work overseas as a tour manager for various travel companies and cruise lines. It was not until I was undertaking research for my book that I found out that in our congregation was a gentleman who was in Bomber Command during the war. That veteran is Jim Latimer and during his time in service with the RAF he undertook a staggering forty-six missions as a bomb aimer on Halifaxes. It is quite incredible that he has been moving among us as a quiet, polite and unassuming veteran who talks very little about the war years. He and his wife Jean were married at St Paul's Church on 27 March 1948 and have been attending ever since, making them the longest-serving parishioners in the church at around seventy remarkably loyal years. To know them both and to be the only person to have interviewed Jim about his wartime service makes the story even more interesting, and the way our paths have crossed has led to this great and valuable addition to my book.

So here is the story of Jim Latimer. His profile was one of the last I worked on for the book and helped bring *The Last Heroes* to a very good conclusion, coming full circle back to my local area in North Manchester and with whom, as I mentioned earlier, I have links with St Paul's Church, where the Rev. Lisa Battye has been very kind and helpful in assisting me in locating veterans through the church network within the Diocese, some of whom are now in this book and others I intend to include in any future book I write.

Jim began his service when he joined the RAF in mid-1942 in Edinburgh, at 18 years of age. Soon after that he was sent to be trained safely in the far away country of our Commonwealth ally, Canada, on a massive programme known as the British Commonwealth Air Training Plan. This ongoing initiative helped supply the much-needed and highly skilled new manpower to service the needs of an ever-growing Royal Air Force. It also helped to replace the high casualties sustained in the air war on many fronts, especially those of Bomber Command in their ongoing offensive over Europe. Jim graduated as a bomb aimer, or air bomber as they were also known. He went through training and courses at various Royal Canadian Air Force stations, learning many of the essential skills that would be required for his new job during active service. This included an armaments course at Fingal, a navigation course at Port Albert, and a moving

St Paul's Church, Moor
Lane, Salford.

target air bomber course at Jarvis, all in the province of Ontario. This training
was completed on Ansons.

After Jim had passed these courses he returned to the UK by October 1943
and then went on to do more extensive flight crew-related training, such as a ship
recognition course at RAF Skeabrae in Orkney, Scotland, combined bombing
exercises at RAF Mona in Anglesey, and a water dinghy and parachute course
at RAF Moreton-in-Marsh in Gloucestershire. This was followed in April 1944
with further exercises and armament training on the twin-engine Wellington with
21 OTU, also at Moreton-in-Marsh. This led to the next big natural progression
that would complete his training and make him completely ready for active service,
conversion training from the Wellington to the four-engine Halifax Mark III at
the 1652 Heavy Conversion Unit based at RAF Marston Moor in Yorkshire. Jim
completed that big step over a two-month period from late May until late July
1944 and was now ready to actively engage the enemy. The extent of the training
detailed here shows the extensive and rigorous process that air crew had to go
through before having to do it for real in the extremely dangerous conditions and
with the extra perils that they faced in active combat missions and operations. Even
after this long and meticulous training, a great many air crews did not survive past
their first few missions.

Jim first went into action with No. 102 Squadron on 28 July in Halifax MZ798
and then on 30 July 1944 in MZ772. He was involved in air operations to soften

102 Squadron badge with the motto *Tentate et Perficite*, meaning 'Attempt and Achieve'.

up dug-in German positions to help Allied troops who were struggling in the Villers–Bocage area in Normandy during 'the Battle of the Hedgerows'. These would be the first of a remarkable forty-six active combat operations that would see him in action over France, Holland and Germany.

Jim first of all flew from RAF Pocklington in Yorkshire from late July until late August 1944, then transferred to No. 462 Squadron, No. 4 Group, at RAF Driffield in Yorkshire from August until December 1944. He finished operational flying with No. 462 Squadron, No. 100 Group, at RAF Foulsham in Norfolk from January to September 1945. After the first missions in France he was involved in day and night bombing missions on military targets in many places, such as Eindhoven in Holland, and multiple targets in Germany including Wilhelmshaven, Hamburg, Koblenz, Bonn, Mainz, Rheine, Dortmund, Mannheim, Neuss and Hanover. Jim was also involved in other interesting missions, such as the attacks on the U-boat pens at Kiel and the infamous Krupp armament works in Essen in the Ruhr Valley, and was a part of many of the 1,000-bomber raids. It was not always bombs that they dropped on some special operations; they released the 'window' anti-radar metal foil or chaff. This acts as a radar countermeasure as it gives the impression of a cluster of primary targets or swamps the radar screen with multiple returns, causing confusion to the enemy which would deploy forces to the wrong place, increasing the chances of operational success and limiting RAF casualties.

The Handley Page Halifax B.III bomber similar to the one that Jim flew in as a bomb aimer over Nazi-occupied Europe.

Usually any full crew or individual crewman who completed thirty missions, or 'a tour' as it was called, would have an extended rest from operational duties. After doing more than one-and-a-half tours of duty Jim was transferred to RAF Leuchars near Dundee in Scotland, which was run by Coastal Command and was where Nos 224 and 233 Squadrons were based. There he was involved in the air-sea rescue service on standby on a rescue boat team. By this time he was a warrant officer and stayed there until June 1946, after which time he was demobbed. This brought to an end the RAF service of this brave young bomb aimer who was only twenty-one when he finished serving his country.

Jim now briefly recalls some of the things that happened and that aircrew went through during his service:

46 Bombing Missions Over Nazi-Occupied Europe

Many things happened when we were out on missions, as you would expect. We regularly came under enemy attack of one kind or another. We lost a lot of brave airmen who were our friends, three friends of mine I really remember were lost on different operations. On one occasion I saw one go down. We were both on the same mission and I saw his plane when we were just over the target; he was on the starboard side of me and when I was looking at his plane this Focke Wulf 190 came right up behind him and blasted him and I saw it going down and that was it, my friend gone! When we flew on the daytime 1,000-bomber raids with the Americans over Germany there were a lot of losses but more so for them because they stayed in tight formation and got picked off much more. We were in a looser formation so we could take much better evasive action and stood a better chance! Over Germany we experienced constant and heavy anti-aircraft fire and frequent Luftwaffe attacks, bad losses. I do think of them, our lads; it comes back especially around Remembrance Day.

So to conclude writing about Jim I think it is very fitting to say that this humble gentleman whom I have known for some time now has lived according to the motto of his former No. 102 Squadron, *Tentate et perficite*, meaning 'Attempt and achieve'.

Additional Information and Life After Service

- ❖ **Rank at end of service:** Warrant officer.
- ❖ **Medals and honours:** 1939–45 Defence Medal, 1939–45 War Medal, 1939–45 Star, France–Germany Star.
- ❖ **Post-war years:** After the war Jim had various jobs such as running a newsagents and later selling leather goods until his retirement in 1991 aged 68. He married Jean in 1948 and they have four children, ten grandchildren and six great-grandchildren.
- ❖ **Associations and organisations:** None.

Squadron Leader Allan Scott DFM

Served with: 124, 603, 1435, 122 Squadrons, Fighter Command, Royal
    Air Force
Service number: 143726
Interviewed: Wem, Shropshire, 24 May 2016

Service History and Personal Stories

- ❖ **Born:** 27 July 1921, Ainsdale, England, UK.
- ❖ Allan Scott served an incredible thirty-five years in the RAF. He is the last Battle of Malta fighter pilot ace of the Second World War and was awarded the DFM for valour in combat.
- ❖ He scored a total of six confirmed kills, of which five were in Malta, and three of those whilst giving fighter cover to assist convoy WS 12S during Operation Pedestal in August 1942.
- ❖ He completed three tours of duty as a fighter pilot: first from the famous RAF Biggin Hill in Kent, the second from RAF Luqa in Malta, and the third from RAF Ford in West Sussex.

❖ Later, as a test pilot, Allan flew more than eighty types of prototype aircraft running
   from the propeller to the jet age during that huge period of change in aviation.
❖ Amazingly, at the age of 95, he still flies at his local airfield in Shropshire, and recently
   in 2017 he again flew in and took the controls of a Spitfire from his wartime airfield
   at Biggin Hill.

A great example of a man who belies his age, Allan has led an action-packed
life, and still does. Flying is truly in his blood, from when he fought in aerial
combat over Britain and Malta, becoming an ace in the process, through his
days as a test pilot on more than eighty different types of aircraft, right to
the present day, when he keeps his hand in with some local weekend flying
from Sleap Aerodrome in Shropshire. He is another shining example of the
generation that helped save Britain at that most critical time. We finish the
Air Force section with the thirty-five-year RAF service history of Squadron
Leader Allan Scott DFM.

His career in the RAF began when he joined at the age of 18 in March 1940
at Padgate, Warrington. After this he was sent for basic training to an ITU (Initial
Training Unit), which was based at Tranance Hotel, Newquay. Allan was then sent
to RAF Woodley in Berkshire, home to No. 8 EFTS (Elementary Flying Training
School) to learn basic flying skills on Miles Master aircraft; he had completed the
course by May 1941. It was at RAF Woodley that the legendary Douglas Bader
lost his legs in a terrible flying accident in 1931.

Allan's training then intensified as he progressed on to the Hurricane to learn
more fighter pilot skills at RAF Hullavington in Wiltshire, which was home to
the No. 9 (Pilot) AFU (Advanced Flying Unit). He was there from May to July
1941, and after completing his training and gaining his wings, he was ready for
the real thing.

He was soon posted to 124 Squadron at the famous RAF Biggin Hill for
his first operational tour of duty, defending the skies over southern England
for nearly a year until June 1942; during this time he scored his first victory
when he took down a Junkers Ju 88 dive bomber over Clapton-on-Sea on
17 December 1941, and had a shared kill on 30 April 1942 (a Messerschmitt
Bf 109). During this period there were still many large German air raids against
British cities taking place.

Allan's next operational tour of duty the following month took him into another
hard combat zone: the skies over the besieged island of Malta, where aerial combat
raged almost every day in what was then one of the most bombed places on Earth.
He would be there from July until December 1942, based at RAF Luqa, first with
603 Squadron and then, after it was disbanded, 1435 Squadron, which absorbed
the pilots and Spitfires of the disbanded squadron. It was during that time when he
was in many engagements with aircraft of the Luftwaffe and the Regia Aeronautica

Italiana that he scored a further five kills and became an ace – any pilot who scored five or more victories in combat.

Allan scored three of his Maltese victories while giving air support to a very important convoy aiming to resupply this strategically vital island; the air battles he was involved in helped get that convoy through and keep Malta's lifeline open. The mission was given the name of Operation Pedestal. This convoy, numbered WS 12S, took place between 10 and 15 August 1942 and consisted of fourteen fast merchant vessels and their valuable cargo. It was considered so important that it was given an escort of four aircraft carriers, two battleships, seven light cruisers, thirty-two destroyers, and air cover that was made up of seventy-four fighters and twenty-eight torpedo bombers. The air presence was later supported by Spitfires from squadrons based on the island, including Allan's 1435 Squadron. Unfortunately, with constant enemy attacks from bombers and fighters, motor torpedo boats, heavy and light cruisers, and submarines, as well as the presence of heavy minefields, the convoy suffered heavy casualties. It lost thirteen vessels in total, which included the aircraft carrier HMS *Eagle*, the cruisers *Manchester* and *Cairo*, the destroyer *Foresight* and nine merchant ships; in addition, more than 500 merchant and Royal Navy sailors and airmen were lost. Only five of the original fourteen merchant vessels eventually made it to the Grand Harbour in Malta. The losses were so bad that some equated it to the tragic PQ17 Arctic convoy that was decimated by the Germans only a few weeks earlier, in July 1942, with the terrible loss of a third of all its ships. However, the ship that was carrying arguably the most important cargo – aviation fuel – an American tanker with British crew named SS *Ohio*, did manage to make it through. This shipment helped keep the Maltese air offensive against Axis shipping going and threw the island a vital lifeline. Although it was costly in terms of men and material, the operation was actually a strategic victory: the Royal Navy and Merchant Navy, with the support of the RAF, had saved Malta.

The badge of 603 Squadron with the very apt motto *Gin Ye Daur* – 'If you dare'.

It was during these events that on 13 August Allan shot down an Italian Breda Ba 88 bomber, and this was followed by two Messerschmitt Bf 109 kills, before the convoy finished on 15 August. Later in the month he got another Bf 109 and the same in October 1942, bringing his total to six kills, one shared and six probables, leading to Allan being awarded the DFM (Distinguished Flying Medal) for valour in combat.

In December this second operational tour of duty was over and, after some well-earned leave,

Allan's next important trip would be to Buckingham Palace in early 1943 to be awarded his DFM by King George VI. It was while at the Palace waiting for the ceremony to begin that Allan crept off for a quick cigarette and was caught by a young Princess Elizabeth who, as Allan put it, 'Politely admonished me for smoking and not being where I should be at that time'. When Allan next met the now Queen Elizabeth II it was at an event seventy-two years later, in July 2015 in Scotland. It was here at the Edinburgh HQ of the Royal Auxiliary Air Force's 603 Squadron that he reminded the Queen about their last meeting: 'It raised a smile.'

In a break between operational flying Allan was posted to 58 OTU (Operational Training Unit) at RAF Grangemouth, Stirlingshire, where he was given the job of testing various marks of Spitfire to see if they were airworthy to use as training aircraft. This was from February until September 1943, after which it was time once again to return to front-line flying. He was posted to 122 Squadron at RAF Ford, West Sussex, and was involved in giving fighter escort cover for the 2nd Tactical Air Force and US 8th Air Force bombing missions over Germany. These took them right into the heart of Berlin. During his final operational tour of duty from September 1943 until June 1944, Allan had to swap his beloved Spitfire for the American P-51 Mustang, which he flew giving top cover during these dangerous missions.

This final tour finished for Allan on 6 June 1944 and a new career direction in the RAF began thereafter: as a test pilot. After training in Beford, he was posted to many RAF MUs (Maintenance Units), where he tested more than eighty types of aircraft from mid 1944 until the early 1960s. These would include, in numerical order, No. 5 MU at RAF Kemble, Gloucestershire; No. 27 MU at RAF Shawbury, Shropshire; and No. 39 MU at RAF Colerne, Wiltshire.

Another fascinating posting that Allan would undertake while a test pilot was when he was seconded to RAF Aston Down, Gloucestershire, at that time home to No. 20 MU and the civilian No. 2 ATA Ferry Pool, to which he was loaned. While there, Allan recalls:

> There were many times that if required we would test up to ten different types of aircraft a day before handing them over to the very capable ATA pilots – mostly women – who would then fly them on to their allotted squadrons. The ATA did a very good job keeping our squadrons supplied with the vital front-line aircraft that were needed to continually take the war to the enemy.

During his years as a test pilot Allan flew a whole range of aircraft, from fighters to bombers and propeller to jet aircraft, as aviation moved into the jet age. These included the Lancaster, Halifax, Blenheim, Whitley, Hastings, Hurricane, Mosquito, Typhoon, Fairchild, Tiger Moth, Vampire, Meteor, Tempest, Corsair, Hornet, Buckingham, and also helicopters like the Wessex and Pioneer.

All this dangerous flying on what were mainly prototypes or new versions of these aircraft meant that it was a very dangerous job, and as you would expect Allan experienced some close shaves. For example, while at RAF Shawbury in 1946 Allan's Mosquito developed an engine problem and he just managed, by skilful piloting, to clear No. 1 Hanger by a few feet and avert disaster. For this he was awarded the RAF Green Endorsement accolade for safely landing in difficult circumstances, and Scott's Corner was born. A plaque is still there to commemorate the event. But Allan was not so lucky on 21 October 1953 while doing an acrobatic display in a Tiger Moth at RAF Turnhouse, near Edinburgh. Here he had a serious crash that left him temporarily blinded and needing plastic surgery for facial reconstruction, along with serious injuries that put him out of action for two years. True to form, when he had recovered and returned to flying, the first aircraft he got into was a Tiger Moth – talk about getting straight back into the saddle! In this case it really was from the horse that thew him.

As part of our conversation, Allan told me just what it was like to be a fighter pilot:

A Fighter Pilot in the Heat of Battle

I always felt that I flew instinctively. In aerial combat you had to remember that you were moving at hundreds of miles an hour and things could and did change in a split second. But there were three major things you always had to do in the heat of battle: namely have your eyes on the aircraft in front of you that you were pursuing, be aware of what was around you in the sky at any given time and keep checking your rear as well so that an enemy aircraft didn't drop on to your tail and get you. Not easy – as the saying goes, you needed eyes in the back of your head! Something I learnt to do that really helped keep me alive and engage my targets effectively was to always attack on a turn, making it very hard for your target to take evasive action quickly and also very difficult for anyone behind you to engage you properly. Also never stay straight in an attack or you could very easily become the victim. I learned to apply these things very early on, from when I was at Biggin Hill and we first started to attack large formations of incoming German bombers and their escorting fighters in what was still at that time a real Battle for Britain and the skies above it. Then I carried that experience on to Malta where we really had some seriously hard-fought engagements with the Germans and Italians. We inflicted some heavy casualties upon them but we also took heavy casualties too. I remember once in Malta we lost five pilots in just over a week; that's five friends gone – very difficult but you learned to live with it, as many have rightly said, because we had no choice. It was a very sad fact of war and one that all too often was our reality. I guess my tactics must have worked, though – after all, I am still here, and for that I am very grateful. I still enjoy flying when I can at my local airfield at Sleap, and this year went again to relive that wonderful experience of flying in a Spitfire from the Biggin Hill Heritage Hanger at my old wartime airfield where I had a go at throwing her around a bit, and I plan to be around until I am a hundred as I also have a flight booked for then.

Allan's varied career continued: in 1962 he worked for the Inspectorate of Radios on the Handley Page Hastings transport aircraft as a second pilot and he was also involved in the testing of new communications equipment on board this aircraft. This job took him to various places such as Hong Kong and Singapore. By 1967, while at RAF Odiham, Hampshire, he was promoted to squadron leader. He still flew various aircraft when possible, which in 1971 included the RAF front-line Cold War fighter, the Mach 2 Lightning.

In 1975, while at RAF Benson, South Oxfordshire, Allan retired from the RAF, ending a staggering thirty-five years of service to his country. For three and a half decades Allan flew the United Kingdom's best aircraft, from the iconic Supermarine Spitfire to the supersonic BAC Lightning, proving without doubt that he still had the 'heart of an ace'.

Additional Information and Life After Service

- ❖ **Rank at the end of service:** Squadron Leader.
- ❖ **Medals and honours:** DFM, 1939–45 Defence Medal, 1939–45 War Medal, 1939–45 Star, Aircrew Star with France–Germany Bar, Africa Star with '42–43 Bar, Malta 50 Years Commemorative Medal.
- ❖ **Post-war years:** After returning to civilian life Allan worked for Wimpey Homes as a property salesman in the Abingdon-on-Thames area in Oxfordshire and retired in 1984. He married Pat in 1947, whom he met while stationed at RAF Shawbury. They were together for sixty-five years. They have one son and three grandchildren.
- ❖ **Associations and organisations:** RAF Benevolent Fund, Sleap Aero Club.

4

Intelligence and the Secret War

The intelligence war was by its very nature one that was fought covertly and as such should be known as the 'Secret War'. It was undertaken by each of the services at all levels, as it was by all the nations involved in the the war, and was more crucial than ever before in helping turn the tide in favour of the Allies and bringing about an eventual victory. In this overview we look at some of the organisations involved in achieving this that were part of that 'Shadow Service'.

Bletchley park – the cryptography work carried out at this Government Code and Cypher School (GC&GS) establishment near Milton Keynes in Buckinghamshire was central to the breaking of the German Army, Navy and Air Force Ultra codes, named Enigma after the machine that the Nazis used to send their top-secret scrambled messages. It was here that staff also broke the Lorenz cipher, the coded messages sent by the German Lorenz machines for top-level communications between Hitler and the German High Command in Berlin and the Army High Commands elsewhere in the field of operations. The work at Bletchley Park made a vital contribution to the final outcome of the Second World War. More related information about this can be found within the veterans' profiles in the section that follows.

MI5 and MI6 – There were other organisations operating secretly in order to help the British and Allied war effort under the Secret Intelligence Service (SIS), namely MI5 (UK internal security threats and counter-espionage) and MI6 (UK external security threats), whose origins can be traced back to the Secret Service Bureau established in July 1909. MI5 (Military Intelligence, Section 5) set up a network of double agents that were used very successfully throughout the war to feed misleading information to the Abwehr, the German secret service. Each agent was assigned a case officer from within the counter-espionage branch to monitor every aspect of their handling. This was under the supervision of the Twenty, or Double-Cross, Committee, which included a small inter-agency committee that was created to liaise with and share intelligence with other relevant departments that had a vested interest in national security.

The Manor House at Bletchley Park, part of the GC&CS home of British code-breaking during the Second World War.

MI6 (Military Intelligence, Section 6) also did very important intelligence work under its various departments, or sections as they were known. They were Section V, to liaise with the security service (MI5) on counter-espionage reports from overseas stations; Section VII, economic intelligence to deal with trade, industrial and contraband; Section VIII, radio communications to contact operatives and agents overseas; Section N, to exploit the contents of foreign diplomatic bags; Section D, to conduct active covert operations in time of war including the Home Defence Resistance Scheme in case Britain was invaded; and the Special Operations Executive (SOE), which carried out sabotage operations in Nazi-occupied territories. The SIS, with its closely shared remit, was linked and present with the GC&CS at Bletchley Park. We now look at veterans who each played their own intricate, varied and very important part within this most secret war.

Flight Lieutenant John Lomas

Served with: Royal Air Force, Bletchley Park, Hut 3, Ultra Intelligence
Service number: 157263
Interviewed: Croydon, London, 1 October 2016

Service History and Personal Stories

- ❖ **Born:** 13 December 1920, Stockport, England, UK.
- ❖ John joined the RAF in January 1941 and wished to utilise his German language skills. After an interview at the Air Ministry he was accepted and trained for a special job that included decoding.
- ❖ He was posted at Bletchley Park from April 1941 to October 1943, working with Ultra Intelligence first at Hut 15 then at Hut 3, where he translated the intercepted German Air Force Enigma codes.
- ❖ This work put him at the very centre of the code-breaking operations and would lead to him meeting Alan Turing and witnessing the only visit of Winston Churchill to Bletchley on 6 September 1941.
- ❖ After this he was sent by Bletchley to work 'in the field' as an Ultra liaison officer to the RAF's 329 Wing in Algeria, 276 Wing and US 15th Air Force in Italy, and 164 Wing in Burma. These postings were from October 1943 until April 1946.

During the interview process for this book I couldn't help but think how interesting it was that all the very different realities, personal histories and extremely varied experiences that the veterans had were all playing out and overlapping simultaneously under very different conditions and circumstances throughout the course of the Second World War. And here I was capturing some of these incredibly important stories first hand more than seventy years later, putting them together like parts of a secret code or pieces of a giant jigsaw puzzle to help us see the bigger picture. Each of these pieces is represented by a veteran who has chosen to share his or her story, some for the first time since those significant events took place, and in doing so they have given me the privilege of being the first person their stories have been shared with in their entirety. This has given great richness to the book, and provided some great scoops as well. The remarkable story of John Lomas is a fine example of these things: he was at the very heart of one of the most vitally important and highly secret parts of Allied intelligence gathering at the now famous Bletchley Park, and he kindly chose to talk to me about his unique experiences in another great first-time interview.

To find and interview someone who was at the very epicentre of the code-breaking, deciphering and translating of Ultra intelligence information at Bletchley Park was truly mind-blowing. At the heart of all that went on at the GC&CS was the vital work carried out in 'the huts'. Those that John cited as being most important were numbered 3, 4, 6, 7 and 8, and these dealt with the interception, translation and collation of information related to the Enigma codes and communications of the German armed forces. This work has been credited with potentially saving hundreds of thousands of lives of Allied servicemen and women in all theatres of the conflict. It was also credited with having a profound influence on the direction and eventual outcome of the war, potentially by shortening it by at least two years. This was quite simply a massive contribution on all levels, and playing his part with his German language skills in Hut 3 was John Lomas.

John joined the RAF in January 1941 at RAF Cardington in Bedfordshire. He did his basic training in Great Yarmouth and was then sent to RAF Penarth in South Wales to do a course in airman's pay and allowances. After that he was posted to the RAF Accounts Branch at RAF Wilmslow in Cheshire, a job John recalls as being terribly boring and one that he wanted to change as soon as he could. This opportunity came when he saw a notice asking for German speakers to work as 'Computors', which John could only ascertain meant working collating information in one way or another. It sounded interesting, even intriguing, so he applied for the job as he had already studied German to a good level at Macclesfield Grammar School before the war. John was sent to the Air Ministry in London and interviewed by Josh Cooper, who he found out later was a high level code-breaker. There he was tested by reading a paper in German about 'radio location', the early technology later known as radar. After being told he had passed, John was

The highly complex German Enigma machine, which had a staggering 158 million, million, million possible settings to choose from each day, making code-breaking a long, difficult and daunting process for the Allies.

sent to Rugby in Warwickshire to do a course in German Air Force codes. It was the outcome of this course that led to him becoming part of RAF Intelligence and being posted to Bletchley Park from April 1941 until October 1943.

At Bletchley John started by working for a short time in Hut 15, which dealt with Signals Intelligence and Traffic Analysis (SIXTA). From here he would send selected essential information to his Bletchley counterpart in Malta. After this, in June 1941, John was moved to Hut 3. He stayed there until early 1943, when his section was transferred to Block B, Room 145, Air Section. His job in both places was the translating of intercepted Luftwaffe Enigma codes. After translation he would make a summary of the information, put the interceptions in order of priority, and then make sure they went to the correct individual or high command. During his time at Bletchley John would meet Alan Turing and most of the top code-breakers. He would also witness the visit of Winston Churchill on 6 September 1941.

John was then chosen for some different intelligence work out in the field, but before he was assigned to these special postings he had to become a commissioned officer and so was sent to RAF Cosford on an officers' course, where he attained the rank of pilot officer. In October 1943, he was sent covertly in plain clothes with his RAF uniform in a separate bag through Lisbon in neutral Portugal, and on via Gibraltar and Rabat, Morocco, to Algiers, Algeria. There he would become the Ultra liaison officer between RAF HQ and RAF 329 Wing and Bletchley. This posting lasted six months until April 1944, when he was transferred to Conversano, near Bari in Italy, where he continued his work, this time for and between RAF 276 Wing, 15th US Air Force and Bletchley, until May 1945. His job during both assignments was to receive top-secret Ultra reports from Bletchley and pass the information on German land and air movements to the Allied air forces, who would put it into their operational planning to achieve maximum success in their ground and air offensives.

John stayed on in Italy until July 1945, then returned to the United Kingdom. His next posting was as liaison officer between RAF 164 Wing in Rangoon, Burma, and Bletchley, a post in which he stayed from October 1945 until April 1946. He and others were listening in on radio traffic from different areas around Asia where insurgencies were springing up and also from the Chinese communists, after which he reported anything of interest back to Bletchley. Once 164 Wing was closed down, in April 1946 John was transferred to Singapore, where he did similar liaison work with the Army until June of that year. He then returned home again and Bletchley Park and the RAF released him in late June 1946. John, by then a flight lieutenant, was demobbed at RAF Hednesford in Staffordshire and went back to civvy street, keeping the details of his work on Ultra a secret for many decades to come.

John was privy to what was happening at the centre of Ultra intelligence gathering at Bletchley and shared them with me:

Insights and Aspects of Life at Bletchley Park

After I had been in Bletchley a short time a man came for me and said come with me for a walk round the lake. And as we walked he introduced me to the secrets of Enigma, that we were decoding the German Air Force's most secret codes and the chat we got from that was known as Ultra, meaning Ultra secret Ultra Intelligence. It is the most important thing in the war, the most secret thing in the whole war and is never to be discussed outside of your own little area. You are never to discuss it with anybody else at all, and it's so secret that Churchill said that he would shoot with his own hand anybody who talked carelessly about the decoding of Enigma.

The man was Peter Lucas, head of the Air Force interception section in Hut 3, known as SALU after the men who developed the unit, Mr Saltmarsh and Mr Lucas. This was the unit John was assigned to. John then went on to share other recollections:

As we were listening in to the German communications every day and they were being decoded and later translated by us we, of course, heard about a lot of operations as they were happening. Sometimes when you heard exceptionally bad things that had happened all you could do is feel very sorry for the servicemen involved because we couldn't do much about it at that point. I remember that particularly being the case with Convoy PQ 17 and Dieppe. You got the Luftwaffe air traffic as they were supporting the attacks and we later heard the full extent of what had happened, that is when the reality of the war came home to us. Other times you received chat about things beforehand or as they were building up. These were things that you could do something about because the information had been intercepted and translated in time to act upon it. This meant, of course, that you could possibly make a difference to the outcome of an operation or a battle and maybe help save the lives of some brave servicemen or women somewhere, which I think and hope we did.

Additional Information and Life After Service

- ❖ **Rank at end of service:** Flight lieutenant.
- ❖ **Medals and honours:** Bletchley Park Commemorative Medallion. Did not claim other official medals.
- ❖ **Post-war years:** Post Office savings bank, Manchester, 1946–47; UK Immigration Service, 1947–80. Ended up as assistant chief of the British Immigration Service. Never married, no children.
- ❖ **Associations and organisations:** No affiliations. Only attended 329 Wing annual reunions.

Leading Wren Jean Valentine

Served with: Women's Royal Naval Service, Bletchley Park, 'Bombe'
    operator
Service number: 72583
Interviewed: Henley-on-Thames, Oxfordshire, 17 April 2016

Service History and Personal Stories

- ❖ **Born:** 7 July 1924, Perth, Scotland, UK.
- ❖ Jean began doing her bit for the war effort at the age of 15, working as a volunteer in soldiers' canteens in her home town of Perth in Scotland.
- ❖ Volunteered for the Wrens at the age of 18 and after basic training was chosen to work at the top secret establishment of Bletchley Park.
- ❖ Stationed in Hut 11 as a Bombe operator on Alan Turing's 'Bombe' code-breaking machines between September 1943 and March 1944.
- ❖ Worked to find each day's settings on the rotors of the German encryption machine, the Enigma, in order to help break those codes and obtain the vitally important information within them.

❖   Later went on to work on a Bletchley outstation in Columbo, Ceylon, now Sri Lanka, from May 1944 until September 1945 as part of a team that manually broke the highly secret Japanese meteorological codes.

Bletchley Park's important work in the past and the legacy which is maintained today is an ongoing asset to the nation. It was at this top-secret location in Buckinghamshire during the Second World War that the Government Code and Cipher School (GC&CS) studied, worked upon and created methods that allowed the Allies to decipher the military codes and ciphers such as the Enigma and Lorenz of the Germans, and also those of the Japanese and other Axis nations and their armed forces. By intercepting and decoding their highly sensitive communications, they were able to pass on the 'Ultra' information to the relevant people and chiefs within the government and intelligence community. This in turn was passed on to the high-ranking commanders of the Allied forces out in the battle zones of various theatres of war, who were then able to use the information to carry out operations in such a way that led to eventual victory over the Axis Powers. Bletchley Park's work was simply that vital and a massive game changer in the bigger picture of this global conflict.

Bletchley Park was also the birthplace of the information age, with the invention of the code-breaking Turing–Welchman Bombe and Flowers' Colossus: the world's first electronic computer. From there also came the seed of what today is GCHQ – Government Communications Headquarters – the heart of the intelligence-gathering community in the UK. We have continued to reap the benefits of Bletchley Park from its inception in 1938 right through to today's internet age.

At the height of its operations there were 12,000 people working at and passing through Bletchley Park on any twenty-four-hour rotation. We now follow the story of just one of those people: Bombe operator Jean Valentine.

At the age of 15 a young lady by the name of Jean Valentine already felt moved to do her bit for the war effort, and so in between helping with chores at home for her mother she volunteered and gave time working in soldiers' canteens in her home city of Perth in Scotland. This she did for three years until July 1943 when, at 18 she was old enough to officially join up and contribute to the war effort by becoming part of the Women's Royal Naval Service (WRNS, or Wrens). After basic training at Tulliechewan Castle in Balloch, Dunbartonshire, Jean was then sent to Earls Court in London and after being interviewed was selected for a very special top secret posting. Once briefed, and having signed the Official Secrets Act, Jean was then sent to an outstation of Bletchley Park in Adstock, Buckinghamshire, for training on a machine called the Bombe, which had been devised by Alan Turing and Gordon Welchman to find each day's settings on the rotors of the German Enigma machine. Once these settings had been found the messages could be successfully intercepted and decrypted, and their translated contents used for the highly valued information that was held within them.

Then from September 1943 until March 1944, while billeted at Steeple Clayton in Buckinghamshire, Jean was sent to work at the heart of Bletchley Park in Hut 11 on one of the Bombe decryption machines, of which there were five in that particular hut. It was here that through her work she directly played her part and helped contribute towards the code-breaking efforts at Bletchley Park, or Station X as it was also known, which as Jean found out later in life played such an incredible part in the outcome of the war. However, her contribution to this kind of work was far from over when Jean was selected to go and join a team based in a Bletchley Park overseas outstation in Colombo in Ceylon, which was tasked with breaking the very important Japanese meteorological codes that helped guide and dictate the military movements of the Imperial Japanese forces.

For this Jean had specialist training in Japanese codes and ciphers at Bletchley Park while being put in the very nice billet of Woburn Abbey. Once this was finished her posting took her out to Colombo for fifteen months from May 1944 until September 1945, during which time two very significant events happened. First, the team was successful in intercepting, deciphering and breaking the Japanese codes, and second, Jean met and married Clive, who was a Seafire pilot with the Fleet Air Arm. After this she returned home to the UK and was demobbed at Chatham, Kent, in October 1945, bringing to an end an exceptionally interesting wartime service in which her clandestine work helped the war effort in many ways. It was not until the mid-1970s, with the release of the first books about Bletchley, that Jean felt free to talk about her wartime experiences.

I asked Jean to share with me some of her memories regarding her very special and secretive wartime work. She told me:

Part of the Code-Breaking History of Bletchley Park

It was interesting being at Bletchley Park. I didn't know how interesting it was going to be all these years on. People had never heard of it but we who were there were told you must never speak about this and I don't know anybody who did. Churchill described it as 'the goose that laid the golden eggs and

never cackled'. We were told what to do, we were disciplined to do what we were told, and we did it! However, all that has climbed out of the woodwork now and everybody knows more about Bletchley Park than I do quite honestly.

The Bletchley Park and its Outstations badge was awarded to the veterans of this top-secret establishment, with an engraving on the back reading, 'We also Served'.

A recreation of Alan
Turing's Bombe at the
Bletchley Park Museum.

I was very inquisitive about how such a big operation with so many people could
be kept so secretive, and how well that was done. Jean explained:

> You knew the people you worked with and you knew nobody else. When you
> went for your meal you mixed with people who worked in other huts but you
> never in any way discussed what you were doing or what they were doing for
> that matter, I assume we were all told to do that. I enjoyed being part of it and
> it would have been nice to talk about it, but however you couldn't.

During one of our conversations I asked Jean to describe in more detail her work
on the Bombe in Hut 11:

> We wanted to win this war and so whatever we were able to do we did. When I
> first began working on Alan Turing's Bombe I found it to be staggering. When
> you look at it you can see it has 108 drums and that is equivalent to thirty-six
> German Enigma encryption machines, whose codes we were trying to break. It
> had a choice of three rotors out of five and it just had be found out which rotors
> were being used and what the starting letters were, and just think about this: the

Enigma machine was capable of 158 million, million, million possibilities and also the rotors and starting letters were changed each day, so we had to set up the Bombe anew every day, drums at the front and the plugs at the back. You can start to imagine the sheer size of the task faced by the 'Bombe' and by those trying to break the enemies' codes on a daily basis at Bletchley Park, but we were successful in this endeavour.

Additional Information and Life After Service

* ❖ **Rank at end of service:** Leading Wren.
* ❖ **Medals and honours:** 1939–45 War Medal, 1939–45 Defence Medal, Bletchley Park and Outstations Commemorative Medallion.
* ❖ **Post-war years:** From just after the war until the 1970s Jean's husband, Clive, worked in the aircraft industry for BOAC and de Havilland. This meant that the family lived in many places over the years, such as Burma, Karachi, Bombay and the UK, and during this time Jean concentrated on bringing up her family. In 1970–72 they lived in Brussels, Belgium, and Cologne, Germany, where she worked for Viking Tyres as an office manager. After returning to live in Marlow, Buckinghamshire, Jean continued to work for Viking Tyres as part of its marketing team and also travelled around Europe as a saleswoman for the company. Later they settled in Henley-on-Thames and for about fifteen years she worked on a voluntary basis as a guide at Bletchley Park. Jean was married to Clive for sixty-three years and they have two daughters, six grandchildren and three great-grandchildren.
* ❖ **Associations and organisations:** Royal British Legion, Henley branch.

Sergeant Bernard Morgan

Served with: Royal Air Force, Code and Cipher Unit, No. 83 Group
   Control Centre
Service number: 1697478
Interviewed: Crewe, Cheshire, 6 August 2016

Service History and Personal Stories

- ❖ **Born:** 7 February 1924, Manchester, England, UK.
- ❖ Bernard joined the RAF on 7 February 1942. After training he was posted to RAF Swanton Morley in Norfolk, where he worked on a flight control trainer, doing beam approach training (BAT) refresher courses for pilots.
- ❖ While there he saw and applied for a job as a code and cipher operator in early 1943. After special training he was posted to a mobile intelligence unit as part of the No. 83 Group Control Centre, with the Second Tactical Air Force.
- ❖ On D-Day Bernard landed at Gold Beach and later used the Type X encryption machine to decipher incoming coded messages from the front, requesting air support as the Second TAF moved through France, Belgium, Holland and Germany.

❖   Bernard deciphered the top secret message about the German Surrender early on
    7 May 1945, and was one of the very few in the world to know about the end of
    the war in Europe before it was officially announced.
❖   After the war in Europe finished, Bernard was posted to RAF Delhi in India as a clerk.
    In Delhi he met Mahatma Gandhi, one of many famous people he has met in his life.

At 6.30 p.m. on 6 June 1944, twenty year old Bernard 'Taffy' Morgan arrived as
part of the Allied D–Day invasion force on Gold Beach in Normandy with a very
special RAF mobile intelligence code and cipher unit. They brought with them
a highly secret piece of equipment to do a very special job: this was the Type X
encryption machine, similar in part but much bigger than the German Enigma
machine. For this young man, seeing a body-strewn beach and being in the line of
fire was very daunting indeed, but he had to stay focused as he had a very important
job to do. Bernard was responsible for deciphering the specially coded messages
that would arrive from the front line requesting the air support that the units on
the ground urgently required in the heat of battle. It was a great responsibility for
Bernard and the other men; they had to act quickly as it could mean the difference
between life or death for many soldiers who were being engaged by the enemy.

    Bernard's diverse service career began on his eighteenth birthday on 7 February
1942 when he joined the Air Force at RAF Padgate, Warrington. He was sent to
Blackpool for basic training, which was undertaken on the town's streets and seafront,
partly under the watchful eye of his physical training instructor and already well-
known footballer Stanley Matthews. Bernard himself would later become a successful
athlete, running as part of the RAF athletics team. Weapons training followed at
the nearby requisitioned Rossal Public School in Cleveleys, and once all this was
completed he received his first posting to RAF Swanton Morley, Norfolk. There he
worked as a flight control trainer for Airspeed Oxford aircraft using beam approach
training (BAT) on refresher courses for RAF pilots to help them land aircraft in bad
weather using the beam approach system. Later in that posting Bernard had to type
up the daily routine orders (DROs); this would not be the last time the RAF would
utilise the clerical skills he had gained from his time as a clerk on the railways. It was
while he was at this RAF station that he saw a job advertised for a code and cipher
operator. This really interested Bernard and he applied for it, and so began a new
adventure in his service career. He was interviewed at RAF Oxford in early 1943,
after which he was sent on an NCO course at RAF Cardington, Bedfordshire, and
upon finishing was awarded the rank of sergeant. Next was a code and cipher course
at Harberton House, Oxford, with No. 5 Radio School. Once this specialist training
was completed, in September 1943 he was posted to an RAF mobile code and
cipher unit, No. 83 Group Control Centre under No. 83 Group Main HQ, which
was part of the Second Tactical Air Force. He joined the unit at RAF Paddlesworth
near Folkestone and it was here he was introduced to and trained on a secret piece

of equipment, Type X. He would work on this until the end of the war in Europe. Bernard now gives us an overview and insight into his work as a code and cipher operator deciphering highly sensitive intelligence information:

Top Secret Type X Machine

My training as an RAF code and cipher operator using the Type X machine was done by the sergeants of our mobile unit, the No. 83 Group Control Centre. We functioned and were organised like this: we had Bedford covered trucks and each acted like a mobile office with a different function, each supporting the other in our work; we even had our own power generators. Two trucks had wireless operators collecting incoming coded messages from front-line Army units requesting air cover. These scrambled messages came in sets of five letters and pages of these were passed on to our truck, where we had two Type X machines set up. We had to have new settings every day that were taken from a codebook and then set on five rotor wheels like the ones you see on an Enigma machine. I would then type in the coded messages; these would pass through a big drum on one side of the machine and the plain text would come out of the drum on the other side on long tape. I would then put them together to create a full message and get them off ASAP to our air operations officer in the next truck. He would then look at his big plotting map to see where the RAF squadrons were and contact the ones that were closest and able to give the air cover the quickest. We had to be fast; people's lives depended on it. We did our best to help the boys out there. Looking back I am very satisfied with my contribution in the war, but the greatest honour must be given to the pilots.

After months of training around the south coast of England, Bernard took part in Operation Overlord and on D-Day he landed on Gold Beach, Normandy, as part of that force of liberation. From there he and his unit assisted the Allies with air cover as they pushed on through France, Belgium, Holland and finally into Germany, where the war ended for him in a place called Schneverdingen near Luneburg Heath, Lower Saxony. It was there that Bernard received and decoded a top secret cipher that was quite simply one of the most famous and important military transmissions sent during the war. It arrived in the early hours of 7 May 1945 and stated that 'the German war is now over'. Bernard was one of the few people in the world at that moment that knew about this momentous event and historical news, but he was not allowed to say anything until it had been officially announced as this news was still, for twenty-four hours at least, highly secret.

Bernard's diverse career continued when he was later sent by the RAF to give clerical support for an RAF pageant that was being held at the Royal Albert Hall in London on 19 and 20 September 1945 to celebrate the end of the war, for which he worked closely with Richard Attenborough. After this he was posted to RAF Delhi in India from November 1945 until November 1946, working as a clerk in

A Type X encryption machine similar to the one used by Bernard.

A copy of the famous top secret 'surrender message' given to me by Bernard.

B/CAST   V   X Q F   XQF 0/10   ''IMMEDIATE''
T   SELF
FROM   ALO GCC   070915
TO   ALO ALL WINGS LESS 39 WING
QQY BT

C B G 1 . THE GERMAN WAR IS NOW OVER . AT R H E I M S LAST
NIGHT THE INSTRUMENT OF SURRENDER WAS SIGNED WHICH IN EFFECT
IS A SURRENDER OF A L L PERSONNEL OF THE GERMAN FORCES ALL
EQUIPMENT AND SHIPPING AND ALL MACHINERY IN GERMANY . NOTHING
WILL BE DESTROYED ANYWHERE . THE SURRENDER IS EFFECTIVE SOME TIME
TOMORROW . THIS NEWS WILL NOT BE COMMUNICATED TO ANYONE OUTSIDE
THE SERVICE N O R TO MEMBERS OF THE PRESS

BT   070915

May. 1945. (83.G.C.C.)

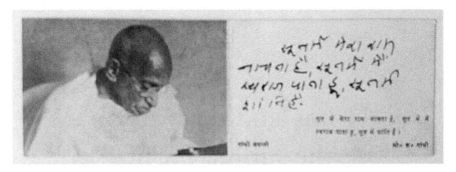

The signed message from Gandhi to Bernard given during their meeting in October 1946, one of the famous people he met. Others have included Winston Churchill. Bernard Montgomery, The Queen and Prince Phillip, Prince Charles and Camilla, and David Cameron.

the Central Registry. It was while based there that he was invited to attend a peace and prayer meeting on 11 October 1946, where he met and spent some time with Mahatma Gandhi. After India, Bernard returned to the UK, officially finished his service on 24 November 1946 and was demobbed in February 1947.

Through his service as a code and cipher operator Bernard made a valuable contribution to the Allied war effort. These great efforts are summed up well in the words of Monty in a message to the troops before D-Day:

'To us is given the honour of striking a blow for freedom which will live in history, and in the better days that lie ahead men will speak with pride of our doings.'

Field Marshal Bernard Law Montgomery

Additional Information and Life After Service

❖ **Rank at end of service:** Sergeant.
❖ **Medals and honours:** Legion d'Honneur (French Government), 1939–45 Defence Medal, 1939–45 War Medal, 1939–45 Star, France–Germany Star, Dutch Liberation Medal. Civilian awards consist of the Special Long Service Award from the Football Association in 2011 and Lifetime Achievements Award from East Cheshire County Council in 2016 for services to football.
❖ **Post-war years:** Bernard went back to work as a clerk on the LMS Railways for another thirty-five years until retirement in 1982. He was involved with Crewe Alexandra Football Club for sixty-six years from 1947–2014 as turnstile staff co-ordinator. Married to Brenda in 1950–2001, they had one daughter, two grandchildren and one great-grandaughter.
❖ **Associations and organisations:** Normandy Veteran Association, Stoke on Trent; Made Crewe Alexandra honorary vice president in 2004.

5

Home and the War on the Home Front

The Home Front was so important in its contribution to the war effort that it deserves to be called the 'Fourth Service', and that service took many forms. Without its overall and very significant contribution the war could not have been won. The idea of a Home Front comes from the mass mobilisation of civilians to support a war effort and this was first implemented in Great Britain in the First World War. During the Second World War the nation's labour was mobilised once again.

While the civilian population pulled together to play its part in winning the war it was itself under constant bombardment from the Luftwaffe and suffered attempts to starve it by the actions of the German U-boats and Navy. It had to draw its manpower from whoever was available, regardless of age, sex or ability, as most of the regular servicemen and women were drawn away to fight the enemy.

Many jobs that were once held by men who were now at war were now taken mainly by women, who did an equally good job. This in time would bring about profound changes regarding a woman's role in society, as more than half a million women went into uniformed services and millions more into other vitally important jobs. Countless men and women at home did their bit and faced many dangers and hardships, while in many cases their loved ones were serving far from home. To quote the words of a veteran I spoke to regarding this: 'Those who worked and waited also served.'

This they did and in so many organisations, capacities and occupations, such as those working for Air Raid Precautions (ARP) as air raid wardens and fire watchers, Auxiliary Fire Service (AFS) as fire fighters and fire engine drivers, Emergency Medical Service (EMS) as ambulance drivers and orderlies, and in hospitals as nurses and hospital orderlies, and the Air Transport Auxiliary (ATA) as pilots, engineers, various ground crew and clerical staff.

They also worked under the Ministry of Agriculture in all aspects of food production in organisations such as the Women's Land Army (WLA) and the Timber Corps, under the Ministry of War Production in the factories as riveters making aircraft, as machinists making parts for everything used by all the services, and down the mines as 'Bevin Boys'; the roles were vast for both sexes. All who were involved played an equally significant part in keeping the country fed, supplied and functioning internally. They did so while heeding the advice to 'Keep calm and carry on'.

Reflecting that diversity of service, we now hear from some of those veterans who made that vital contribution on the Home Front from 1939 to 1945, each playing their own very important part.

Air Raid Warden Betty Lowe MBE

Served: Air raid warden, Civil Defence Service
Interviewed: Salford, Lancashire, 17 August 2014

Service History and Personal Stories

* ❖ **Born:** 26 August 1908, Salford, England, UK
* ❖ Betty lived through and experienced the two biggest conflicts of the twentieth century and of our world history, the First and Second World Wars.
* ❖ As a child of 8 during the First World War she witnessed Germany's new terror weapon, the Zeppelin, as it flew low over her area in Salford on a bombing mission.
* ❖ During the Second World War, in addition to her regular job, Betty was an air raid warden as part of the Air Raid Precautions for the Civil Defence Service.
* ❖ Additionally, Betty was the longest-serving Girl Guide in Great Britain, with more than ninety years in the organisation, and also served for more than forty years in the Women's Royal Voluntary Service (WRVS), continually giving her time freely for others around her.
* ❖ Among her many awards for service to the community were the MBE in 1996, the Mayor's Citizen Award in 2007 and the Point of Light Award in 2014.

When I interviewed Betty in 2014 at Beechfield Lodge Care home in her native Salford this wonderful lady was an incredible 105 years old and had lived through and witnessed more than a century of British history. Betty, officially the oldest resident of Salford, had memories that stretched back over two world wars and was one of the few people alive in the United Kingdom who had memories and stories from both world wars. She vividly remembers at the age of 8 in 1916 seeing a German Zeppelin flying low over Salford on its way to bomb somewhere near Manchester. In the Second World War, Betty was assigned as an air raid warden to help direct people from their offices to shelters during air raids and did her bit to contribute as part of the Civil Defence.

Her story is one of long service of helping others and, while doing so, breaking a few records along the way. Betty was Britain's longest-serving Girl Guide, starting at the age of 11 in 1919 and putting in more than a staggering ninety years of service, during which time she went on to be Girl Guide leader and later became vice president of Guiding for Greater Manchester West. In recognition of her service she was made an honorary Lifetime Guide in the Trefoil Guild. In her normal working life Betty was an invoicing clerk for various companies for sixty-two years, mainly for Morris and Ingram in Salford where she worked throughout the war years. Later on she ran a launderette in Pendleton until her 'official' retirement, but as we know she carried on working during and long after that, giving more than forty years' voluntary service to the Women's Royal Voluntary Service at Hope Hospital in Salford. She worked there one day a week in the canteen until the age of 105, and she also continued to volunteer at her care home, Beechfield Lodge on Eccles Old Road, Salford, where by all accounts she baked some of the best cakes you could ever wish to taste.

'Too many people think of volunteers as a means to an end, as cheap labour. True voluntary service is nothing of the kind. It is, in fact, the gift of a thoughtful person of their skill, their energy and their time,' said Lady Stella Reading, founder of the Women's Voluntary Services.

Betty was never married and did not have children, so she channelled all the energies of her life into continually helping and giving to others around her. This was rightly rewarded in 1996 when she was appointed MBE by the Queen at Buckingham Palace for her lifelong services to the community. In 2014, when David Cameron presented her with the Point of Light Award given to honour those who have made an exceptional difference to their community, he said of her: 'She had lived and breathed serving others.' Running through the middle of all this was the Second World War, where Betty continued to go to work throughout the Blitz and where she served as an air raid warden dealing with whatever hardships and dangers the war years threw at her. It was this kind of determination shown by her and many others like her that kept the country running and maintained the Home Front during those very difficult years.

Because Betty's memories reach so far back into the twentieth century, we are given a truly unique opportunity to hear recollections from the Home Front from each of the world wars:

The First World War and Zeppelins Over Salford and Manchester

What I can remember is we were all playing outside and this noisy plane came over and they said it was a Zeppelin and it wasn't like our aeroplanes. It was quite a heavy-looking thing and it was quite low and after a while all the mothers came out and dragged us all inside and told us that we hadn't to go outside until it had gone, but they never let us out again that day. It came over Owens Square in Salford.

The opportunity to talk face-to-face with one of the few people left in Great Britain who could give a first-hand account of witnessing a Zeppelin during the First World War just captivated me. I asked Betty to tell me more about the experience:

As children we thought we were looking at 'Flying Sausages'. Nobody had ever seen anything like it before, it was like seeing something from another world. Because of this we were watching it for a long time, going I think towards Manchester. No one, including our parents, really knew what this was or what it was doing there, until later that is when it was dropping bombs on people!

Twenty-five years later, as a grown woman, Betty was again experiencing the enemy in the sky over Salford and Manchester. This time it was as an air raid warden, where she was actively involved in helping and directing people away from the danger:

An Air Raid Warden in the Second World War

You became an air raid warden when you reached a certain age but before that we used to leave our houses during an air raid and have to go to shelters ourselves. People used to come down and tried to make things better by brewing tea and bringing cakes. Later I was working at Morris and Ingram and I had to go because we had to do war work and I took a man's job so the lad could go in the Army. They never employed women before the war but when the war broke out that all changed. When the sirens went I was doing my air raid job in the office at St Ann's Rosary School on Liverpool Street. As the raids came I had to dash to the offices and call the people out and we had to tell them where to go and stand with our bucket and the syringe for dealing with incendiary bombs. All we could really do then was hope for the best and wait until it was all over, there were times when Salford and Manchester got bombed very heavily. One

An artist's impression of a First World War German Zeppelin on a mission.

Firemen in action during the Manchester Blitz. It was scenes of devastation like this that Betty regularly saw as a Fire Warden for the Civil Defence Service during the Second World War.

of those times was during the Christmas Blitz on Manchester in 1940. The city was on fire and the glow could be seen from miles away. Salford was very close by and the inferno was seen by most people, and parts of the city were smouldering for days after. They said it was like a firestorm in the centre, this was because of the kind of bombs the Germans were using. Lots of our local people were killed. Poor souls they didn't deserve it, no one deserved it, that's the terrible thing about war, anyone could get it, here today, gone tomorrow. The generations that have come since are so lucky, they've never seen or had to experience anything like that. Most of them don't know they're born.

I was cherishing every moment sitting with someone who had lived through such huge changes in the history of our country, a witness to times, people and events long gone and an England almost unrecognisable to the one of her childhood. So I asked Betty more about her memories of times gone by, starting with her time as Britain's longest-serving Girl Guide:

I began when I was eleven and a friend in my street said will 'I go with her,' so I went and I have been a guide ever since, about ninety years now. We used to take them camping and all sorts, any road I am still a member of the Trefoil Guild; it's for all the people who have been guides all their lives and we do things to help the guides if they need it. And I still help out at Hope Hospital every Thursday as well, go at 12.30 and back about 4.00.

Betty went on to say about past times:

The kids get looked after better now than when we were kids. At Christmas whatever you got you loved, you see, but now you don't get enough is what most think. My dad used to drive a horse and cart for the corporation in Salford and fix the stones on the streets that got worn down from the horses and the like. He had no time for motorists. When we had the trams we used to have to go into the middle of the road to get a tram, nothing like that now. It was a bit dangerous with everything coming at you. It's a completely different world now, some things for better and some things for worse, there you go.

Near the end of the interview I could not help but ask Betty what she thought the secret to a long life was and she told me:'Working and keeping your mind busy.'

However, in this case I think there was also something else that contributed to Betty's longevity and something that I have seen in all the veterans that I have interviewed. It is summed up perfectly by the inscription on her Women's Voluntary Service Medal that simply reads – 'Service before self'.

Additional Information and Life After Service

- ❖ **Rank or job upon finish of service:** Air raid warden.
- ❖ **Medals and honours:** MBE, Women's Voluntary Service Medal, Mayor's Citizen Award, Point of Light Award.
- ❖ **Post-war years:** Continued to work at Morris and Ingram as an invoice typist and clerk, and later had her launderette. She devoted her spare time to helping in the local and wider community through the various organisations, as mentioned in greater detail earlier. Although Betty did not marry and had no children, she had a big extended family of nieces, nephews, great nieces and nephews, and great great nieces and nephews.
- ❖ **Associations and organisations:** Honorary member of the Trefoil Guild.

Riveter and Driller Susan Jones

Served: Factory worker, A.V. Roe & Co. aircraft manufacturers (Avro)
Interviewed: Manchester, Lancashire, 21 November 2014

Service History and Personal Stories

❖ **Born:** 26 April 1923, Manchester, Lancashire, England, UK.

❖ For the duration of the war, Susan (pictured in above wartime picture on left) worked as a riveter and driller for the aircraft manufacturer A.V. Roe & Co. (Avro) at Ivy Mill in Failsworth, where she was known to be the fastest riveter on the night shift.

❖ There she worked riveting together many of the different body parts used in lots of aircraft types including the famous Manchester, Blenheim and Lancaster bombers.

❖ She also worked as part of the Civil Defence, taking on the additional tasks and responsibilities of being a fire watcher and first-aider at her factory.

❖ In 2012 Susan featured in a documentary with Ewan McGregor called *Bomber Boys* about those involved in various aspects of Bomber Command during the war.

Susan gives a very different account from the Home Front, this time from the perspective of a factory worker involved in the construction of many types of aircraft, mostly bombers, at one of the many factories under overall control of the Ministry of Aircraft Production, headed by Lord Beaverbrook. This local girl was well prepared for the tough war work she would undertake, having started her first job at the age of 14 in 1937 as a parceller in a Co-op laundry and in 1938 as a machine worker in the Marlborough cotton mill in her home area of Failsworth. Her wartime service gives an insight into another aspect of the war, one that reflects everyday hard-working people doing their bit, in this case in a factory of the industrial north.

Susan worked for aircraft production company A.V. Roe at Ivy Mill in Failsworth. She was there throughout the entire course of the war as a riveter and driller putting together vital components including the fuselage, inner and outer skins, bomb doors, ailerons, flaps and other parts for many types of aircraft such as the Anson and for Bombers such as the Blenheim and the aptly named Manchester, the forerunner to her favourite aircraft, the Lancaster. At the factory she did both day and night shifts but later opted to do only night so she could work with her friends. It was during that time that she earned a reputation for being the fastest riveter on the night shift, capable of doing at her best output more than fifty rivets per minute.

After completion, the various parts were then taken by road to the Avro plant at Woodford Airfield, near Stockport, where they were put together to help make the aircraft. During the course of the war some 3,000 Lancasters were assembled there in the same way that other aircraft production companies did elsewhere. After construction they would then normally be flown by members of the Air Transport Auxiliary to a depot for arming and then later on to their allocated squadrons.

While at the Avro factory Susan also became part of the Civil Defence Service when she took on the additional task of fire watcher as part of Air Raid Precautions, and a further role of being a first-aider. Fire watch was carried out mostly from the rooftops of the factories and buildings where people worked. It was during some of those watches that Susan witnessed the terrible firebombing in the Manchester Blitz of Christmas 1940.

The hard work of those in factories of all kinds up and down the country was a massive and very important contribution to the war effort. People such as Susan helped to keep the armed forces supplied with the essential materials to keep fighting, in the same way those in the Land Army helped keep the country fed. These vital industries were largely responsible for us being able to sustain and eventually win a very long and arduous six-year war. The hugely significant role that those on the Home Front played in the overall victory cannot be stated enough.

Women played a huge part in this during the war and successfully undertook every type of work at all levels in order to keep the economy going and replace the men who were serving in the armed forces. They served in every capacity, including the factories where they built ships, aeroplanes and munitions and worked as riveters, machine workers and engineers. The scale of women's involvement and contribution can be seen by the government figures from late 1943 that showed in 1939 women's employment in the UK was about 5.1 million (26 per cent of the workforce) but by September 1943 this had risen to 7.25 million (36 per cent of all women of working age). Forty-six per cent of all women aged between 14 and 59 and 90 per cent of all able-bodied single women between the ages of 18 and 40 were engaged in some form of work or national service by this time.

From among these many millions of vitally important female war workers we now concentrate on the experiences of just one, Susan Jones, who worked out of sight of most people to produce essential aircraft for the RAF. Susan told me with great Lancastrian humour of her time working for Avro:

A Factory Worker on the Home Front in Wartime Britain

Well the workforce was thrown together with all sorts of people from everywhere. They used to bring men and women from County Durham and from all over Geordieland, you know, and some from Mansfield and all that, from all over the country. They used to bring them in to help with the war work. Oh the things that happened and the stories I could tell you about the day-to-day life and goings-on at the factory. Honest to God, without a word of a lie, I hated that job when I first went there but it finished up that I had five of the best years of my working life. They was absolutely brilliant, I loved every minute. You would clock on, pick up your rivet gun and get to work. Long hours working away in your dungarees behind blacked-out windows, as they of course had to be. Pretty hard graft but you did have a sense that you were contributing to something important as we all were during those years. I was very sad when I walked out of those factory gates for the last time. I whispered goodbye and had a tear in my eye but still have the great memories of years well spent.

Part of Susan's time at the factory was spent mainly building and putting together the famous Lancaster bomber, and I asked how it felt to be part of that history:

Well at first as I say when I started there it was just a job, it was a job that I had to do and I went out and earned my money and did my bit you know. But since then I have felt proud and humbled to think that I was part of a legend like the Lancaster Bomber that played such a big part in the war.

It was Susan's incredible riveting speed during the war that later led members of her family, who are actively involved in Second World War re-enactment, to lovingly nickname her 'Rosie the Riveter', after the famous poster girl used for recruitment of women into industry in the US during the war. In 2012 Susan was also part of a documentary narrated by Ewan McGregor called *Bomber Boys*, which covered

Susan in the centre at a Lancaster reunion in 2014.

those involved with the Lancaster. In it she demonstrated with great accuracy seventy years later, at 90 years of age, how to rivet metal plates together, and gave the actor a telling off for not doing it properly!

Additional Information and Life After Service

- ❖ **Rank or job upon finish of service:** Riveter and driller.
- ❖ **Medals and honours:** 1939–45 Defence Medal.
- ❖ **Post-war years:** After finishing six years at A.V. Roe & Co. Susan went on to work in a number of places from 1945 until her retirement in 1996. These were mainly in a familiar factory environment with companies such as Howarth's cotton mill and Morgan Ebonite and Co., both in her local area of Failsworth, where she was employed as a machine worker. Later she was a shop worker at Middleton and Mellor, a sheet metal company, in Newton Heath. These jobs incorporated her great skill and speed with various machinery and drilling equipment. In 1947 Susan married Albert Jones, a former Royal Navy sailor who had served on HMS *Faulknor* during the war in various theatres including the Arctic convoys to Russia. They were married for forty years and have two children, three grandchildren, five great-grandchildren and one great-great-grandchild.
- ❖ **Associations and organisations:** Royal Naval Association and HMS Faulknor Association (in memory of her late husband); Battle of Britain Memorial Flight (linked through Susan's work on the Lancaster); Member of IWM Veterans North, and along with her family actively part of the Friends of the 40s re-enactment group.

'We Can Do It!' The famous Second World War poster depicting Rosie the Riveter, from whom Susan got her nickname.

Land Girl Dorothy Hewitt

Served: Agricultural worker, Women's Land Army
Interviewed: Stalybridge, Lancashire, 15 March 2016

Service History and Personal Stories

- ❖ **Born:** 12 April 1925, Ashton-under-Lyne, England, UK
- ❖ Dorothy started work as a mill girl aged 14 in a mill and dyeing works in Carrbrook Village near Stalybridge, Lancashire, in 1939.
- ❖ Wanted to help the war effort and volunteered and joined the Women's Land Army (WLA) on her 18th birthday in April 1943.
- ❖ Sent to Reaseheath Agricultural College in Nantwich, Cheshire, in 1943 to learn new skills in agriculture and horticulture.
- ❖ Ministry of Agriculture sent her to work as a land girl for the WLA for the Hardern Family at Mill Lane Farm in Cranach, Cheshire.
- ❖ Worked for two-and-a-half years as a land girl, during which time she had to adapt to a totally new way of life and work. She became an 'adopted' member of the Hardern family, and still maintains links with them to this very day.

Lancashire lass Dorothy Hewitt started work on her 14th birthday on 12 April 1939 at the Calico printing and dyeing works in Carrbrook village, near Stalybridge, as a finisher of dyed materials. Four years later, Dorothy joined the Women's Land Army at her earliest opportunity, on her 18th birthday on 12 April 1943. The new life and work that Dorothy was about to encounter as a land girl in the countryside of Cheshire was a million miles away from that of being a mill girl in her previous industrial setting in Lancashire. It would bring with it a wealth of interesting and funny experiences mixed with hard work in this new, very different and at first very challenging environment.

To prepare and give her the basic skills that were going to be needed for this new life, Dorothy was sent to Reaseheath Agricultural College near Nantwich, Cheshire, which in her words was 'the place everybody was sent to have their rough edges knocked off'. After a month of agricultural, horticultural and livestock training, the Ministry of Agriculture put Dorothy with the Hardern family at Mill Lane Farm, in Cranage, Cheshire. This is where Dorothy would spend the next two and a half years until November 1945, working with and becoming part of that family. It was also during this period of huge change in her life that she would meet her future husband, Reginald Hewitt, who was serving in the RAF at nearby RAF Cranage.

During the war the varied roles that women played on the Home Front and the hard work that they did in many places from the factories to the land played a huge role in maintaining the survival of our country during those difficult war years. Not only does an army march on its stomach, as the old saying goes, but as we all know well, so does the nation as a whole. With this in mind the important contribution of the Women's Land Army cannot be stated enough. This was especially at a time when Nazi Germany was trying to starve out our nation with the use of submarine warfare to destroy as much of the merchant fleet as possible by sending millions of tonnes of vital food and raw material supplies to the bottom of the ocean. The Women's Land Army was originally founded in the First World War, but was re-formed just before the start of the second under the control of the Ministry of Agriculture. At its head was Lady Denman, who was a leading figure in the Women's Institute Movement, and the WLA had its HQ based at her home, Balcombe Place in Sussex.

By the time Dorothy had joined, in 1943, there were more than 80,000 women working in the WLA, who were affectionately known as land girls. The Women's Land Army was a civilian organisation that also included the Timber Corps, where around 6,000 women were employed to cut down trees and work in saw mills. The WLA was a big organisation that was very well directed, regulated and inspected. It had representatives in each of its seven regions and fifty-two county offices; it had its own magazine, *The Land Girl*, and also its own song, which went: 'Back to the Land, we all must lend a hand, To the farms and the fields we must go, There's a job to be done, Though we can't fire a gun, We can still do our bit with the hoe.'

The WLA, with its land girls and timber girls, continued to serve the country until 1950 when it was disbanded around the time rationing finished.

The girls were expected to do most of the jobs required to run a working farm. This, of course, involved very hard and dirty work and long hours. Dorothy now shares with us various insights and experiences about her work:

A Land Girl During the Second World War

I was very lucky when I went to work for Mr and Mrs Harden on their farm in Cranach near Middlewich. Some girls lived in hostels and went to different farms every day or every week, I stayed with my family all the way through from start to finish. I settled in and it was very different to what I was used to and was very hard at first, but I got used to it after some months and we managed the farm very well after that. I did all sorts of jobs like milking the cows, looking after all the other kinds of livestock, making silage in a big silo. I also drove a tractor for ploughing because I couldn't handle the big working horses, I was only a small girl you know. We also had to do ratting to find and kill rats, and gathering the crops at harvest time, which was very long hours because it was what we called 'Double Summertime' and was light until almost 11 o'clock at night. But that was very interesting because we had a lot of different hired help at harvest time and for potato picking and times like that. We had all sorts such as patients from Cranage Hospital, boys from a reform school in Holmes Chapel, we had personnel from RAF Cranage. At one time we had two German prisoners from the nearby POW camp and even a conscientious objector. A right old mix of people we hired to help us.

Dorothy continued to share with me more interesting and funny stories from the Home Front and life on the farm, delivered in a charming and humorous way with a great Lancashire accent to boot:

When I was eighteen I wanted to join the Women's Land Army so I went off into Manchester to the office and applied. I was 7½ stone and 5ft 2in and I didn't think I would be suitable. They must have been very short of Land Army girls as they eventually decided yes and they had to make me special trousers because the uniform wouldn't fit! Then I got my Land Army instructions and ended up working on Mr and Mrs Harden's farm and during my time there many funny things happened. Well let me tell you some of them, starting with the Silage Silo. In the first few months that I was there we were doing silage. Now I don't know if people are aware but it was stored in a large concrete tunnel, and the boss told me we were going to have boys from the remand home and you will be in the

Land girl Dorothy at Mill Lane Farm, Cheshire.

silo with six of the boys and I will be carting the wet grass up with the other six! Well I didn't feel very happy about this and I thought: 'I don't know if I want to be in the silo with six boys from a remand home.' Anyway I thought, 'Well I've got to do it but what happens if they start any funny business?' So he said: 'What have you got in your hand in that silo?' I said: 'My fork, my pitchfork.' 'Right,' he said. 'If they start any funny business you stick that in them and shout as loud as you can and we'll come and help.' But you know they were great, worked hard and were no bother at all those lads.

A couple of other funny things I remember. When we were doing harvest and had the patients from Cranage Hall Hospital working with us, they had health problems but not the physical kind, you know the other kind. Anyway you had to really watch some of them because they would try and sneak away behind the bushes and get up to all sorts when they could! It were quite embarrassing you know. Another time when we were ratting in the farmyard I was with the whole family and Mr Harden lifted up a shed and the rest of the family and me stood with farm implements ready to bash anything that came out. Well a giant rat shot out and ran right over my feet, I had never seen anything that big before, the size of a dog it were. I screamed, jumped on Mr Harden's back but he was stuck in that position because of his lumbago. His back had gone and he had me swinging off him and not letting go, can you just imagine it, like something from a comedy film. We laughed a lot about that later and have done over the years when looking back. We had some right funny times.

Dorothy went on to tell me about the strong bonds that were formed with the Harden Family and how they have continued for over seventy years to this very day:

I was godmother to two of their three sons and they still come to visit me regularly. The elder one will be eighty-two and the younger one seventy, and one of my daughters was bridesmaid to the eldest son.

It is a great and long-lasting legacy that means that Dorothy's wartime story continues to this very day.

Additional Information and Life After Service

* **Rank or job upon finish of service:** Land girl/agricultural worker.
* **Medals and honours:** WLA Official Issue Badge – Second World War; WLA and Timber Corps official badge.
* **Post-war years:** After leaving the WLA in November 1945 Dorothy married Reginald in December of that year, after which she became a housewife and mother. In 1957 Dorothy returned to work as a cook at Ridge Hill Junior School, Stalybridge, where she remained until her retirement at the age of 60 in 1985. She was married for sixty-three years, has two daughters and one grandaughter.
* **Associations and organisations:** Royal British Legion, Stalybridge Branch 1995–2008.

3rd Officer Pilot Joy Lofthouse

Served: Civilian Pilot, Air Transport Auxiliary
Service number: W149
Interviewed: Cirencester, Gloucestershire, 15 February 2016

Service History and Personal Stories

❖ **Born:** 14 February 1923, Cirencester, England, UK.

❖ Joy worked at Lloyds Bank in the Cotswold town of Cirencester in 1939–43, first as an accountant then as a cashier. However, she sought much more adventure in life.

❖ Joined the Air Transport Auxiliary at the age of 20 after seeing a recruitment advert in the *Aeroplane* magazine.

❖ Trained to fly at Thame in Oxfordshire and then stationed at No. 15 Ferry Pool at Hamble near Southampton for the delivery of most of her aircraft.

❖ Learned to fly eighteen types of aircraft as an 'ATA Girl' and delivered them to various RAF stations and maintenance units around the country from 1943 until 1945.

❖ Achieved a class 3 rating and was able to fly fighters, which included the legendary Spitfire, and other types up to the twin-engine Anson.

When I interviewed Joy Lofthouse in the Cotswolds in February 2016 I realised how lucky I was to be able to spend time with one of only three female pilots from the Air Transport Auxiliary still with us in the UK at that time. This charismatic lady shared with me her experiences and insights into a unique civilian organisation that delivered a great and vital service that kept the RAF supplied and effectively running throughout the war. Without the ATA the job of the RAF in Fighter, Bomber and Coastal Commands would have been a lot harder, as their resources would have been stretched to the limit. Every civilian trained pilot that flew and delivered aircraft as part of the ATA meant one less pilot that potentially had to be taken from the front line to do the same job. This made a huge difference during a time of real national crisis such as the Battle of Britain, when every pilot was needed to fight in a battle that could change the outcome of the war and the destiny and fate of the country.

All this was made possible by the volunteer men and women from twenty-five countries including the United Kingdom and United States of America, and those in South America, the Commonwealth and occupied Europe that came forward to fill the ranks of the ATA, and who served in a difficult and sometimes dangerous job while delivering a staggering 309,000 aircraft of 147 types to various RAF and Royal Navy stations during the war years. They also ferried vital supplies and manpower and acted as air ambulances both in the UK and overseas. The ATA's total pilot complement comprised 1,152 men and 166 women. Other aircrew included 151 flight engineers, nineteen radio officers and twenty-seven ATC cadets, and there were 2,786 ground crew. Some 173 were killed, one of whom was the famous pioneering aviatrix Amy Johnson CBE, who was the first woman to have flown solo from England to Australia in 1930. She died while ferrying an Airspeed Oxford aircraft in January 1941. Each of the pilots and engineers that flew came from very different backgrounds, and among them was Joy Lofthouse, whose story we now follow.

Joy worked in the Cirencester Branch of Lloyds Bank as an accountant and later cashier from 1939 until 1943. Wanting to contribute to the war effort and also have more excitement than in her previous job, she chose to follow her sister Yvonne in joining the ATA, which she did in December 1943 after seeing an advertisement in the *Aeroplane* magazine. Excitement it was indeed as it could not have been further removed from her life working in a bank. Joy soon found herself up in the clouds as she was trained at the ATA Pilot Training School at RAF Thame in Buckinghamshire. Having qualified by early 1944, Joy was then posted to No. 15 Ferry Pool at Hamble, between Southampton and Portsmouth, which was one of eventually twenty-two ferry pools throughout the UK that were used to transport aircraft of every description as, when and where needed. It was this adaptability that gave rise to the ATA's mottos, the official *Aetheris Avidi* ('Eager for the Air') and the unofficial 'Anything to Anywhere'.

During her service, Joy learned to fly eighteen types of aircraft and obtained a Class 3 rating to fly single-engine aircraft such as the legendary Spitfire, Hurricane and Mustang through to light twin-engine aircraft such as the Anson. She flew all these and in the process became a 3rd officer, equal to the rank of pilot officer in the RAF. Joy now shares with us different aspects of her time in the service:

Life in the Air Transport Auxiliary

In the ATA we were civilians in uniform paid for by the ministry of Aircraft Production. We were trained at Thame and also at a smaller place called Barton-le-Clay in Bedfordshire, where under instruction we learned many flying skills. Then you went on a six-week secondment to another ferry pool to learn how they were run and I went to Cosford, where my sister was already based and fully trained. Then back to Thame where we converted on to the Harvard and later on to the school's Spitfire, which was faster than anything you had ever flown before. It wasn't until you had got your wings, flown the Spitfire and moved to your permanent base that you became a 3rd officer.

We then spoke about some of the day-to-day things that an ATA pilot had to do and cope with once fully engaged at their allocated ferry pool:

Joy Lofthouse, left-hand side, upper row, nearest the propeller.

In the Hamble restroom hall around forty women would wait to be allocated their work for the day. The hatch would open and you would be handed a 'chitty' with your flight instructions, and if you hadn't flown that aircraft type before you would follow the Ferry Pilots' Notes. That was our Bible, which was a guide book of about 250 loose leaf sheets that covered every aircraft that was in operation with the Air Force and the Fleet Air Arm.

You would turn to the page you wanted and there it would tell you the essentials you needed for flying that particular aircraft. Sometimes you would be faced with an aircraft you hadn't flown before and so you had to learn the vital information you required very quickly from your notes before flying. Sometimes you might only have thirty to forty minutes to read, learn and then fly as you had to get a move on and deliver those aircraft. Also there were obstacles to overcome with navigation as well. We flew with no radio contact and minimal navigation equipment as in most cases it hadn't been fitted, so we used maps, visual aids such as coast lines if possible, and if needs be follow railway lines as they would lead you to reference or checkpoints, which would take you to your final destination. Anything that could help, not an easy task at all. We were a resilient lot and one of our mottos was 'Anything to Anywhere', and this is exactly how we worked. There were documented occasions where the ATA flew, delivered and landed aircraft to RAF airfields where their highly trained RAF pilots were not even flying that day due to adverse weather conditions. All in all I think we did very well to deliver what they needed when they needed it.

Later in 1945, Joy was moved to Sherburn-in-Elmet near Leeds, where she would fly aircraft up to Scotland to be delivered to the Fleet Air Arm. These were to be put on aircraft carriers and go out to the Far East for the intended invasion of Japan. However, when the war finished in September 1945, Joy was informed that her contract would be coming to an end. It was during that month that she last officially flew as a pilot for the ATA. However, in a lovely ending to this story, Joy once again took to the sky in May 2015 where she calmly took over the controls and flew a twin-seater Spitfire seventy years after her service had finished. Not bad for a lady who was 92 years old at the time. I think it about sums up that amazing generation of veterans.

When we spoke another time about the book and the importance of gathering veterans' stories for posterity, Joy gave me this wonderful saying that sums up everything: 'If all is forgotten, all is for nothing'.

Lord Beaverbrook, head of the Ministry of Aircraft Production, gave an appropriate tribute at the closing ceremony that marked the disbanding of the ATA at its White Waltham headquarters near Maidenhead in Berkshire on 30 November 1945:

Without the ATA the days and nights of the Battle of Britain would have been conducted under conditions quite different from the actual events. They carried out the delivery of aircraft from the factories to the RAF, thus relieving countless numbers of RAF pilots for duty in the battle. Just as the Battle of Britain is the accomplishment and achievement of the RAF, likewise it can be declared that the ATA sustained and supported them in battle. They were soldiers fighting in the struggle just as completely as if they had been engaged on the battlefront.

Additional Information and Life After Service

❖ **Rank or job upon finish of service:** 3rd officer.
❖ **Medals and honours:** Official ATA Issue Badge.
❖ **Post-war years:** Joy married her first husband, George, in 1946, and as a housewife raised her family and then returned to work as a teacher of English and Maths for children with learning difficulties from 1971–85. Joy was then married to her second husband, Charles, for thirty years and went on to be a supply teacher from 1985–2000, when she retired. They have two sons, one daughter and one grandchild.
❖ **Associations and organisations:** Air Transport Auxiliary Association; Project Propeller; member of the Spitfire Association; honorary member of the Aeronautical Society.

Draughtswoman Stella Rutter

Served: Draughtswoman, Vickers-Supermarine Aircraft Company
Interviewed: Havant, Hampshire, 9 February 2016

Service History and Personal Stories

- ❖ **Born:** 15 September 1923, Havant, England, UK.
- ❖ After finishing art school in Portsmouth, Stella obtained a position working as a tracer at the HMS Excellent drawing office on Whale Island in 1940.
- ❖ Later that year she went on to be employed as the first draughtswoman at the Vickers-Supermarine aircraft company near Winchester, where she worked for the rest of the war holding that unique position.
- ❖ There Stella made very detailed technical drawings of the different marks of Spitfire that were mass produced in the UK and went into action in every theatre of the Second World War.
- ❖ In June 1944 Stella was chosen to host a top secret party for Montgomery and Eisenhower to calm the nerves of many of the senior officers involved in the

imminent invasion of Europe, and worked directly under Major General D.A.H. Graham during the event.

❖   Stella was given 100 per cent top security clearance as she was to become one of the few who knew that 'Tomorrow was D-Day' and was sworn to secrecy for sixty years about the highly secretive gathering.

Stella Rutter comes from a very artistic family so it should come as no surprise that her artistic talents led to her becoming the only female draughtswoman working at the Vickers–Supermarine Aircraft Company during the war. These talents stem from and were nurtured and influenced by her father, Charles Broughton, who was vice principal of Portsmouth Art College, from her second brother, Eric, who was a qualified architect and one of the special duty architects assigned to look after the dome of St Paul's Cathedral on fire watch during the London Blitz, and her mother Nora, who was very creative at home. All of this led to a very interesting career, some unique wartime experiences and a great contribution from a woman in what was a very male-dominated environment and line of work during the war years.

It all began in 1939 when Stella attended Portsmouth Art College, and after completing her technical drawing course, where she learned the art of tracing and draughtsmanship, Stella took the job as a tracer in 1940 at the HMS *Excellent* drawing office on Whale Island in Portsmouth. This was home to the naval headquarters and front-line training units of the Royal Navy. While there, Stella helped draw up the plans for upgraded parts of the well-known battleship HMS *Belfast*, which was one of the Town Class cruisers and the flagship of Bombardment Force E that supported the allied landings on Juno and Gold beaches on D-Day. The following year Stella secured an interview at Vickers–Supermarine, the aircraft company responsible for the development and manufacturing of, among others, the famous Spitfire. She was successful, and in March 1941 began work in the chief draughtsman's office at its Hursley Park site near Winchester. There her job was to draw the masters of the assembly drawings of the Spitfire on fine linen. These were prepared by the three other men in her office and finalised by Stella with her also correcting any defects. After this her drawings would be printed and used as a manufacturing guide for the assembly of the various versions or marks of Spitfire that were being made at the Vickers–Supermarine factory in Southampton.

Stella remained employed in that office until the end of the war under Joe Smith, the head of Supermarine, Gerald Gingell, the technical publication manager, and Lovell Cooper, chief draughtsman. There she worked as the only woman amongst nearly 100 draughtsmen and got paid the same £3 equal weekly rate as they did, something that was quite unheard of for a woman in the Great Britain of 1941. Stella also worked on the technical drawing of other important and well-known

An example of a Spitfire built by Vickers-Supermarine, for whom Stella drew the technical plans at Hursley Park in Hampshire.

aircraft that Vickers-Supermarine produced, such as the Seafire (the naval version of the Spitfire flown from aircraft carriers). This work was, of course, undertaken in great secrecy and the Hursley Park site was one of the various parts of Supermarine production that had been dispersed to different locations after intense Luftwaffe bombing on the main site at Woolston in Southampton. The main lesson learned there was not to have all parts of your production process in one place, especially the technical drawing and development parts, in case the whole lot gets destroyed during enemy action, as it nearly did.

Before D-Day General Montgomery and General Eisenhower wanted to hold a formal get-together, a party of sorts, to calm the nerves of the top commanders who were going to be directly involved in Operation Overlord, the Allied invasion of Western Europe. Montgomery knew Joe Smith and phoned him to ask if he knew of a woman who could deal socially with large groups of men and be trusted to keep her mouth shut, to which Joe replied: 'I have one young lady to whom I give a security level as high as my own, 100 per cent.' All of this Stella found out later.

At 10 a.m. on Saturday, 3 June 1944, while working at her draughtboard, Stella was summoned into the office of chief draughtsman Lovell Cooper. There she was introduced to Major General D.A.H. Graham, who made a very important request for Stella to host the top secret gathering of high-ranking officers in an underground Nissen hut in the grounds of Hersley Park that night, and said that if she accepted she would be sworn to secrecy about anything she was told or overheard at the gathering. Such was the gravity and importance of what she was about to undertake that evening, and the very sensitive information she could potentially hear, Stella accepted, and in doing so became confidante to one of the most secret get-togethers of the war, which she has only begun talking about in recent years.

Stella now shares with us the details about that very special evening:

Tomorrow is D-Day

Montgomery had been in many battles before and he knew what the night before a battle was about and how important it was, and how anybody involved in seniority of that would be shaking with nerves. So he approached Eisenhower, who had never been in that position before, and told him that they needed to have an informal party of sorts on an official basis on the night before D-Day for all of these commanders, and in order to maintain an air of calmness we had to have a lady be a hostess. And he then asked Joe Smith whether he had a lady he could trust with 100 per cent security and I was chosen. The party was held in a covered Nissen hut in Hursley Park Forest next to his camp. I went on a jeep and had to go through three lots of security and eventually arrived and was greeted by Major General Graham, who took me into the hut and showed me around. There were tables full of every kind of food imaginable, and as we walked down the hut there was a man finishing laying out the tables and he said to him, 'Would you leave that please,' and when the man had gone and we were alone he said: 'Tomorrow is D-Day and that is why you are here,' and he briefed me as to what was to happen. At that moment I had become privy to one of the biggest secrets of World War Two and that was a huge responsibility for a woman of my age. There was great trust being put in me, one which I never betrayed and always kept for many decades that followed.

From that moment Stella, a 20-year-old draughtswoman from Hampshire, knew the enormous gravity of what she had been told, and she knew that if she said anything that it could potentially cost the lives of thousands of servicemen, a massive responsibility she carried from that instant and never spoke about for sixty years. Later Stella told me more about the party:

I was requested to help all of these commanding officers to eat, drink, dance, sit down and meet other officers who would be on the their right and left on the battlefield, and meet them and know them by sight. I think approximately sixty-two other officers were in attendance and Major General Omar Bradley turned up as well, and as a hostess I was, of course, introduced to and worked with them all.

The party took place on the evening of 3–4 June and D-Day was originally scheduled to go ahead the following evening, the 4th, into the early hours of the 5th, hence Stella being told 'Tomorrow is D-Day'. As history recalls, it was cancelled that day due to bad weather but successfully went ahead one day later on 6 June. As a result of Stella knowing all about this she was informed that she was put on the B.I.G.O.T list for those who knew about the 'British Invasion of German Occupied Territory', which meant anyone on it was not allowed to leave the British mainland for twelve months and was closely watched by the British Secret Service during that time. This all goes towards making a very interesting and very different wartime story indeed.

Additional Information and Life After Service

- ❖ **Rank or job upon finish of service:** Draughtswoman.
- ❖ **Medals and honours:** Vickers-Supermarine Workers Badge.
- ❖ **Post-war years:** After finishing at Vickers-Supermarine in 1945 Stella worked for a year as a clerk at the Portsmouth College of Art. In 1946 she married Sydney Rutter in Havant. They had two daughters and Stella concentrated on bringing them up and being a housewife for many years. During that time Stella was a producer of plays for a theatre production company in Bedford called The Chameleons. Later she became a teacher at the White House Private School in Bedfordshire for six years and retired in the 1980s. Stella is also an author, who had three books published between 2007 and 2015. She has three grandchildren and two great-grandchildren.
- ❖ **Associations and organisations:** First chairman of the Central Region of the Spitfire Society and later made a patron of the same society in 2012; member of the Royal Air Force Association.

Machine Operator Lilian Grundy

Served: Capstan lathe worker, A.V. Roe & Co. aircraft manufacturer
(Avro)
Interviewed: Manchester, Lancashire, 29 August 2014

Service History and Personal Stories

❖ **Born:** 10 March 1923, Manchester, Lancashire, England, UK.

❖ Lilian started work as a mill worker aged 14 in Prestwich cotton mill near Heaton Park in 1937. This began a lifelong association working mostly on machines in mills and factories around north Manchester.

❖ During the war Lilian worked as a machine operator on capstan lathes, producing small intricate parts required for use in the Lancaster bomber.

❖ Her wartime service took place at an A.V. Roe factory in Newton Heath, Manchester, working on long night shifts from 1941 until 1945.

❖ The love of her life, George Grundy, was a Lancashire Fusilier who was shot in the arm by a sniper and captured near Dunkirk in 1940 while serving with the British Expeditionary Force. Lilian waited five long years for his return, after which they married.

Lilian Grundy, née Clague, is a great example from the Home Front of 'those who served whilst waiting'. Throughout the war there are many great stories of enduring love between people who met under all sorts of circumstances and despite the adversity of the times their love for and loyalty to one another survived and continued, in most cases for the rest of their lives. This lovely intertwined tale demonstrates just that and covers the service years of Lilian and her childhood sweetheart, George. While Lilian served her country at home undertaking the hard work of a factory worker on lathes, George served his country overseas in the Army. After his capture near Dunkirk in 1940 they continued to maintain their contact and their adoration for each other through Red Cross correspondence in the hope that if the war was won by the Allies, they would one day be reunited. After five long years of patient waiting on both sides, that dream came true in 1945 and as soon as possible after his repatriation George and Lilian tied the knot, bringing to an end one long story and starting a new one that would allow their devotion to one another to continue and to remain unbroken over the next five decades.

It was quite normal in the much harder days of the 1930s and 1940s Britain that most children would finish their education at the age of 14 and go straight into work. This is what Lilian did when she began work as a mill worker winding bobbins at Prestwich cotton mill at the back of Newton Street near Heaton Park, Manchester, in 1937. This began an association that Lilian would have with mills and factories on machines of one kind or another for most of her working life. After finishing at Prestwich mill aged 17 in 1940 the next job took her to Messrs Hall and Bros, who were confectioners based at a factory in Whitfield. She stayed for nearly fourteen months as part of the production line wrapping sweets until called up for war work aged eighteen in July 1941. Lilian's wartime work would be with aircraft manufacturer A.V. Roe at its factory in Newton Heath. This was one of many factories it ran in the north-west and some of the work undertaken there was to make various smaller precision parts for aircraft, mainly the Lancaster. These had to be crafted on lathes and it was work that required constant attention to detail over the long working hours and shifts that wartime factories required for the constant output that fed the war effort. Lilian worked there on twelve-hour night shifts, six nights a week from when the war was in full swing in July 1941 until after it finished in November 1945. Like the other Avro worker featured in this book, Susan Jones, Lilian has always been very proud to be associated with the famous Lancaster bomber.

George Grundy met Lilian Clague, later Grundy, in August 1939 in St Mary's Park in Prestwich. George became a Lancashire Fusilier, first in the Territorial Army in 1938 and later, aged 19, in the regular army at the outbreak of war in September 1939. As Private Grundy (3450470) he served in the Salford 1/8th Battalion L.F.s when they were sent as part of the BEF to Belgium and France in

April 1940. The 1/8th Battalion was incorporated into the 4th Infantry Brigade, which was part of the 2nd Infantry Division. During the Battle of France, the 1/8th, along with various other battalions, was overrun by German troops on 26–27 May 1940 around the village of Locon while attempting holding actions in the retreat to Dunkirk. After this George, who had been injured, was to become a prisoner of war for the next five long years in Stalag VIII B, which later in 1943 was renamed Stalag 344. The camp was located near the town of Lamsdorf in the province of Silesia in Eastern Germany, where he was Prisoner 16632.

The long years of captivity seemed like an eternity for the couple but they were able to send and receive letters through the International Red Cross, and because of this Lilian was able to know that George was still alive as a POW and patiently waited for his safe return, which came in May 1945. Soon after being reunited, the couple were married on 2 June 1945 in a white wedding at their local church, St Hilda's in Prestwich, where Lilian was a 'Victory Bride', which meant they did not have to pay for the wedding, only for the 7s 6d licence fee. George was finally demobbed in April 1946 in Manchester. The couple went on to a long, happy and successful married life with children and later grandchildren and were together for fifty years until George passed away in March 1996. While he was alive, they continued their wartime connections through the 1940 Dunkirk Association, going on pilgrimages to Dunkirk, where they met Charles de Gaulle, and in Belgium, where Lilian danced the waltz with King Leopold of Belgium. They also attended numerous Dunkirk-related events in the United Kingdom in the years when George was a standard bearer for the association. This, along with their enduring love and commitment to each other, is what makes this such a delightful story.

Lilian now shares with us some vivid wartime recollections:

Wartime Factory Work and Waiting Five Years for Her Sweetheart

When I was called up after saying no to the Land Army because I was scared to death of mice and I didn't like horses, which wasn't much good, I eventually had a letter to go for an interview at the A. V. Roe factory at Briscoe Lane in Newton Heath. Before I knew it I was on a capstan lathe, which was a machine for making smaller aircraft parts. The lad who was there before me left it with a note that said: 'I want this machine, capstan lathe, back in the same order as I left it. I have gone in the Navy. Good luck to you.' and I thought: 'I'll say a little prayer for the lad, I didn't know him, I hope he'll come back all right, I'll never know.' And I was there from July 1941 until 1945 in November, I did my share. I was on nights and it was twelve hours' hard graft. It was incredibly hot in summer with all the heat from machines and the like and in winter you had a scarf under your boiler suit and I don't know how many jumpers I had on. I don't know if

George and Lilian on their wedding day.

I had two pairs of knickers on, probably, it were that cold, everybody was the same. They had big doors open on to the Newton Heath railway at the back, and they used to take the bomber parts through and on to it and my machine, No. 8, was right by that big door and boy it was freezing in the winter. But in the summer I used to think: 'Isn't that lovely,' when you saw the moonlight coming in. You'd come out smelling terrible from the machine and you had to be careful 'coz big pieces of the aircraft were passing you through the main way in the middle of the machines and the continual noise was unbelievable. Also the mist as we used to call it, which was the fine oil, was in the air everywhere and used to cover you and you would breathe it in and it would even be on your food. But you did what you had to do because you knew it was important and that you were contributing to the war effort, and that's really all that mattered in the end: to do your bit to help the men out there defeat the Nazis. I always remember when D-Day was announced on the wireless in the canteen. We all thumped the table, stamped our feet and cheered, then everybody stood up and recited the Lord's prayer out loud together and said God bless them all, the brave boys fighting and dying at that very moment, and there wasn't a dry eye in the place!

An example of the wartime correspondence between Lilian and George sent from Stalag VIII B, Christmas 1941.

We then went on to talk about waiting all those years for her beloved George. Lillian said:

> He got home a week before the war ended because the Americans had already liberated his camp and repatriated him, and it felt like he had been away forever. We got married within a short time, after all we had waited five years to see and be with each other once again. We did, of course, have to spend some time getting to know one another once more because in that time we had both become a bit different. He came back obviously changed by the experiences of five years in a German POW camp. That is to be expected – who wouldn't be after such an ordeal? And you couldn't play the song Silent Night because he used to get upset. It reminded him of many Christmas times in the camp where they used to miss their families, cry and say: 'Why are they not coming for us?' I guess things like that always stay with you when you are in such extreme conditions. I think he had a bit of what they call today post-traumatic stress disorder, not surprising though after all those years in captivity. Very hard on anyone something like that, bless him. But he was the man I fell in love with and I still loved him and him me. We must have done – after all, we spent the next fifty years together.

Additional Information and Life After Service

- ❖ **Rank or job upon finish of service:** Machine lathe worker.
- ❖ **Medals and honours:** 1940 Dunkirk Veterans Association Women's Medal.
- ❖ **Post-war years:** Lilian worked for a number of companies after leaving Avro in November 1945 up until her retirement in 1985, including a return to Messrs Hall and Bros, and later at Jazz Smith dry cleaners and private house cleaning jobs around north Manchester. George was a Post Office driver. They have two daughters, three grandchildren and one great-grandchild.
- ❖ **Associations and organisations:** 1940 Dunkirk Veterans Association; Royal British Legion, Swinton Branch.

Stenographer Joy Hunter MBE

Served: Secretary, PA and stenographer, Cabinet War Rooms, Westminster
Interviewed: Guildford, Surrey, 2 May 2017

CABINET WAR
OFFICE
WESTMINSTER

Service History and Personal Stories

- ❖ **Born:** 15 September 1925, Brockmoor, England, UK
- ❖ During the war Joy worked for the Cabinet War Office at Churchill's highly secretive War Rooms under Westminster, the epicentre of British military strategic planning, and in close proximity to Winston Churchill.
- ❖ Joy was privy to some of the highest level military information of the war and as a secretary with top level clearance helped type the D-Day battle orders for the Allied Supreme Command.
- ❖ On VE Day, 8 May 1945, she was among the huge crowds who gathered at Buckingham Palace to celebrate and to see the Royal Family on the balcony to mark the end of war in Europe.
- ❖ In July 1945 Joy was chosen to go as part of an elite secretariat to accompany Churchill and his diplomatic mission at the Allied victory conference in Potsdam, Germany.
- ❖ While there, Joy met American president Harry Truman and Soviet leader Josef Stalin, and was at the British victory parade in Berlin on 21 July 1945. She also visited the ruins of Adolf Hitler's Reich Chancellery.

Joy Hunter's wartime service led to her being at the heart of some the most historical places and events of the latter part of the conflict, from Churchill's secret underground command bunker in London to the remains of Hitler's Reich Chancellery in Berlin. I first saw Joy while watching a documentary to mark 100 years of the Imperial War Museum, where her story was one of those featured. Immediately I thought how amazing it would be to have a woman with such a unique background and special narrative to add another very different dimension and insight into the war alongside the other varied veterans' stories in the book. So I was very happy when the Imperial War Museum very kindly helped to arrange an interview with Joy, during which I found out much more about all that she did during and after the war and about her many incredible experiences and achievements.

At seventeen, Joy's parents sent her to train as a secretary at a very good private establishment, Mrs Hoster's Secretarial College, near Stamford in Lincolnshire. For the six months that Joy was at the college, between June and December 1943, her tuition fees were £90, a huge amount of money for her parents to find back in 1943, especially when they only had the salary that her father earned as a vicar. However, one way or another they did it and the jobs that Joy would get as a result of this changed the direction of her life and would lead her into a very different kind of war service. Mrs Hoster's was set up to specially train and prepare young ladies for jobs in some of the most important key areas in the government, civil service and other prominent places, and also to act as a form of employment agency to supply and place these highly trained young women into those jobs. Even while Joy was training at the college, a job placement came up at 10 Downing Street, which she turned down and instead stayed on to successfully complete her training, something she felt she owed to her parents for their hard work and sacrifices to get her there. Doing this also meant that her fully completed training included becoming a stenographer, giving her the ability to transcribe speech in shorthand at high speed, around 100 words per minute, which was a valuable skill to have for any workplace as a secretary or personal assistant. These were both jobs that Joy would go on to do in some very interesting places indeed.

The notification of job offers came from Mrs Hoster in the form of a 'pink slip', and so Joy's work life began at the age of 18 after being interviewed by Miss Brown, head of secretarial services at the Cabinet War Office in Whitehall, London, where she was offered employment as a typist. Her first assignments there were from January until May 1944, beginning in a typing pool of sixty or so girls. Soon after, Joy was chosen to work as a PA to Major General West at Richmond Terraces, Whitehall, as part of the British Control Commission, where post-war planning was already taking place even prior to the invasion of Europe. Then, in May 1944, Joy was transferred to the Cabinet War Rooms under Westminster. It was here that Winston Churchill and the British military top brass spent most of their time and from where some of the biggest decisions and most important battle planning of the war took place. It was the epicentre of the Cabinet War Office and where all the heads of services came and went and briefed Churchill, and where most of the British war effort was directed from. It was where all the latest intelligence poured into and orders went out of, and for more than twelve months, from May 1944 until July 1945, it was Joy's workplace.

In that huge underground military bunker and labyrinth Joy worked an average eight- to ten-hour day, sometimes longer, and was part of a team of twelve in a special room that operated twenty-four hours a day and was always guarded by two armed marines. The team would receive hourly updated intelligence reports on the progress of the war and had to type up whatever was given to them as quickly as possible so it could go out to whoever and wherever required within the command structure and hierarchy. Being privy to such high-level intelligence information meant having to sign the Official Secrets Act, not talking to anyone about where you worked and exactly what you did, and never keeping a diary, as any such information could, of course, compromise operations and potentially threaten the lives of thousands. This was brought home in a big way when Joy was given the job of typing the D-Day battle orders for the Allied High Command, which would have been given to the top commanders planning Operation Overlord, the invasion of Normandy, and the later intended liberation of Western Europe and eventual destruction of Nazi Germany. At the moment Joy read and typed up the order of battle for the invasion, this information included the disposition of Allied divisions, the units involved, the number of men involved, the beaches where they would land, and essentially their overall battle plan. This was information so sensitive that it was at the same level of Bletchley Park. Joy processed and typed this up at around eighty words per minute and when she left work, carried in her head what few in the nation knew at that time.

It was thanks to good people such as Joy who did not say anything, that operations such as these succeeded and the war was eventually won. When it ended, Joy and her parents celebrated by joining the huge crowds that were recorded by the newsreels of the time celebrating on the Mall and in front of Buckingham Palace on VE Day on 8 May 1945. They witnessed Winston Churchill, whom Joy saw and talked to during the course of her work in the War Rooms, with the Royal Family, who from the balcony of the palace acknowledged and joined with the people in this most historical moment. As the news of the time said: 'We are living in the midst of many great events, we know that in the days when war seems remote and far away these will be historic pictures, they will tell another generation how England celebrated Victory in Europe Day.' So true, and Joy was there and a part of it all. However, it would not be the last great event that she would be a part of because later on Joy was chosen as one of the elite secretariat that was a part of the diplomatic mission that accompanied Winston Churchill to the Allied post-war conference at Potsdam in Germany, where the division of and post-war structure of Europe was finally agreed upon.

It was there that Joy was part of more historical moments, such as meeting American president Harry Truman and Soviet leader Josef Stalin at a dinner party during the Potsdam Conference. This, along with already spending time with Churchill on a few occasions, meant that Joy had met 'the Big Three', as they were known, the most powerful leaders in the world at that time. Also, while there, Joy was at the British victory parade in Berlin on 21 July 1945, in the crowd opposite where Churchill took the salute and reviewed many British units including the famous 7th Armoured Division 'Desert Rats'. Another interesting moment for Joy was being taken to the Russian sector and visiting the Reich Chancellery, which lay in ruins, and along with the other members of the party taking parts of Hitler's conference table, which lay in pieces all over the floor, and medals and other memorabilia that no one else cared about that lay among the debris of war in the shattered centre of power of the defeated Nazi regime.

We now hear from Joy, who shares with us some of the fascinating moments she experienced and lived through during the war:

Being Present at some Fascinating Parts of the Second World War

In early May 1944 I was told I was to go and work downstairs. I had no idea what 'downstairs' meant because nobody knew it existed. Nothing was ever discussed whilst working; we didn't even know the names of our colleagues in the main building, but I soon found out it was Churchill's War Rooms. Down there it had strip lighting and was very stuffy, not very good air conditioning, we were very closely monitored and if we wanted to go to the washrooms we were timed and we had to be escorted, and very military precision times for everything. The work down there was immediate because it was a hub of information and our section was called the Joint Planning Secretariat. We were responsible for three senior officers from the services and, yes, I did help type the D-Day battle orders. Every hour there were reports from all three services from all around the world. Wherever they were they would send reports into the War Cabinet Offices. We also had immediate knowledge of where any air raids had been and what the casualties were. Because of all this information we had to sign the Official Secrets Act as you do working in a government service, as they still do today. We would see Churchill sometimes, you would know when he was around because you would smell his cigar. He would stop to talk occasionally when we passed him in the corridor, and I think he liked to talk to regular people because he was surrounded most of the time by military types.

As it is so rare to talk to someone who worked in close proximity to Churchill during the war and met him on a few occasions in a true working environment,

'The Big Three' – Churchill, Truman and Stalin – at the Potsdam Conference, all of whom Joy had met.

I went on to ask Joy if she had any specific or special stories regarding the Prime Minister during her time at the Underground Cabinet War Rooms:

Well there is one which is quite good, even though I have told it to others before, but maybe you've not heard it. Sometimes we had the real treat of watching a film with Churchill, he enjoyed old films and we had a room down there with an old reel projection set up. We would, of course, have to wait for Churchill to arrive before it began. On this particular occasion we were waiting quite a long time, then we could smell the telltale cigar smoke, which meant he was on the way. Then the door flew open and there was Winston Churchill in his dressing gown, with a cigar in one hand and a drink in the other and he merrily announces: 'Winnie's here, let it roll!' Much to the amusement of everyone there. People seem to like that story.

Being so interested in Joy's unique wartime experiences and how they gave her access to so many historical people of the time, both civilian and military, I said meeting her was for me like connecting with history because she was a part of that incredible history, to which she kindly replied:

But you are part of history too, because when you are my age, which I hope you will be, there will be people coming to you saying: 'Did you do that, did you interview so and so? You met that man who was 92, my goodness me fancy doing that, capturing all that.'

Those inspiring words epitomised all that I have been doing since 2014, capturing history, and to hear it from a veteran who really understood the importance of it meant a lot to me. This perfectly encapsulated the drive behind *The Last Heroes*.

Additional Information and Life After Service

- ❖ **Rank or job upon finish of service:** Secretary, stenographer and PA.
- ❖ **Medals and honours:** MBE in 2013.
- ❖ **Post-war years:** After the war, Joy's working life continued to be varied and extremely interesting. Here is a brief summary from 1945 until 2013. After return from Potsdam until mid-1946, Joy was PA for Professor Lionel Robbins, Head of the London School of Economics, then became secretary to the Archbishop of Canterbury, Jeffrey Fisher in 1946–49. While bringing up a young family Joy gained many qualifications, including a degree and BA in teaching, and she typed manuscripts from home in the 1950s and 1960s for additional income, during which time she also worked for the National Book League. She then became a full-time teacher of religious education at Guildford Girls County Grammar School, Surrey, from 1971–73, followed by being

an RE teacher at St Bede's Church Mixed Secondary School in Redhill, Surrey, where she eventually became an assistant head teacher by 1981. After that Joy worked for the NHS as a health education advisor, putting together and delivering health education programmes throughout the UK until 1993, when she 'officially' retired aged 68. However, after this Joy went on to work voluntarily two days a week for Age Concern in Guildford for a further twenty years as a manager until 2013, when at 88 she did really retire. That same year Joy was awarded an MBE for her tireless charity and community work with many associations such as the Mothers' Union, Girl Guides and Age Concern. While doing all that Joy also managed to complete a masters degree in Applied Theology through Oxford University, where she graduated with a distinction aged 74 in 1999. Joy married Noel Hunter in 1949; they had three children and Noel sadly passed away of polio in 1956, after which Joy successfully brought up her children – another huge credit to her – and now has eight grandchildren and ten great-grandchildren.

❖ **Associations and organisations:** Mothers' Union and the Girl Guides.

Connecting with History

Our veterans are all around us, they walk among us, we pass them in the street, unaware in most cases of what they have done for us. They are our next-door neighbours, our parents, our grandparents, our friends, the elderly people in care homes up and down the country. These most amazing people have lived through much harder times than we have ever seen, and experienced terror and destruction on a scale not known by the generations that have followed since 1945.

It was their service in wartime and their hard work in peacetime that laid down the foundations for this great country, which is still one of the best in the world to live in for so many reasons including the opportunities it offers and the freedom it gives people who are born here and those who come from elsewhere. We as a nation should not forget that we owe a lot of this freedom to the wartime generation who sacrificed and endured so much for this country and who unfortunately are becoming fewer in number every day.

The times they have lived through, the things they have seen and experienced, the history they were a part of and contributed to in so many ways is what helped to forge the post-war country that we now live in and still reap the great benefits of in so many ways. It is these things that we should remember, be very grateful for and thank them for, while we still can.

Every time I shake or hold the hand of a veteran I feel that I am truly connecting with the last living history of that time and place. I feel very humbled and privileged and it makes every interview a very special experience and lovely memory.

Gary Bridson-Daley

The author Gary Bridson-Daley with 105 year old veteran Betty Lowe 'Connecting with History'.

Veterans' Poetry and Songs

Peaceful Reactions to the Experiences of War

These additional pieces of poetry and song lyrics have been added because they are very moving expressions and personal representations of the thoughts and feelings of some of the veterans interviewed during the making of the book and throughout the project.

They show in a very peaceful way various responses to the often traumatic experiences of war, and in doing so add a further and very interesting human dimension to the book and those within it.

Each piece is accompanied by background information regarding that particular work and the veteran who gave it for use in the book.

My mouth shall speak of wisdom; and the meditation of my heart shall be of understanding.

Psalm 49:3

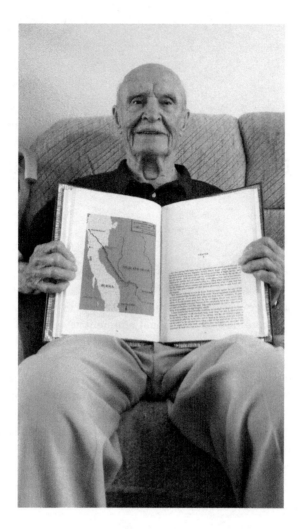

The Haunting

When I spent the day with Jack P. King, survivor of the Death Railways, I was so impressed with all his many forms of artistic impression including his prolific output of nearly 100 pieces of quality poetry, that I asked him if he would write a piece about his wartime experiences especially for my book. The result is this incredibly moving and aptly named piece called 'The Haunting', which is about a visitation from his friends who were victims of the horrific events on the River Khwae, who returned to tell him to keep the memory of what happened there alive so that the world will never forget. It was written on 30 October 2016. Note that in the poem the word 'benjo' means latrine.

I am honoured to have this included in *The Last Heroes*. It is unique as it is the only piece that has been specifically written by a veteran for inclusion here, and Jack is also the only veteran to contribute and have two pieces of work featured in this section. As you will see, and I think will agree, it is crafted from the mind and delivered by the hand of a very talented man, 94-year-old Jack P. King.

The Haunting

When all the world is dark and still
The ghosts slide silent from the hill,
And gather whispering in the gloom
To crowd around me in my room;
Why are they here? Why do they roam?
Skeletal phantoms, far from home?

From the jungle dense and green,
Where creepers weave their tangled screen,
There we lie in slimy clay
Never to see another day;
Can you yet hear the pick-axe ring?
Remember songs we used to sing?

Do you remember the bed bugs' bite?
The mosquitos' whine throughout the night?
Harsh, shouts of fierce and brutal guards, crack of bamboo clubs,
Of rags and tags for clothing and *benjo* in the shrubs.
Hard and heavy labour on rice and watery stew?
This was our lot, the phantoms cried; 'It was the same for you.

Ah, you're still living, we are not, our mouths are stopped and still,
But yours is free to tell the world; so tell it how you will;
Please let them not forget us in our graves so far away,
The freedom which you hold so dear were paid for with our day;
You and I were soldiers then and keen to strike a blow
For King and flag and Home Land against a vicious foe.'

The phantom figures shuffled off as moonlight lit the hill.
My room was empty as before and all was quiet and still,
Had I really seen these things or was it just a dream?
For in this life of rush and care, things are not what they seem;
No, they were real, these phantoms, and all they said was true,
And I just keep their hopes alive by telling this to you.

Jack P. King, Royal Artillery and POW 'Death Railway',
River Khwae, 1942–45

Palette

Stella Rutter came from a very artistic and creative family. Her father, Charles Broughton, was vice principal of the Southern College of Art in Portsmouth, her brother was one of the architects on fire duty in the dome of St Paul's while the blitz of London was going on, and Stella became the only draughtswoman in the drawing office at Vickers-Supermarine. There she drew up plans used in the production of many aircraft, including the famous Spitfire. This creativity also extended to poetic writing; the piece featured here is called 'Palette' and fuses together in words colours and nature within the bigger picture of time, space and human emotion, all of which reflect thoughts from the Home Front during wartime Britain.

Palette

Golden is the sunset sparkling with splintered light
Taking wing to flying thoughts masking all in its might.
Blue is the colour bold far in infinite space
Boosting with endless patience complicated actions of the race.
Green is the swaying grass that covers all the land
Bending, flowing in the wind timeless as the road of sand.
Red is the flame of hope that glows within my heart
Engulfing all that lies therein waiting to play the part.

Stella Rutter, Draughtswoman, Supermarine,
UK, 1940–46

Shores of Normandy

This song, sung in the style of a calm sea shanty, is a very powerful composition by Jim Radford, Normandy veteran, professional shanty singer, song writer and peace campaigner, who is still very much involved with the organisation Veterans for Peace. It directly reflects his feelings and emotions of being a 15-year-old boy who was a galley hand on the rescue tug *Empire Larch* when he witnessed and experienced the horrors of the invasion of Normandy first-hand on 6 June 1944. Jim sang this beautiful and very poignant song to a packed Royal Albert Hall on 6 June 2014 on the seventieth anniversary of D-Day and received a standing ovation. He still travels all over the world to perform at many different kinds of festivals and gatherings to spread his message of remembrance, peace and reconciliation. (View his Albert Hall performance and his Veterans for Peace work online).

Shores of Normandy

In the cold grey light of the sixth of June, in the year of forty-four
The Empire Larch sailed out from Poole to join with thousands more.
The largest fleet the world had seen, we sailed in close array,
And we set our course for Normandy at the dawning of the day.

There was not one man in all our crew but knew what lay in store,
For we had waited for that day through five long years of war.
We knew that many would not return, yet all our hearts were true,
For we were bound for Normandy, where we had a job to do.

Now the Empire Larch was a deep-sea tug with a crew of thirty-three,
And I was just the galley-boy on my first trip to sea.
I little thought when I left home of the dreadful sights I'd see,
But I came to manhood on the first day that I saw Normandy.

At the Beach of Gold off Arromanches, 'neath the rockets' deadly glare,
We towed our blockships into place and we built a harbour there.
Mid shot and shell we built it well, as history does agree,
While brave men died in the swirling tide on the Shores of Normandy.

Like the Rodney and the Nelson, there were ships of great renown,
But rescue tugs all did their share as many a ship went down.
We ran our pontoons to the shore within the Mulberry's lee,
And we made safe berth for the tanks and guns that would set all Europe free.

For every hero's name that's known, a thousand died as well.
On stakes and wire their bodies hung, rocked in the ocean swell;
And many a mother wept that day for the sons that they loved so well,
Men who cracked a joke and cadged a smoke as they stormed the gates of hell.

As the years pass by, I can recall the men I saw that day
Who died upon that blood-soaked sand where now sweet children play;
And those of you who were unborn, who've lived in liberty,
Remember those who made it so on the shores of Normandy.

Jim Radford, Merchant Navy, Rescue Barges,
1944–45, Royal Navy 1946–54

Peace and Love

Every time I have met Sam King he seems to have a very calm and peaceful air about him, and this I think is due in a very big way to the strong Christian faith that he has carried with him throughout his life, in both wartime and peacetime. This also comes out when he talks about his wartime and life experiences and says on many occasions 'by the grace of God', to which he really does attribute all the good things that have happened in his life.

Sam shared with me and gave me permission to quote this lovely verse, as I am happy all veterans included in the poetry and song section have done. These words helped guide him through many trials and tribulations over the years, and reflect to a large extent what he feels life should contain more than anything else.

Peace and Love

All the way my saviour leads me,
Cheers each winding path I tread,
Gives me grace for every trial,
Feeds me with the living bread.
Though my weary steps may falter,
And my soul athirst may be,
Gushing from the rock before me,
Lo, a spring of joy I see.
This my song through endless ages:
Jesus led me all the way.

Sam King MBE, RAF, Ground Crew,
UK 1944–47 and 1948–52

The Ballad of the Bearded Brigade

This Submariners poem from Phil Wilcox, merchant seaman and later submariner, is about life under the ocean waves, and about the hard work involved and the heavy duty maintenance and problems down in the torpedo rooms and other areas below on a submarine in active service in wartime.

It was there that the hard-pressed crew were checking out and working on the torpedoes nicknamed 'fish' and other machinery for leaks and other seagoing problems under adverse conditions. All these tales delivered in submariners' speak with reference to the things they knew from their working environment give a great window into their underwater world.

The Ballad of the Bearded Brigade

Way down beneath the waves
There are your galley serfs and slaves,
Disappearing at their master's wish
To haully, haully back on fish,
Lo and behold there is much training
Gnashing of teeth and much complaining.

Drip tins filled in record time, overflowing into mine
Clear decks for action lower tower cry, to aimers and corner slave,
Those too tired to lend a hand in this happy, happy land,
Hell what am I doing, slipping, let me carry on with dripping
With this weary tale of woe that was a fish that would not go.

I went from fore end all the way flying, left upon the desk was lying
Friday's sausages, mouldy mash and every single bit of gash,
Up came floorboards from the trenches, out came low tide, tools and wrenches
Tackle and turn gauge bars too, turning band and what a view,
In accordance with the Master's wish, slaves suffer slowly upon the fish.

Into fore end it came creeping, all bunged up with rust and leaking
Then they say you've to try and fix it, with a ya puncture outfit,
But they could not find a hole coz the good load shot high up the pole
Having patched it up with bits of tin and downing tools their hands shut in,
Low tide flustered, rage ensued, suck the fish, black up the tube.

Back came gash and what a view, tackled antennae and bow too
Low tide tools and all his wrenches, back went floorboards on the trenches,
Put back big fixers, spuds and lockers, getting ready for his supper,
I've carried out his Majesty's wish and wish their heads to dream of Fish!

Phillip Wilcox, ABST Submariner, HMS *Supreme,*
South-east Asia, 1943–45

The D-Day Dodgers

This is a song given to me by John Clarke reflecting his feelings and those of many servicemen from the hard-fought Italian Campaign. He recalls that when the radio announcements came through about the D-Day invasion saying words to the effect 'Today the Liberation of Europe has begun', that they were very saddened to hear this because, as John said: 'We had already been fighting in Europe to liberate Europe, and had been doing so for over eight months and at great cost and suffering to many involved.' During the Italian Campaign between September 1943 and April 1945 approximately 46,000 died and 300,000 were wounded.

It was this disillusionment that led them to write a song that was a cynical take on events in the Italian Campaign, as it seemed to many veterans of these battles that the others outside must have thought they were on holiday or not doing much in their 'side show', which, of course, was far from the truth. Their song was called 'The D-Day Dodgers' and was sung to the tune of the wartime favourite, Lili Marlene.

The D-Day Dodgers

1) We are the D-Day Dodgers, out in
   Italy,
Always on the vino, always on the Spree,
8th Army Skivers, and the Yanks,
We live in Rome, we dodge the tanks,
For we are the D-Day Dodgers, out in
   Italy.

2) We landed at Salerno, a holiday with pay,
Jerry brought his bands down, to play us
   on our way,
They showed us the sights and brewed
   up tea,
We all sang songs, and the beer was free,
For all the D-Day Dodgers, out in Italy.

3) Naples and Casino were taken in our
   Stride,
We didn't go to fight, we just went for
   the ride,
Anzio and the Sangro, were all a farce,
We did nought at all, we had a day
   pass,
For we are the D-Day Dodgers, out in
   Italy.

4) Once we had a blue light, we were
   going home,
Back to dear old Blighty, never more to
   roam,
Then someone whispered, in France
   you'll fight,
We said 'blow that'. We'll just sit tight,
For we are the D-Day Dodgers, out in
   Italy.

5) If you are in the mountains, amidst
   the snow and rain,
You'll see rugged crosses, some which
   bear no name, (Quietly)
Heartbreaks and toil and soldering done,
The lads beneath, they slumber on,
For we are the D-Day Dodgers, out in
   Italy.

6) Then on the way to Florence, we had
   a lovely time,
We ran a bus to Rimini, right through
   the Gothic Line,
Soon to Milano we shall go.
When we've chased Jerry, beyond the Po,
For we are the D-Day Dodgers, out in
   Italy.

7) The years have quickly passed, today we're old and grey,
But still we remember, this our special day,
When all the lads and lasses are gathered here,
To sing the songs and drink the beer,
For we are the D-Day Dodgers, who fought in Italy,
For we are the D-Day Dodgers, who fought in Italy.

John Clarke MBE, Black Watch, Tunisia–
Italy–Greece–Palestine, 1943–46

The Debt

Jack P. King was a twenty-five-year career soldier of the Royal Artillery from 1937–62 and was serving in the 31st Battery, 7th Regiment, Coastal Artillery, when he became a prisoner of war after the fall of Singapore on 15 February 1942. He then spent the next three and a half years in brutal incarceration at the hands of his vicious and cruel Japanese captors, when he was beaten, became diseased and was suffering from malnutrition while working as slave labour on the infamous 'Death Railway'.

Despite all this, and probably as a means of therapy and as a peaceful reaction to it, Jack became incredibly creative in many ways. He is a gifted writer with twenty-five books published, including his autobiography of his service years called *A Magic Shadow Show*.

He is also a prolific painter, a composer of pieces of music, and a talented poet with nearly 100 pieces of poetry on various subjects written to date. One of those, 'The Debt', has been included here. It describes the previous lives of those pensioners who younger generations see at a bus stop and in the street without knowing what these people have gone through, did and gave for their country.

The Debt

1) See the poor old lady
At the windswept bus stop
Huddling so tightly in
Her threadbare clothes?
Once she manned a table
As they plotted hostile planes in,
Picking out the targets,
For our boys in blue.

2) See the old man shuffling
Down the grey and grubby alley
Eyes red-rimmed and rheumy,
Sunken cheeks so white,
He was once a gunner
On an ack-ack gun site
Watching through the hours
Of the war-dark night.

3) See those hands so knobbly,
Gnarled and crooked and veiny,
Shoulders hunched and humpy,
Sad eyes cast down?
That man sailed the icy seas
On the russian convoys,
Little children mock him
As he shambles round the town.

4) See the old folk queuing
At the pension counter?
There's no way of knowing
What their eyes have seen.
Many have so little,
But their pride won't let them
Ask for help or favours
Because of what they've been.

5) Brash and cheeky youngsters
Dressed in jeans and trainers
Seldom know what hunger
Or true hardship means,
Heedless of the old folk
With their fading memories,
Never know the debt they owe
To such as these.

Jack P. King, Royal Artillery and POW 'Death Railway',
River Khwae, 1942–45

Grandad

This piece entitled 'Grandad' was written by the youngest grandchild, now adult, of veteran Cyril Tasker for his nintieth birthday in 2013. It seemed like a very poignant addition to this section of the book as it is all about honouring our veterans and this piece reflects the gratitude from a younger generation to an older one, again a very valuable link between the past and the present and a very nice contribution from a different angle.

Cyril Tasker was in the 716 company, Royal Army Service Corps, attached to the 9th Battalion, 6th Airborne Division. He dropped into Normandy on D-Day in a Horsa glider near Ranville, and soon after he linked up with Major Howard's Paras at Pegasus Bridge. As a supply driver he went on to see action at front lines everywhere from the Merville battery, through Normandy and on into Belgium, where he was involved in the Battle of the Bulge, on to Holland and finally Germany, where he was one of the troops who linked up with the Russians in Vismar on Germany's Baltic coast. After this he went with the 6th Airborne Division to serve in policing duties in Gaza, Palestine.

Grandad

People have you heard the news, Cyril is 90 today.
He looks not a day over 80, I hear you all say.
So what do we know, about this Cyril chap?
Well we know that in the summer, he wears a nice white cap.

Married to Jean, his lifelong soulmate.
Laughing and joking, together they are great.
They do everything together, rarely seen apart.
After 65 years, she has stolen his heart!

There is one thing about Cyril, that we know for sure.
That he was a hero, in the Second World War.
Everywhere he goes, he is greeted with cheers.
He even invited Belgian people, round to his house for beers!

He always has upon him, his magic piece of string.
A natural entertainer, though I'm not sure he can sing!
A Dad, Grandad and Great-Grandad as well.
Everyone enjoys hearing, the stories he tells.

So there you have Cyril, a very special man.
As his youngest Grandchild, I'm quite a big fan!
I've now come, to the end of my rhyme.
Grandad I hope that you have, a wonderful time.

HAPPY 90th BIRTHDAY! Xx

A good quote from Cyril to finish, one of his favourites: 'Let hope fill the years to come and memories gild the past.'

Cyril Tasker, 6th Airborne Division, Normandy–Battle of
the Bulge–Palestine, 1944–46

Archibald McIndoe, plastic surgery pioneer who successfully treated many badly burned airmen.

The Guinea Pig Anthem – McIndoe's Army

When war was looming the British Government, having seen the use of the Fascist air forces during the Spanish Civil War, realised that the next war would involve aerial combat on a much bigger scale. This would in turn produce many airmen in need of treatment for burns, and with this foresight they set up the Emergency Medical Service in hospitals outside central London to deal with this anticipated problem. One of these specialist hospitals was the Queen Victoria Cottage Hospital in East Grinstead, where Archibald McIndoe and his first-class medical team formed the burns centre.

Once the Battle of Britain was raging in 1940, Hurricane and Spitfire pilots suffering from burns began to arrive and were starting to receive a new treatment called plastic surgery. A lot of these new techniques were being pioneered by McIndoe and his team, which in time made this hospital at East Grinstead world-famous and eventually led to him becoming Sir Archibald McIndoe.

As the war raged on, Bomber Command's operations increased significantly and as a result so did their casualty rate, known to be some of the worst of any of the services engaged in combat during the war. This meant that the emphasis switched from burned fighter pilots to burned bomber crews. Among these, due to his horrific accident, was gunner Jan Black-Stangryciuk.

During the war some of these burned pilots formed a special club called the Guinea Pig Club, the name meant to emphasise the nature of the experimental treatment they were undergoing at the time. There were 649 Guinea Pigs at the end of the war: 80 per cent were Bomber Command crews; from the overall figure 62 per cent were British, 20 per cent Canadian, and 18 per cent Australian, New Zealand and other mixed nationalities.

Jan, whose story is featured in full in this book, is one of the very few Second World War Guinea Pigs left in the United Kingdom. After recovering from his terrible injuries he went on to serve in the Polish 300 Squadron, completing eighteen operations. He remembers the great appreciation and respect that McIndoe and his team earned, not just for the surgery they performed but also because their care extended way beyond that. Especially McIndoe who, he recalled, was like a brother and a confidant who listened to their fears, and as an advisor helped prepare them for civvy life outside and after their RAF service, very important indeed for those servicemen who had to live with serious disfigurement and the prejudices that could be experienced as a result of it.

The Guinea Pig Club is still in existence today, working hard to support the few Guinea Pigs that are left with the services of an honorary plastic surgeon and financial help for the widows. They also help keep the memory alive of what was achieved through the next generation of relatives. This they do with His Royal Highness Prince Philip, Duke of Edinburgh KG, as their president.

They have their own song, known mainly to those who are affiliated to the club in some way but little known outside of that. Jan, a Polish Bomber Command veteran and Guinea Pig, shared it with me during conversations with him, and so with permission I have included the piece in this section of the book as it meant a lot to those veterans who were able to rebuild their lives after horrific injuries, and who paid such a high price in the service of our country.

Per ardua ad astra (Through adversity to the stars), motto of the Royal Air Force.

The Guinea Pig Anthem

We are McIndoe's army,
We are the Guinea Pigs
With dermatomes and pedicles,
Glass eyes, false teeth and wigs.
And when we get our discharge
We'll shout with all our might:
'Per ardua ad astra'
We'd rather drink than fight.

John Hunter runs the gas works,
Ross Tilley wields the knife.
And if they are not careful
They'll have your flaming life.
So, Guinea Pigs, stand ready
For all your surgeons's calls:
And if their hands aren't steady
They'll whip off both your ears.

We've had some mad Australians,
Some French, some Czechs, some Poles.
We've even had some Yankees
God bless their precious souls.
While as for the Canadians
Ah! That's a different thing.
They couldn't stand our accent
And built a separate wing.

We are McIndoe's army,
We are the Guinea Pigs
With dermatomes and pedicles,
Glass eyes, false teeth and wigs.
And when we get our discharge
We'll shout with all our might:
'Per ardua ad astra'
We'd rather drink than fight.

Jan Black-Stangryciuk, RAF, Polish No. 300 Squadron,
rear gunner, Europe, 1942–45

Until Much Later

During the war Frank Tolley served with the RAF on Lancaster bombers as a bomb aimer and was part of No. 625 Squadron. He completed twenty-two missions, mainly over Germany, which included the well-known and now controversial air raid on Dresden that took place on 13 and 14 February 1945. Due to the nature of the raid it has been to a greater or lesser degree in the minds of those who took part ever since.

Fifty years after the Second World War Frank's eldest grandson enquired about the part Frank had played and asked him what he thought about killing people. It was a very thought-provoking thing to be asked and a difficult, soul-searching question to answer.

After some thought, Frank later produced this written piece in response, which allowed him the opportunity to work through his thoughts and feelings in relation to Dresden and his time on other missions with Bomber Command.

Until Much Later

1) In nineteen-forty I joined the RAF,
Not for a laugh nor for fun,
But because War had begun.
For one who dared, I was scared,
Up there in the sky – Hoped I would not
    die …

2) Later, in a Lancaster Bomber's nose,
Looking down for the target markers.
There! To port, the targets lit.
Skipper and engineer see it too
And the aircraft's nose is altered by ten
    degrees.

3) I call, 'Open bomb doors' and report
'Still too far starboard: Left-left;
Left-left and again Left-left.
Keep it steady now, Steady, Steady.'

4) With target under bomb sight's cross
So, 'pear switch' pressed;
Bombs all go.
There! Below it's all aglow.

5) When I call 'Close Bomb doors.'
All the crew seems more composed –
When navigator directs skipper,
'Change course, compass three-twenty
    degrees.'

6) Now we're returning to base.
Will a fighter give chase;
Will there be more 'flak'?
All crew hope, maybe pray –
we will again see Lincoln Cathedral
when night becomes day.

7) No thought or prayer for those we've
    killed –
UNTIL MUCH LATER.
Only that another Operation has been
    fulfilled.

8) Then at last, the War is over.
And a thankful feeling that life is a 'Bed
    of clover'
and I am proud to have become a
    father.

9) But now for UNTIL MUCH LATER!
Thoughts return of targets bombed
And wondering how many children,
how many mothers did we kill?
In our participation to eliminate
    The Nazi ill.

Frank Tolley BEM, RAF, No. 625 Squadron,
bomb aimer, Europe, 1940–45

Farewell to the Skies

Ken 'Paddy' French was very determined to do his bit during the war and came all the way from County Cork to do so, making him one of only a few Irishmen from the Republic of Ireland to be a fighter pilot in the Royal Air Force Fighter Command.

He flew as a Spitfire pilot with No. 66 Squadron RAF from 1941 until demobbed in 1946, seeing active service in the skies over the UK and Europe. There he gave air cover for various ground missions, including the Normandy D-day landings, and on into France, Belgium and Holland.

I was fortunate after interviewing and spending a lovely day with Ken that he allowed me to quote a nice verse, special to him from among the various pieces in his own book. It is effectively a pilot's 'Farewell to the Skies', about a pilot who loved his flying days and was sad to say goodbye to them, but he was left with happy memories of his time in the RAF and the many close friendships forged whilst there. It is a short piece full of sentiment and a lovely addition to this poetry section.

Farewell to the Skies

In skies so blue where once we flew
To many angels high,
The Hurricanes no longer fly,
Nor Spitfires fill the sky.
We flew with boys becoming men
How lucky you and I were then
To fly those planes that served our ends,
And fly with men who were our friends.

Ken French, RAF Spitfire Pilot, No. 66 Squadron,
UK and Europe, 1941–45

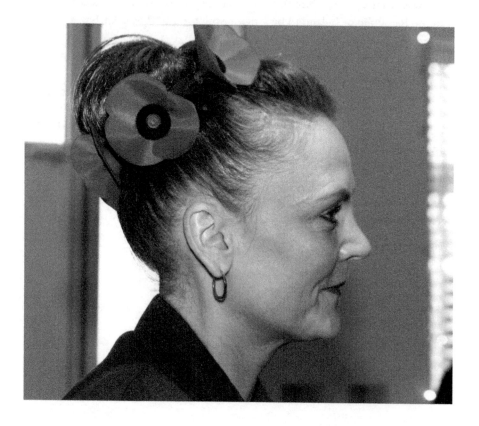

Remembrance Anthem

This piece is a song by a friend of mine, professional singer Sarah Dennis, AKA the veterans' sweetheart, and it is a tribute to the veterans of all conflicts called the Remembrance Anthem – A Debt of Gratitude. Sarah and myself have been working on our own different projects but with the same theme and goal running throughout, to honour our veterans. With this in mind we have helped and supported each other when and where possible. An example of this is in the title of the song with the words 'A debt of gratitude', which was inspired by this book and its aims.

Sarah is working on an incredible project called the 'Tour of Remembrance', which aims to raise £1 million for a number of veterans' charities over the 2014–18 period (and possibly beyond), which also coincides with the centenary remembrance events of the First World War and other important Second World War anniversaries. To find out more about her amazing work and her aims in more detail, go online and search under 'Tour of Remembrance'. Sarah's work extends into many areas, from her singing at charity events through to resources for education to teach the importance of remembrance in schools.

Remembrance Anthem

We Will Remember Them – A Debt of Gratitude

There is no finer love than they showed
There is no deeper debt of gratitude our nation owes
We will remember them as poppies fall
With each crimson petal they heard the call

They gave their lives for us that much we know
They sacrificed for us that we may grow and live our lives in peace and happiness
God sent your guardian angel on their shoulders to rest

Remember them as poppies fall
Remember them they heard the call
They gave their lives for you and me
So we live happily happily free

There is no finer love than they showed
There is no deeper debt of gratitude our nation owes
We will remember them as poppies fall
With each crimson petal they heard the call

We will remember them land air and sea
They sacrificed for us for you and me
We'll sing our song for them throughout the land
And with honour and compassion pray more children understand

Remember them as poppies fall
Remember them they heard the call
They gave their lives for you and me
So we live happily happily happily happily free

Written and Composed by the veterans' sweetheart,
Sarah Dennis

Casualties of War

The Last Heroes has at its core the message of remembrance and extended thanks to all those who have served in all conflicts. It is with this in mind that we now look briefly and focus on the casualties of both the First and Second World Wars who were returned to the United Kingdom on what was sadly their last journey.

During the world wars, Britain served as an island fortress for all manner of things pertaining to the armed forces. In both conflicts it was well placed geographically in relation to most areas of engagement and theatres of war; as a result of this it was used as a place for equipping and training troops and as a launch pad for land, sea and air operations.

It was also the place that acted as a major centre of military medical care for many thousands of servicemen and women who were wounded, fell victim to disease or were injured in some way during service of one kind or another, both at home and overseas.

Many of the servicemen buried in the United Kingdom were killed in action. However, a great number were wounded or contracted disease while on active service overseas and were brought back to Britain for hospital treatment or convalescence before succumbing to their injuries or illness.

It was the choice of the serviceman or woman's family to lay their relative to rest wherever they wished, and as a result of that today the graves of more than 170,000 men and women who served in the armed forces during those conflicts can be found in churchyards and cemeteries throughout the United Kingdom.

Some burials form war grave plots, but most are scattered throughout cemetery grounds. In all, British and Commonwealth war dead are buried or commemorated in almost 13,000 different locations across the country.

Lest We Forget

They shall grow not old,
as we that are left grow old.
Age shall not weary them,
nor the years condemn.
At the going down of the sun
and in the morning

We will remember them

For Those Who Never Returned

The stories in this book are of those who did survive this conflict. Many others did not; they paid the ultimate price for our freedom. To honour them I include these very fitting tributes.

The Kohima Epitaph

When you go home
Tell of us and say
For your tomorrow
We gave our today

The Ultimate Sacrifice

They were among those who at the call of King and Country left all that was dear to them. They endured hardness and faced danger, and finally passed out of the sight of men by the path of duty and self-sacrifice, giving up their own lives that others might live in freedom.

Let those who come after see to it that their names be not forgotten.

Their Gift To Us

They all gave something, Some Gave All.

D-Day 75

A piece I wrote seventy-five years to the day whilst in Normandy to mark this very special D-Day anniversary in 2019. Lightly edited later on another important Second World War Anniversary on 1 September 2019, eighty years to the day since the Nazis invaded Poland, triggering the Second World War

D-Day 75

D-Day 75 and I am with those still alive
Veterans of Normandy 6th June 1944 who did survive
They who endured the hell of that day
Returning to honour the fallen, many respects they pay

Now in their 90s they come once again to join their pals who didn't make it
Their friends who died in that hell to smash the Nazi evil and break it
I go to Normandy 75 years to the day to again let 'The Last Heroes' know
That what they did will never be forgotten in 'Overlord' that bravest show

To the Last of the 'Greatest Generation' I pay tribute in words
and poems abound
So that your deeds will be remembered even when you're no longer around
Leaving a legacy for those yet to come
Letting them know it was their freedom that you won

Again I say Thank You and God Bless You All for a job well done.

Gary Bridson-Daley
6 June 2019
Normandy, France

V.E. Day

A poem written to commemorate the 75th anniversary of V.E. Day and all it stands for, and to remember the sacrifices of the entire nation to make it so.

V.E. Day

V.E Day 75 years On
Celebrating a Victory so comprehensively won
Good over evil, Nazism and oppression defeated, Rightly So!
Freedom restored at great cost didn't you know?

Mighty forces arraigned against each other
Life and death conflict in the global family, brother fighting brother
Sad and senseless slaughter, yet incredible bravery on land, sea and air
Stopping a tyrannical danger so mankind can live a lasting peace that is just
and fair!

Now we pause to recall this important history and give a sigh of relief
If that wartime generation hadn't given so much, it would have been a world of
horror beyond belief
Thank God good prevailed so that all those sacrifices weren't in vain
Lets hope that future generations will never have to face the same

To those now in their twilight years thank you for all you have done
Look back with pride and know that when danger was all around you stood
firm and didn't run
From 39 to 45 six years of hardship and war was thrown at you all
But you rose to the challenge, destroyed the evil of fascism and were left
standing tall

Over seven decades on with an anniversary to lift the spirits and warm the heart
Remembering all who came forward when called, each playing a vital part
Army, Navy, Air Force, Special Forces, Intelligence and Civilians too
On the front lines, in the fields and factories, everyone saw it through

The stresses, the strains, the losses, the pains, despite it all everyone battled on
Standing up for the greater good until the final victory was won
Along the way making history that echoes on through the years
Such as the Battle of Britain, Dunkirk, D-Day and so many others, along with
their hopes and fears!

A conflict like no other with names that leap out of history books, and faces that
appear on TV screens
Churchill, Montgomery, Eisenhower, Stalin, Roosevelt and Rommel
Even hated Hitler and Mussolini won't be forgotten it seems
Great British names like the Lancaster and Spitfire, Vera Lynn, Turing and
Bletchley, did us all proud
But let's not forget the everyday man, woman and child, the faces in every crowd

The last who are with us now and those in spirit too
They made Great Britain Great, and in dark times pulled this country through
On May the 8th 2020 and on any other V.E Day that we celebrate
Please don't forget, if it wasn't for the courage of the allied forces from all nations
Ours may have been a very different fate

So break out the Union Jacks and may there be street parties galore
And the victory that was brought to Europe, let us share it once more
Show we are still proud of past times and victories hard won
Join hands and minds with all generations for remembrance and fun

As it was in '45, may it be once again, smiling faces and church bell chimes
Happy people recalling and enjoying triumphant times
Long live in the psyche of the nation a day as important as this
A moment where we jointly shine and unite in pride and bliss!

Gary Bridson-Daley
26 November 2019
Salford, Greater Manchester

Sacrifices Never Forgotten

I wrote this poem to further honour the veterans of all conflicts from the past to the present day, both the British and those who came from all over the globe to stand by us and fight with us in times of national and world crisis, to remember the sacrifices they have made and still continue to make to this very day. This includes a further dedication to all those brave people who have sacrificed in every way in the various front lines of the battle against Covid-19; thank you, each and every one of you.

Sacrifices Never Forgotten

We will remember them
All those who served, who live and who have died
Who went on to long lives
Or were cut short and were denied

They who in our country's hour of need
Came forward to protect and in many ways did bleed
Preserving our very way of life and all the values we hold dear
Democracy, liberty and freedom so that we can be free of fear

Men and Women through many conflicts did answer this country's call
With heads held up high can now stand up tall
From every corner of this sceptre'd isle and from beyond they came
At times of great national danger again and again

Many made the ultimate sacrifice and so remain forever young
Echoing in time like the songs they once sung

And in the minds of their loved ones they will never fade
Next to their surviving brothers in arms they do parade

Others live on and fight the battle every day
Still carrying the pain in every way
Re-living dreadful moments from way back when
For it is as real now as it was then

Forget them not, those near us and those who have passed
Those who died in battle and those ageing who did last
For 'A Debt of Gratitude' is what we owe them all
So may the Last Post forever sound
And in remembrance may the poppy's red petals forever fall

Gary Bridson-Daley
9 July 2016
Extended dedication 2020

Allied aircraft flying over the USS *Missouri* at the surrender ceremony in Tokyo Bay, 2 September 1945.

Hope for a Better Future

At 9.08 a.m. on Sunday, 2nd September 1945 in Tokyo Bay, Japan, the unconditional surrender of Imperial Japan took place on the US battleship *Missouri*, bringing to an end almost to the day six long years of war. Leading this historic occasion was General Douglas MacArthur as Supreme Commander of the South-west Pacific Area.

After Japan signed, the representatives of the United States, China, Britain, USSR, Australia, Canada, France, the Netherlands and New Zealand all added their signatures and this twenty-minute ceremony heralded the end of the most devastating war in human history. As if in recognition of this, the sun burst out through the low-lying clouds.

The other great recognition of this being one of the most historic moments in world history were the very poignant words of General MacArthur during the course of the ceremony, which reflected the hopes, thoughts and feelings of millions of people throughout the world who had experienced or been involved in this most destructive conflict.

These words are as important and as relevant now as they were then, and as such seem like a very good addition to help conclude this book as they epitomise the hope for a better future to which we still aspire and dream of in the turbulent world we live in today. These were his words:

> It is my earnest hope, and indeed the hope of all mankind, that from this solemn occasion a better world shall emerge out of the blood and carnage of the past – a world founded upon faith and understanding, a world dedicated to the dignity of man and the fulfilment of his most cherished wish for freedom, tolerance, and justice.
>
> Let us pray that peace now be restored to the world, and that god will preserve it always.
>
> *General Douglas MacArthur*
> 2 September 1945

Acknowledgements

To conclude the journey ... A very big thank you to all the amazing people, veterans and everyone else who helped in every way to make this book a reality, and who made my personal journey from start to finish so special, memorable and full of enlightening, humbling and wonderful moments. I feel truly honoured to be contributing in some small way to the preservation of such hugely important history.

Gary Bridson-Daley, 2020

The author would also like to thank the following people, organisations, associations and charities whose help and co-operation contributed in making this book possible and is greatly appreciated.

All at Broughton House for ex-servicemen in Salford, Michael Shanahan at the Royal Chelsea Hospital in London, Manchester Evening News, Royal British Legion, Imperial War Museum North, Dr Jolly and Rimi Bhatia and the Sikh Community of Manchester, Malcolm Solomons and the Jewish Museum of Manchester, Peter Devitt and the RAF Museum London, Norman Warwick and All Across the Arts in Rochdale, Helen Richardson at the Diocese of Gloucester, John and Victoria Phipps at D-Day Revisited, Chris Cherry, Joanna Mrugas and Heathlands care home in Prestwich, Cindy and Maz, Mark Cunliffe of Manchester Airport Festival of Remembrance, Heike Watzal, Rev. Lisa and all at St Paul's Church Moor Lane, Salford, Robert and Lynne Moseley, Katherine Lynch and the staff at Bletchley Park, Arthur Belzuik and the Polish Airmen's Association, Carole Whorwood of the Dame Vera Lynn Children's Foundation, Peter Carroll and Rajbahim Tumbahangphe of the Gurkha Peace Foundation, David Jones and Shoreham Aircraft Museum, Bob Marchant and the Guinea Pig Club, Caroline at Aces High, Roberto Zavattiero, Serge Averbukh, Andrew Collis, Howard Mason at BAE Systems Heritage Department, John Webster and the Air Transport Auxiliary Association, Gary Stewart and the Recognize Black Cultural Heritage Association,

Neil Flanagan and the West Indian Association of Service Personnel, The Airborne Assault Museum RAF Duxford, Alicia Powell and the IWM London, Milton and Millie Brown and Kirklees Local TV Ltd, George Lane and the Manchester Airport Chaplaincy, Jim McMaster and the Submariners Association, Claire Wright at Trafford Veterans MESS, Julian Hoseason, Nikos Paliousis, Christopher Barbarski & Wojtek Deluga and the Polish Institute and Sikorski Museum, Jacques Weisser and AJEX (the Association of Jewish Ex-Servicement and Women), Stan Mackenzie and the Royal Tank Regiment Association, Greater Manchester Branch, Group Captain Patrick Tootle and the Battle of Britain Fighter Association, Paul Campbell and the Biggin Hill Heritage Hangar, Air Commodore Charles Clarke and the 619 Squadron Association, Squadron Leader George 'Johnny' Johnson, Wing Commander Tom Neil, Sarah Dennis and the Tour of Remembrance, Linda Fisher and Shoulder to Soldier. To all others who have helped along the way, thank you all.

All military insignias, logos and crests from all services on the MoD portal and through historical branches 'Reproduced with permission of the MoD'. With special thanks to all at the DIPR.

Historical decommissioned insignia, logos and crests: Crown copyright, MoD. Courtesy of Air Historical Branch (RAF) and Crown copyright, MoD. Courtesy of Royal Naval Historical Branch.

All the families of the veterans for their kind assistance and the veterans themselves for permission to use all materials included in this book, such as poetry, information, photos, documents provided.

Very special thanks to Alan Meltzer and Helen Kay for their kindness and support, and for being there throughout this long and very eventful journey.

Additional heartfelt thanks to Dame Vera Lynn and Susan Fleet for their very kind and continued validation of 'The Last Heroes' and my 'Debt of Gratitude' Project.

To contact the author about *The Last Heroes* please email **bookoftheveterans@gmail.com**. You can also find the 'A Debt of Gratitude to The Last Heroes' page on Facebook, and follow the author on Twitter, @bridson_daley.

Gary Bridson-Daley hails from Manchester and has always had a keen interest in world history, especially the Second World War. Working as a tour manager in travel and tourism for over fifteen years led him to extensive worldwide travel and exposure to many countries and cultures. This, along with a deep respect for the freedom bought for us by the efforts and service of Second World War veterans, inspired him to begin the 'Debt of Gratitude' project and to publish it in the form of *The Last Heroes* in order to honour those who served and to capture their precious stories for posterity.

ABOUT VETERANS
FOR VETERANS
TO HONOUR VETERANS
BECAUSE TO REMEMBER IS TO HONOUR.

The Last Heroes and its mission to honour our service veterans is supported and further validated by the following organisations, associations and charities from whom the author has received help and cooperation during the making of this book. Thanks to each for their kind, varied and important contributions.

Central Gurdwara Manchester & SIKH Association Manchester

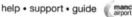